STATE PARKS
of the
NORTHEAST
America's Colonial Frontier

A Guide to
Camping, Fishing, Hiking,
& Sightseeing

VICI DeHAAN

A Cordillera Press Guidebook
Johnson Books: Boulder

9 8 7 6 5 4 3 2 1

Cover design by Bob Schram/Bookends

Library of Congress Cataloging-in-Publication Data
DeHaan, Vici.
    State parks of the Northeast : America's colonial frontier / by
Vici DeHaan.
        p.   cm
    ISBN 1-55566-143-2
    1. Parks—Northeastern States—Guidebooks.   2. Northeastern
States—Guidebooks.   I. Title.
    F2.3.D44   1995
    917.404'43—dc20   94-43534
                                                                CIP

Front cover photograph of Quoddy Head Lighthouse in Quoddy Head
    State Park, Maine, by Eric J. Wunrow.
Back cover photographs of boat, seagull, lobster traps, ox, and cannon-
    balls by Bob Schram.
Back cover photograph of loons by Nancy White-Schram.

Printed in the United States of America by
Johnson Printing Company
1880 South 57th Court
Boulder, Colorado 80301

Contents

America's Colonial Frontier

This book is dedicated to Warren, my patient co-driver, camper, and co-pilot who accompanied me on the many miles needed to put this book together. Our traveling adventures would fill a book of its own.

As a child growing up in Colorado, I first became fascinated with the Northeast during family visits to my grandparents who lived in Watertown, Massachusetts. When I retired from teaching elementary school after thirty-one years, my first goal was to visit the Northeast as a "leaf peeper." Even though I love the golds and reds of our Colorado aspen, they somehow don't compare with the hardwoods when they take on their fall hues. As the brilliant forests spill over the mountaintops, they always remind me of the beauty created by the fairy who painted those wonderful scenes in Walt Disney's movie *Fantasia*. My trip more than surpassed my expectations.

My northeastern research has been done over several years. I've explored the area in a small, private plane, flown in commercially, and rented a car or motorhome, and in 1993, Warren and I came with our pick-up pulling a travel trailer. The sheer number of state parks is much too vast to even attempt to visit them all, so I have endeavored to get a sampling of the parks in each state and completed my research by contacting the various parks and state agencies.

Not only are the state parks jewels in themselves, but they provide access to so many nearby attractions. As I compiled the book, I listed many of these for your own visits.

Naturally, I have discovered many parks that I want to return to for closer exploration. These include Franconia Notch in New Hampshire, Niagara Falls, Oil Creek in Pennsylvania, Watkins Glen in New York, and Gifford Woods in Vermont, to mention just a few.

If history attracts you, the Northeast is one of the best places in the U.S. to visit. Many of the state parks are themselves historic or are located close to historic sites. Here you can get a good sense of how we came to be who we are as Americans. I especially enjoyed touring Gettysburg and Mystic Harbor and walking Boston's Freedom Trail in the company of an informative national park naturalist.

As a marathon runner, I am constantly on the lookout for new and exciting places to train and was never disappointed, particularly when I was able to explore trails through the thick woods. Hiking is a real treat in the Northeast, and I found that totally waterproof boots and insect repellent were an absolute must! The literature available on deer ticks advises visitors to wear clothing that makes their appearance readily apparent. I can truly attest to the fact that these tiny insects are very hard to see and, since some can carry Lyme disease, they should be avoided whenever you spend time in the woods.

For anyone who loves fresh fish, it doesn't get any better than this. Plenty of opportunities abound for you to catch your own, should you be so inclined.

Special thanks goes to Jane Fiske of Rhododendron State Park in New Hampshire for all the in-depth information she contributed.

I hope you enjoy your northeastern explorations as much as I have.

CONNECTICUT

The early Indians referred to Connecticut as Quinnehtukut or "beside the long tidal river." The Connecticut River begins its journey in northeastern Vermont and winds its way through Connecticut, ending in Long Island Sound, making it the largest river in the U.S. without a port located at its mouth. Today the river serves as a major center for marine activity. Two other major rivers in the state are the Thames and Housatonic. The state's largest lake is Lake Candlewood.

The southernmost section of the Berkshires and Taconic mountains extends into the northwestern part of Connecticut. Six-tenths of the state is forest, primarily 60- to 100-year-old hardwoods, providing glorious color in the fall. Much of the forested land is the site of 91 state parks and 30 state forests.

Visitors go to Long Island Sound to enjoy boating and saltwater fishing for bluefish, sea bass, and flounder. During the winter, skiers congregate at Mohawk Mountain State Park near Cornwall. Snowmobilers enjoy their sport in the Litchfield Hills.

Mystic Seaport, where you can see exhibits from the region's early whaling days, is the state's biggest attraction. Groton is often referred to as the "Submarine Capital of the World" and is now home to the submarine USS *Nautilus*.

Much history occurred here, including the adoption of the U.S. Constitution and key events in the Industrial Revolution. Nathan Hale, Benedict Arnold, and Israel Putnam, who told his troops at Bunker Hill not to fire until you see the "whites of their eyes," were all born here.

BEAR MOUNTAIN STATE PARK
1

LOCATION - Bear Mountain State Park is north of Danbury off Connecticut 37. It borders Lake Candlewood, the third largest man-made lake in the world, and is the largest one east of the Mississippi.

ACTIVITIES - At Bear Mountain, enjoy a picnic and go hiking and fishing in Lake Candlewood.

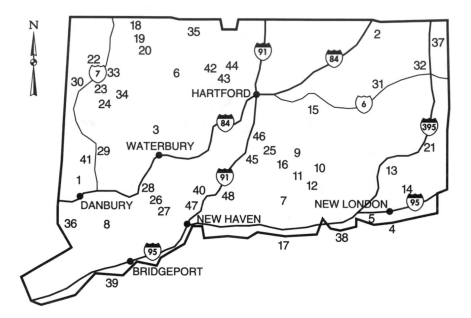

N

18
19
20
35
2
37

22
33
91
84
32

30
7
23
34
6
42 44
43
31
6
HARTFORD
15

24

3
84
15
WATERBURY
46
395

41
29
25
9
21

1
45
16
10
13

28
40
91
11
12
14

DANBURY
26
27
47
48
7
NEW LONDON
95

36
8
NEW HAVEN
5
4

95
17
38

BRIDGEPORT

39

In Danbury, tour Charles Ives's Birthplace, 5 Mountainville Avenue. From I-84, take Exit 2 or 4. This home of the Pulitzer Prize-winning father of modern music was built in 1790. Attend outdoor symphonies, jazz and folk concerts. Tours are given Wednesday and Thursday from 2:00–5:00 PM. For information, call 203-743-5200.

Stop by Meeker's Hardware Store on White Street to get a five-cent coke. It's the only hardware store listed in the National Register of Historic Places.

Marcus Dairy on Sugar Hollow Road, Danbury, has a fifties Cruise Night most Saturdays for vintage cars and motorcycle rallies most Sundays. For information, call 203-748-9427.

The Military Museum of Southern New England at 125 Park Avenue, I-84, Exit 3 in Danbury, has an extensive collection of anti-tank weapons and World War II military vehicles and artifacts. It's open May 1–September 30, Thursday–Sunday from 11:00–4:00, and October 1–April 30 by appointment only. Call 203-790-9277.

Attend summer noontime concerts at St. James Church, 25 West Street. It houses the Bulkley Memorial Carillon, the first made in the U.S.

The Danbury Scott-Fanton Museum at 43 Main Street, Exit 5 off I-84, has eighteenth- and early nineteenth-century furnishings and Revolutionary War exhibits in the house, circa 1785. For information, call 203-743-5200. The Tarrywile Mansion at 70 Southern Boulevard is an historic Victorian mansion. For tour hours, call 203-744-3130. Additional Victorian homes are located on Deer Hill.

Play golf at the Richter Park Golf Course on Aunt Hack Road, Danbury. It's rated as one of the top ten public golf courses in the U.S. by *Golf Digest*. For a tee-off time, call 203-792-2550. During the winter, go cross-country skiing here.

The old jail and pre-Revolutionary cemetery at 80 Main and Wooster Street, south of the city center, has oversized cells constructed to house women jailed wearing hoop skirts. P.T. Barnum was jailed for libel, but continued to run his newspaper from here. It's open weekdays from 8:30–4:30.

Incoming pilots can land at Danbury Municipal Airport, located 3 miles southwest of town. No rental cars are available.

INFORMATION
Bear Mountain State Park
Danbury, Connecticut 06801
203-566-2304

BIGELOW HOLLOW STATE PARK

2

LOCATION - The hollow is 2 miles northeast of Union on Connecticut 197.

ACTIVITIES - Launch your boats into Mashapaug Lake, 2½ miles north of Connecticut 197 near Union. Go trout fishing in Bigelow Pond and Lake Mashapaug. Go scuba diving, hiking, and enjoy a picnic.
INFORMATION
Bigelow Hollow State Park
Union, Connecticut 06770
203-566-2304

BLACK ROCK STATE PARK
3

LOCATION - The park is 2 miles west of Thomaston on U.S. 6.
FEATURES - The name "Black Rock" is derived from graphite mined here by early settlers.
ACTIVITIES - Hike the blazed Mattatuck Trail that connects the park to woodland sections of Mattatuck State Forest. Collect arrowheads, go camping in one of 96 sites, and attend nature programs. Go swimming and pond and stream fishing. In the winter, go cross-country skiing and ice skating.
INFORMATION
Black Rock State Park
Tomaston, Connecticut 06787
203-283-8088 (campground office)
203-677-1819 (park office)

BLUFF POINT STATE PARK AND COASTAL RESERVE
4
FORT GRISWOLD BATTLEFIELD STATE PARK
5

LOCATION - Bluff Point is on Long Island Sound southeast of Groton. Follow Connecticut 117 from I-95. Turn right onto U.S. 1, left on Depot Road, and continue under the railroad overpass to the parking area.

Fort Griswold is on Monument Street and Park Avenue in Groton. It's 2 miles from Clarence B. Sharp Highway, off I-95.

FEATURES - The rocky bluff and beach feature a 100-acre tidal salt marsh and upland forest.

Fort Griswold is the site of the 1781 massacre of American defenders by British troops. This historic site commemorates the time when British forces, led by Benedict Arnold, captured the fort, massacred the Continental army soldiers stationed there, and burned New London and Groton.

ACTIVITIES - Hike to Bluff Point and Mumford Point, passing the site of former Governor Winthrop's residence. Go saltwater fishing and enjoy a picnic. During the winter, go cross-country skiing.

Tour Fort Griswold's historic battlegrounds and stop by Groton Monument on the hilltop. Walk through Monument House to see artifacts from the massacre and whaling industry. The park is open Memorial Day through Labor Day from 10:00–5:00, and Labor Day through Columbus Day on weekends from 9:00–5:00.

Tour Ebenezer Avery's house with its weaving room and period furnishings.

Bike an 8-mile bike trail or go hiking on Haley Farm in Groton. Follow Connecticut 215 south to Brook Street where parking is available. Enjoy cross-country skiing during the winter.

Take a river cruise along the Thames River aboard *River Queen II*. For reservations and information, call 203-445-9516. Stop by the USS *Nautilus* Memorial, located off I-95, Exit 86, then north on Connecticut 12, outside the naval submarine base. Walk through the museum to learn about the development of the submarine. Tour the *Nautilus*, the first to cruise under the North Pole from the Bering Strait to the Greenland Sea, decommissioned in 1980. Visit the torpedo room, attack center, and living quarters. For tour information, call 203-449-3174.

Tour Mystic Harbor where the fastest clipper ships were being constructed in the nineteenth century. Pick up a booklet to take a walking tour of Mystic's historic homes from the Chamber of Commerce at 2 Roosevelt Avenue. Stroll through the Mystic Seaport Museum along the Mystic River on Connecticut 27, 3/4 mile south of I-95, Exit 90. Tour the *Charles Morgan*, a wooden whaling ship, the 1882 *Joseph Conrad*, and a fishing schooner. Take a steamboat ride aboard the 1908 *Sabino*, or a windjammer cruise from Whaler's Wharf north of the downtown drawbridge. For reservations, call 203-536-4218.

Tour Olde Mistick Village on Connecticut 27 at I-95. The village is an eighteenth-century-like colonial shopping center. Free concerts are presented Saturdays and Sundays from May–October. For information, call 203-536-4941.

During December, enjoy an old-fashioned Christmas celebration at Mystic Seaport, featuring special tours, holiday decorations, and Lantern Light Tours from Seamen's Inn.

In Mystic, tour Denison Homestead on Pequotsepos Road. It's furnished with Denison family heirlooms representing five distinct eras from 1717–1941. For information, call 203-536-9248. Whitehall Mansion is on Connecticut 27. From I-95, take Exit 90 north. The restored mansion was built in 1774.

Mystic Marinelife Aquarium, 55 Coogan Boulevard, has over 6,000 living specimens of undersea life. Hourly demonstrations of whales, dolphins, and sea lions are presented in Marine Theater. For information, call 203-536-9631.

Incoming pilots can land at Groton/New London Airport, located 3 miles southeast of town. Rental cars are available.

INFORMATION

Bluff Point State Park
Depot Road
Groton, Connecticut 06340
203-506-2304

Fort Griswold Battlefield State Park
Groton, Connecticut 06340
203-445-1729 (park office)
203-446-9257
(Ebenezer Avery House)

BURR POND STATE PARK
6

LOCATION - Burr Pond is 5 miles north of Torrington on Connecticut 8.

ACTIVITIES - At Burr Pond, site of Borden's first condensed milk factory, go hiking on the path around the 88-acre park pond and go fishing, swimming, and boating. Camp in one of 40 campsites in Taylor Brook Campground. During the winter, go cross-country skiing and ice skating.

Tour Hotchkill-Tyler House on 192 Main Street. This Victorian mansion has 16 rooms and an adjacent museum featuring early life in Torrington. For information, call 203-482-8260.

INFORMATION

Burr Pond State Park
385 Burr Mountain Road
Torrington, Connecticut 06790
203-379-0172 (campground)
203-482-1817 (park office)

CHATFIELD HOLLOW STATE PARK
COCKAPONSET STATE FOREST
7

LOCATION - Chatfield Hollow State Park is one mile west of Killingworth on Connecticut 80.

Cockaponset State Forest is adjacent to Chatfield Hollow on Connecticut 148.

ACTIVITIES - Chatfield Hollow State Park, with its natural caves and rocky ledges, offers hikers over 18 miles of trails to explore. Trails range in length from the ½-mile nature trail to 2½-mile Deep Woods Trail. One of the trails goes to a covered bridge. No boating is allowed in Schreeder Pond, but swimming and fishing for stocked trout are permitted. During the winter, go ice skating.

Nearby Cockaponset State Forest has additional opportunities for hiking. You can camp in one of 16 campsites and go fishing and swimming. During the winter, go cross-country skiing and snowmobiling.

INFORMATION
Chatfield Hollow State Park
Killingworth, Connecticut 06419
203-566-2304

Cockaponset State Forest
18 Ranger Road
Haddam, Connecticut 06438
203-566-2304

COLLIS P. HUNTINGTON STATE PARK
PUTNAM MEMORIAL STATE PARK
8

LOCATION - Huntington State Park is north of Redding. Take Connecticut 58 to Sunset Hill Road.

Putnam Memorial State Park is at the intersection of Connecticut 58 and 107 between Bethel and Redding.

FEATURES - Huntington State Park was a gift of Anna and Archer Huntington, a world famous sculptor.

Putnam Memorial State Park contains General Israel Putnam's New England troops' winter quarters used during the winter of 1778–79. Today the site has a restored blockhouse and palisade.

ACTIVITIES - At Huntington, go hiking through the sugar maples, fishing in one of the five ponds, horseback riding, and canoeing. During the winter, enjoy cross-country skiing.

At Putnam Memorial State Park, tour the Columbus Museum to see artifacts from the Revolutionary War. You can also enjoy a picnic, go fishing, hiking, spelunking, and attend military reenactments.

The Mark Twain Library on Redding Road in Redding was originally founded by Mark Twain, who moved here when he was 73.

Saugatuck Valley Hiking Trail is off Connecticut 53 near Redding and is part of Devil's Den Conservancy. It has 15 miles of hiking trails that pass through Redding, Weston, and Easton, and along a dramatic 200-foot cliff above the reservoir. An additional 50 miles of hiking trails are located in the Redding Land Trust. Pick up a map and trail guide at the town clerk's office or library. For information, call 203-938-2551.

Plumtrees School House on Plumtrees Road in Bethel is the last one-room school operated in the country.

INFORMATION
Collis P. Huntington State Park
Putnam Memorial State Park
Redding, Connecticut 06896
203-566-2304

DAY POND STATE PARK
9

LOCATION - The park is 5½ miles west of Colchester off Connecticut 149.

FEATURES - The pond was originally constructed to turn a large water-wheel to power the "up and down saw" of the family sawmill.

ACTIVITIES - The park's dam was restored in 1935 when it was provided with downstream fish ladders to assist migratory salmon on their way to spawn in the pond. Anglers go flyfishing for regularly stocked trout from the eastern shore of the pond. No boating is allowed, but swimmers can swim in the pond.

Hikers can explore old logging roads and foot trails in nearby Salmon River State Forest. The Salmon River flows through the forest and is known for its excellent trout fishing. In early spring, whitewater kayakers and canoers come to run the river. The forest also features a covered bridge, salmon fish ladder, and both big and small game hunting. During the winter, go cross-country skiing.

Comstock Bridge, off Connecticut 16, is one of five remaining covered bridges in Connecticut.

INFORMATION
Day Pond State Park
Colchester, Connecticut 06415
203-566-2304

DENNIS HILL STATE PARK
See under HAYSTACK MOUNTAIN STATE PARK

DEVIL'S HOPYARD STATE PARK
10
GILLETTE CASTLE STATE PARK
11
SELDEN NECK STATE PARK
12

LOCATION - Devil's Hopyard State Park is 5 miles south of Colchester and 3 miles north from the intersection of Connecticut 82 and 156. It's also 3 miles north of North Plain.

Gillette Castle State Park is on 67 River Road off Connecticut 431 at Hadlyme. If you arrive from the west, take the Chester-Hadlyme ferry.

Selden Neck State Park is on an island located near Gillette Castle and is accessible only by water.

FEATURES - Devil's Hopyard is considered to be hallowed ground by the superstitious. Early folklore held that the Devil had a "great eye for wild and rugged scenery," like that found in the hopyard. Another tale tells of the Devil hopping from ledge to ledge in order not to get wet, and the holes left behind were the result of his hot hoofs.

Chapman Falls, located on Eight Mile River, drop 60 feet over a series of steps.

Gillette Castle was patterned after a Rhine fortress and was constructed in 1914.

ACTIVITIES - At Devil's Hopyard, camp in the 27-site campground near the falls from mid-April through the end of September. Go trout fishing in the stream and hike along 15 miles of trails. Boat rentals are available in East Haddam.

Gillette Castle State Park features a 24-room hilltop fieldstone mansion built in 1919 by actor William Gillette, who was known for his portrayal of Sherlock Holmes. The castle is open daily Memorial Day through Columbus Day, and weekends Columbus Day through the last weekend before Christmas. The grounds are open year-round. Enjoy a picnic and go fishing and hiking. Food concessions are available. Rent canoes from North American Canoe Lines at Hadlyme below the castle and go canoe camping.

At Selden Neck State Park you can go canoe camping from May–September.

In East Haddam, attend the Great Connecticut Traditional Jazz Festival in August. Tour Amasa Day House on Moodus Green, Connecticut 151. From Connecticut 2, take Exit 16. The house, built in 1816, was lived in by three generations of the Day family. See period furnishings and family heirlooms. It's open from late May through mid-October Wednesday–Sunday from 1:00–5:00. For information, call 203-873-8144.

Tour historic Johnsonville on Johnsonville Road, an historic nineteenth-century mill village. Tours are offered from late May through Labor Day weekend. See their exhibit with 50 miniature rooms and a carriage collection. For information, call 203-873-1987.

Nathan Hale School House on Main Street, Connecticut 149, is at the rear of St. Stephen's Church. This one-room school is where patriot Nathan Hale taught from 1773–74. It's open Memorial Day through Labor Day weekends and holidays from 2:00–4:00. For information, call 203-873-9547.

Attend performances in the Goodspeed Opera House at Goodspeed Landing in East Haddam. For schedules, call 203-873-8348. The New England Steamboat Line, across the river from Goodspeed Opera House, offers cruises. For details, call 203-345-4505.

For an hour-long round trip via vintage steam train from Essex to Chester, contact the Connecticut Valley Railroad. Its train connects with an optional riverboat cruise at Deep River returning you to Essex. The railroad is reached via Exit 3 from Connecticut 9 onto Railroad Avenue. For timetables, call 203-767-0103. For boat ride information, call 203-767-0119.

Incoming pilots can land at East Haddam Airport where year-round sight-seeing flights and sea plane rides are available. Call 203-873-8568.

INFORMATION

Devil's Hopyard State
366 Hopyard Road
East Haddam, Connecticut 06423
203-873-8566

Gillette Castle State Park
East Haddam, Connecticut 06423
203-526-2336

Selden Neck State Park
203-526-2336

DINOSAUR STATE PARK
See under WADSWORTH FALLS STATE PARK

FORT GRISWOLD BATTLEFIELD STATE PARK
See under BLUFF POINT STATE PARK AND COASTAL RESERVE

FORT SHANTOK STATE PARK
13
STODDARD HILL STATE PARK
14

LOCATION - Fort Shantok is located on the west bank of the Thames River, 4 miles south of Norwich off Connecticut 32.

Stoddard Hill State Park is 5 miles south of Norwich on Connecticut 12.

FEATURES - Fort Shantok is located on the site of a seventeenth-century fortified Mohegan village and burial ground.

ACTIVITIES - Today you can still see remnants of the fort's stone foundation. Interpretive signs on the fort site point out important events in the area. Hike short trails around the grounds, including one around the cemetery. Enjoy a picnic and go freshwater fishing in Tantaquidgeon Pond or in the Thames River for bass and bluefish.

Indian artifacts from the area are at the Tantaquidgeon Indian Museum on Connecticut 32 in Montville. The museum is open summers only.

Stroll through Mohegan Park and Memorial Rose Garden, located east of Norwich off Connecticut 32 on Mohegan Road. The roses are in full bloom from late June through mid-July.

John Baldwin's house, circa 1660, is at 210 West Town Street in Norwich. From I-395, take Exit 82, or from Connecticut 2, take Exit 27. Take a guided tour to see demonstrations of colonial skills. For times, call 203-889-5990.

INFORMATION
Fort Shantok State Park
Norwich, Connecticut 06360
203-566-2304

GAY CITY STATE PARK
15

LOCATION - The park is 3 miles south of Bolton on Connecticut 85.

FEATURES - The name Gay City came from the now-extinct mill town begun here in 1796. The park entrance road follows part of the original Main Street.

ACTIVITIES - Go swimming, picnicking, and hiking. The trails range in length from .8 mile to a 5-mile outer loop. Go fishing, tour the historic site, and during the winter, enjoy cross-country skiing and ice skating.

INFORMATION
Gay City State Park
Hebron, Connecticut 06248
203-566-2304

GILLETTE CASTLE STATE PARK
See under DEVIL'S HOPYARD STATE PARK

HADDAM MEADOWS STATE PARK
16

LOCATION - The park is east of Connecticut 9 in Haddam.

ACTIVITIES - Haddam Meadows is in the river floodplain and is an excellent spot for field sports, picnicking, boating, fishing, and cross-country skiing in the winter.

Cockaponset State Forest, the state's second largest state forest, is nearby on Connecticut 148. Here visitors can go camping in one of 16 campsites, picnicking, fishing, swimming, and hiking the various forest trails. During the winter, go cross-country skiing and snowmobiling.

Launch your boats into Pataconk Reservoir, 3 miles north of Connecticut 148 on Cedar Lake Road. No internal combustion engines may be used in July and August. Access is limited to carry-in boats.

Attend the Quinnehtukqut Rendezvous and Native American Festival at Haddam Meadows in August. It features native celebrations, including wigwam and teepee villages, black power and hawk/knife contests, storytelling, and drum competition.

Tour the Thankful Arnold House, circa 1794–1810. It's on Connecticut 154, from Higganum. From Connecticut 9, take Exit 7. See its eighteenth- and nineteenth-century furnishings and colonial herb and vegetable gardens. It's open Memorial Day through Labor Day on Saturdays and Sundays from 2:00–4:00 or by appointment. Call 203-345-2400.

In Haddam, take a cruise from Marine Park. Camelot Cruises has various options available. For information, call 203-345-8591. Also, Connecticut River Cruises, Inc., offers riverboat rides guided by "Tom Sawyer." For information, call 203-345-8373.

Visit Connecticut Yankee Information and Science Center on Injun Hollow Road in Haddam Neck, off Connecticut 151. The center is on the grounds of a nuclear power plant and has hands-on exhibits, a self-guided nature trail, picnic area, and boat dock. For details, call 203-267-9269.

The Sundial Herb Garden is on Hidden Lake Road at Higganum off Connecticut 81, on Brault Hill Road. It has both a seventeenth-century formal garden and eighteenth-century garden and tea room. Guided tour "Tea Talks" are offered Sundays. Reservations are required. For information, call 203-345-4290.

INFORMATION

Haddam Meadows State Park
Haddam, Connecticut 06438
203-566-2304

Cockaponset State Forest
18 Ranger Road
Haddam, Connecticut 06438
203-566-2304

HAMMONASSET BEACH STATE PARK
17

LOCATION - The beach is one mile south of Madison off Exit 62 from I-95. Follow signs.

FEATURES - Hammonasset Beach is Connecticut's largest public beach facility with 2 miles of white sandy beach.

ACTIVITIES - Camp in the campground with 558 open campsites located in 6 circles. Go boating in carry-in boats from the launch area at Meigs Point. The launch is over a sandy beach, and the water is shallow at low tide. Larger crafts may be launched from facilities in Clinton or Madison. Purchase snacks at either the camp store or snack bar at the end of Beach Road in Dowd's Camp area. Go saltwater swimming, fishing, and water skiing. In mid-April, take a birdwalk to view the spring migration from one of the state's premier birding areas.

Attend concerts on the Town Green in Madison in July and August.

Tour Deacon John Grave House, at Tuxis Farm in Madison, 581 Boston Post Road. Take Exit 61 from I-95. The house was occupied for over 300 years and is one of the town's oldest homes. For touring hours, lectures, and concerts, call 203-245-4798. The Allis-Bushnell House at 853 Boston Post Road in Madison was built in 1785 by Cornelius Bushnell, chief sponsor of the SS *Monitor*. It's open summers. Call 203-245-4567 for information.

Enjoy chamber music at 8:30 PM every Friday evening in August at the First Congregational Church in Madison. For information, call 203-453-1359.

Go hiking or ski touring on blazed trails on Madison Land Trust. Contact Madison Land Trust, P.O. Box 561, Madison, for a map.

To take a cruise to Thimble Islands, go to Stony Creek, 64 Thimble Islands Road. For cruise information, call 203-481-4841.

Incoming pilots can land at Griswold Airport, located 3 miles east of Madison. No rental cars are available.

INFORMATION
Hammonasset Beach State Park
P.O. Box 271
Madison, Connecticut 06443
203-245-1817 (campground)
203-245-2785

HAYSTACK MOUNTAIN STATE PARK
18
DENNIS HILL STATE PARK
19
JOHN A. MINETTO STATE PARK
20

LOCATION - Haystack Mountain is one mile north of Norfolk on Connecticut 272.

Dennis Hill State Park is 2 miles south of Norfolk on Connecticut 272.

John A. Minetto State Park is 6 miles north of Torrington on Connecticut 272.

ACTIVITIES - Drive halfway up 1,716-foot Haystack Mountain and hike the last mile to the summit where you can climb the 34-foot tower to get a great view of Long Island Sound, the Berkshires, and the mountains of Massachusetts and New York. The fall features colorful foliage, and in June you can see an outstanding display of blooming mountain laurel.

Dennis Hill is a 240-acre estate with a unique summit pavilion located at 1,672 feet, providing a panoramic view of the Litchfield Hills. Go hiking, have a picnic, and go cross-country skiing during the winter.

At John A. Minetto State Park, you can enjoy a picnic and go fishing, swimming, hiking, and during the winter, go cross-country skiing and ice skating.

INFORMATION

Haystack Mountain State Park
Norfolk, Connecticut 06058

Dennis Hill State Park
Norfolk, Connecticut 06058

John A. Minetto State Park
Torrington, Connecticut 06759
203-566-2304

HOPEVILLE POND STATE PARK
21

LOCATION - The park is on the Pachaug River, 3 miles east of Jewett City on Connecticut 201.

FEATURES - The Pachaug River was a major fishing ground for the Mohegan Indians. At low water, you can still see the stone weirs that directed the water so that the fish were forced into the center of the stream where they could be trapped.

You can see glacial features, including eskers, sand and gravel ridges left behind by glacial meltwater, and kettleholes, bowl-shaped depressions carved by the melting of ice chunks.

Hopeville Pond is a former woolen mill pond.

ACTIVITIES - Go freshwater fishing and swimming from the beach in the Hopeville Pond, camping in the 82-site campground near the pond, hiking, and picnicking. Purchase concessions at the concession stand on the beach. A general store is ½ mile from the park. Launch your boats into the pond, located 2½ miles north of Connecticut 138.

Pachaug State Forest is adjacent to the park's east side, one mile north of Voluntown on Connecticut 49. Here you can go boating from the ramp, pond swimming, scuba diving, fishing for trout, and boating in Green Falls Pond Recreation Area. Camp in one of 18 sites at Green Falls and take a hike. Narragansett, Quinebaug, Pachaug, and Nehantic hiking trails pass through here. Backpackers can camp in Peg Mill Brook Shelter. Advance reservations must be made. Call 203-376-4075. During the winter, go cross-country skiing, dog sled racing, snowmobiling, and snowshoeing.

Twenty-two additional camp sites are available in the Mount Misery area. Equestrians have 18 campsites available in Frog Hollow Horse Camp. Reservations must be made. Call them at 203-295-9523. Pick up a map of the horse trails through the state forest.

Other hikes in the Mount Misery area include a trail up 441-foot Mount Misery. In early July, walk through the rhododendron sanctuary when the flowers are in bloom. You can also fish for trout, bass, pickerel, and bullhead in Beachdale Pond. Boating access to Beachdale Pond is available from the east side of Connecticut 49, one mile north of Voluntown.

INFORMATION

Hopeville Pond State Park
193 Roode Road
Jewett City, Connecticut 06351
203-376-0313 (campground)
203-376-2920 (park office)

Pachaug State Forest
P.O. Box 5
Voluntown, Connecticut 06384
203-376-4075

HOUSATONIC MEADOWS STATE PARK
22
KENT FALLS STATE PARK
23
LAKE WARAMAUG STATE PARK
24

LOCATION - Housatonic Meadows are one mile north of Cornwall Bridge off Connecticut 7 and southeast of Sharon, along the banks of the Housatonic River.

Kent Falls State Park is 3 miles north of Kent on Connecticut 7.

Lake Waramaug State Park is 5 miles north of New Preston on Lake Waramaug Road, Connecticut 478.

ACTIVITIES - At Housatonic Meadows, go camping in the 102-site campground along the river under the tall pines. Fish for trout and bass with a 2-mile stretch of the river limited to flyfishing. Go hiking and canoeing and enjoy limited cross-country skiing in the winter.

Visitors come to Kent Falls to see its 200-foot cascade, particularly in the spring and fall. Follow the pathway adjacent to the falls. Go freshwater fishing and hiking.

Lake Waramaug is the site of the Women's National Rowing Regatta. Visitors can enjoy a picnic, camp in one of 88 sites, go fishing, boating with paddleboat rentals available, hiking, and scuba diving. The area has no ramp, so boats must be carried to the water. Concessions are available.

Hopkins Vineyard on Hopkins Road in Warren offers wine tasting in a nineteenth-century barn overlooking Lake Waramaug. For information, call 203-868-7954.

INFORMATION

Housatonic Meadows State Park
Cornwall Bridge, Connecticut 06754
203-672-6772 (campground)
203-927-3238 (park office)

Kent Falls State Park
Kent, Connecticut 06757

Lake Waramaug State Park
30 Lake Waramaug Road
New Preston, Connecticut 06777
203-868-0220 (campground)
203-868-2592 (off-season)

HURD STATE PARK
25

LOCATION - The park is on the east bank of the Connecticut River southwest of East Hampton. It's also 3 miles south of Cobalt on Connecticut 151.

ACTIVITIES - Go canoe camping, picnicking, freshwater fishing, hiking, and rock climbing. During the winter, go snowmobiling and cross-country skiing.

Attend the Connecticut River Raft Race in the park in the summer.

Visit Allegra Farm, 82 Young Street, Connecticut 196, to take a hay ride. For reservations, call 203-267-7636. The Comstock covered bridge is on Connecticut 16, near East Hampton/Colchester, and crosses the Salmon River. Go fishing or have a picnic at nearby Salmon River State Park.

INFORMATION
Hurd State Park
East Hampton, Connecticut 06514
203-566-2304

INDIAN WELL STATE PARK
26
OSBORNEDALE STATE PARK
27

LOCATION - Indian Well State Park is 2 miles northwest of Shelton on Connecticut 110.

Osbornedale State Park is one mile northwest of Derby off Connecticut 34.

FEATURES - Despite its name, Indian Well was never used as a well by local Indians and is known for its scenic waterfall.

ACTIVITIES - At Indian Well State Park you can launch your boats into Lake Housatonic from the western side of the lake. Bring along a picnic and go hiking, swimming, and fishing.

At Osbornedale, you can also enjoy a picnic, go for a hike, and fish in the Housatonic River. During the winter, go cross-country skiing or skating on the lighted pond. Take a scenic ride along the Housatonic River, leaving from the nation's oldest train station in continuous use since 1872. It leaves Union Station from the intersection of Connecticut 7 and 44. For schedules, call 203-824-0339.

Osborne Homestead Museum, former estate of Frances Osborne-Kellogg, is one mile northwest of Derby off Connecticut 34, adjacent to Osbornedale State Park. Take a guided tour of the Colonial Revival home with eighteenth- and nineteenth-century furnishings and attend seasonal events. The museum has a good collection of antiques and art. Stroll through the formal gardens. For information, call 203-734-2432.

INFORMATION

Indian Well State Park
Shelton, Connecticut 06878
203-566-2304

Osbornedale State Park
Derby, Connecticut 06418
203-566-2304

JOHN A. MINETTO STATE PARK
See under HAYSTACK MOUNTAIN STATE PARK

KENT FALLS STATE PARK
See under HOUSATONIC MEADOWS STATE PARK

KETTLETOWN STATE PARK
28

LOCATION - The park is 5 miles south of Southbury. Take Exit 15 off I-85. The park extends approximately 2 miles along the east shore of Lake Zoar.

FEATURES - Kettletown got its name from when settlers purchased the land from the Indians for one brass kettle.

ACTIVITIES - Enjoy camping in one of 72 campsites, and go fishing, hiking, and swimming. Attend camper nature programs.

Drive to Southford Falls State Park, 4 miles southwest of Southbury on Connecticut 188, to see the scenic waterfalls on Eight Mile River at the southeast end of the park. Go horseback riding along Larkin Bridle Trail, hiking, pond or stream fishing, and attend interpretive programs. During the winter, go ice skating and cross-country skiing.

INFORMATION

Kettletown State Park
Southbury, Connecticut 06488
203-264-5169

LAKE WARAMAUG STATE PARK
See under HOUSATONIC MEADOWS STATE PARK

LOVER'S LEAP STATE PARK AND GORGE
29

LOCATION - The park is on Connecticut 133 on Lake Lillinonah Road near Bridgewater.

FEATURES - Lover's Leap is the site of an Indian legend of star-crossed lovers who leaped into the gorge.

ACTIVITIES - Come to enjoy the great view from the Bridgewater side of the park and hike the park trails.

Drive past the Red Mill on Connecticut 133, one of New England's most photographed landmarks.

At nearby Lake Lillinonah, north of the park, go boating from the boat launch, fishing, and swimming. For information, call 203-270-2360.

INFORMATION
Lover's Leap State Park
Bridgewater, Connecticut 06752
203-566-2304

MACEDONIA BROOK STATE PARK
30

LOCATION - The park is 4 miles north of Kent off Connecticut 341.

FEATURES - Two peaks located in the park rise 1,400 feet and provide great views of the Catskills and Taconics.

ACTIVITIES - Enjoy fishing in the stream, camping in one of 84 rustic campsites, hiking, and picnicking. During the winter, go cross-country skiing.

INFORMATION
Macedonia Brook State Park
159 Macedonia Brook Road
Kent, Connecticut 06757
203-927-4100 (campground)
203-927-3238 (park office)

MANSFIELD HOLLOW STATE PARK
31

LOCATION - Mansfield Hollow is one mile east of Mansfield off Connecticut 89. It's located below the confluence of the Natchaug, Mount Hope, and Fenton rivers in Mansfield.

ACTIVITIES - Lake Naubesatuck is relatively shallow, so sailboats, canoes, and small powerboats may be launched from the paved boat-launching ramp. Anglers fish for trout, bass, bullhead, and pickerel. Enjoy a picnic overlooking the lake. Swimming isn't permitted since the water is used for drinking by Willimantic.

Hike through former pastures and among stone foundations left behind from early homesteads. During the winter, a 4.5-mile cross-country ski trail circles the northern half of the lake.

INFORMATION
Mansfield Hollow State Park
Mansfield, Connecticut 06250
203-566-2304

MASHAMOQUET BROOK STATE PARK
32

LOCATION - The park is 5 miles southwest of Putnam on U.S. 44.

FEATURES - The region was once inhabited by Mohegan Chief Uncas. Masmaquet is Indian for "stream of good fishing." The present park is a combination of three parks: Mashamoquet Brook, Wolf Den, and Saptree Run. A cider mill, grist mill, and wagon shop once operated at Marcy Hollow. However, the mill dam and pond were wiped out by a flood in 1938. The grist mill still stands, but isn't open to the public.

ACTIVITIES - Camp in Wolf Den Campground with 35 open sites or in Mashamoquet Brook with 20 wooded sites. Both campgrounds have dump stations. Go swimming in the bypass pool where water is removed from the brook and the overflow released here. Go fishing and hiking. Two places to visit include Table Rock and Indian Chair, both natural stone formations.

For additional hiking, go to Natchaug State Forest, located 4 miles south of Phoenixville on Connecticut 198. The forest is known for its horse trails, fishing, riverfront picnic sites, fishing in the Natchaug River, and both equestrian and backpack camping. During the winter, go cross-country skiing and snowmobiling.

INFORMATION
Mashamoquet Brook State Park
Pomfret Center, Connecticut 06259
203-928-6121 (both campgrounds)

MOHAWK MOUNTAIN STATE PARK
33

LOCATION - Mohawk Mountain State Park is 6 miles west of Goshen off Connecticut 4.

ACTIVITIES - Mohawk Mountain State Park and State Forest is spectacular when fall foliage appears. Follow the road to the abandoned fire tower for some great views from 1,783 feet. Have a picnic and go hiking on forest and park trails and along a section of the Appalachian Trail. Go stream and pond fishing and explore their black spruce bog.

Go snowmobiling here in the winter. You can also go snowmobiling or cross-country and downhill skiing at Mohawk Mountain Ski Area.

INFORMATION
Mohawk Mountain State Park
Cornwall, Connecticut 06753
203-566-2304

Mohawk Mountain Ski Area
203-672-6100

MOUNT TOM STATE PARK
34

LOCATION - The park is 3½ miles west of Bantam off U.S. 202.

ACTIVITIES - Hike the one-mile-long trail to the stone tower on top of 1,325-foot Mount Tom. Go swimming, boating in non-motorized boats, fishing, and scuba diving. During the winter, enjoy ice skating.

Tour Haight Vineyard, 29 Chestnut Hill Road, one mile east of Litchfield off Connecticut 118. The vineyard is open year-round and offers guided winery tours on the hour. For information, call 203-567-4045.

INFORMATION
Mount Tom State Park
Litchfield, Connecticut 06759
203-566-2304

OSBORNEDALE STATE PARK
See under INDIAN WELL STATE PARK

PENWOOD STATE PARK
See under STRATTON BROOK STATE PARK

PEOPLES STATE PARK
35

LOCATION - The park is one mile north of Pleasant Valley on East River Road.

ACTIVITIES - Two-hundred-year-old pines in the Mathies Grove provide a great picnic site adjacent to the Farmington River. Go fishing and hiking in the forest. During the winter, go cross-country skiing and snowmobiling.

INFORMATION
Peoples State Park
Pleasant Valley, Connecticut 06063

PIERREPONT STATE PARK
36

LOCATION - The park is off Connecticut 116, north of Ridgefield.

ACTIVITIES - Enjoy a picnic and go fishing and hiking. During the winter, go cross-country skiing and ice skating.

Woodstock Nature Center is at 56 Deer Run Road at Ridgefield/Wilton on Connecticut 7. Take botany walks, go birding, and attend wildlife programs. The center has 148 acres of wetlands, 2 miles of trails, and a boardwalk. For information, call 203-762-7280.

Golfers can play at Ridgefield Golf Club on Ridgebury Road. For a tee-off time, call 203-748-7008.

Weir Farm on Nod Hill Road on the Ridgefield-Wilton line is one of only two national parks that celebrates American art. The 52-acre site includes J. Alden Weir's home and two artists' studios. Take a summer tour or attend a seasonal program. For information, call 203-834-1896 or 203-761-9945.

Aldrich Museum of Contemporary Art is the first museum in the U.S. to devote itself only to contemporary art. Tour its outstanding sculpture garden. Attend concerts, films, and lectures. It's open Tuesday–Sunday from 1:00–5:00. For information, call 203-438-4519.

Attend a play at Wilton Playshop on Louis Lane, Connecticut 33 and 107, near Wilton, from November–May. For information, call 203-762-7629.

INFORMATION
Pierrepont State Park
Ridgefield, Connecticut 06877
203-438-9597

PUTNAM MEMORIAL STATE PARK
See under COLLIS P. HUNTINGTON STATE PARK

QUADDICK STATE PARK
37

LOCATION - The park is 7 miles northeast of Putnam via East Putnam Road. Follow Connecticut 438, East Putnam Road, north from U.S. 44. East Putnam becomes Quaddick Town Farm Road at the Thompson town line.

ACTIVITIES - Go fishing, sailing, and swimming from the beach or launch your boats from the ramp into Quaddick Reservoir. During the winter, go ice skating.

Quaddick State Forest, north of the park, offers hiking trails and picnicking.
INFORMATION
Quaddick State Park
Thompson, Connecticut 06277
203-566-2304

ROCKY NECK STATE PARK
38

LOCATION - The park is on Long Island Sound in East Lyme, 3 miles west of Niantic. Take Exit 72 from I-95.

FEATURES - Rocky Neck State Park is bounded on the west by a tidal river and on the east by a broad salt marsh and features one mile of beach frontage along Long Island Sound.

ACTIVITIES - Take a walk or go saltwater bathing from the white sand beach or follow the area's wooded hiking trails. The trails lead to Baker's Cave, Tony's Nose, and historic sites of the Tannery, Salt Works, and Shipyard.

Come in March and April when high spring tides bring large schools of herring inland to spawn. Go fishing for mackerel, bass, blackfish, and flounder. Go crabbing, scuba diving, birding, or ride the bikeway from the campground to the beach.

Camp in one of 169 campsites, both wooded and open. Attend camper interpretive programs. Concessions and a dump station are available. During the winter, go cross-country skiing.

Visit nearby Harkness Memorial State Park, located 4 miles south of New London on Connecticut 213. The summer estate once belonged to the Edward S. Harkness family and has a 42-room Italian mansion and formal gardens. Enjoy the grounds, have a picnic, and go saltwater fishing. A summer music festival is held July–August. For information, call 203-443-5725.

INFORMATION
Rocky Neck State Park
P.O. Box 676
Niantic, Connecticut 06357
203-739-5471

SELDEN NECK STATE PARK
See under DEVIL'S HOPYARD STATE PARK

SHERWOOD ISLAND STATE PARK
39

LOCATION - The park is 2 miles south of Westport. Take Exit 18 off the Connecticut Turnpike.

ACTIVITIES - Since the park has 1½ miles of beach frontage along Long Island Sound, you can go swimming, saltwater fishing, and scuba diving. Attend interpretive programs and purchase a snack.

Go to the Nature Center for Environmental Activities, a 62-acre sanctuary, to hike the trails.

INFORMATION
Sherwood Island State Park
Westport, Connecticut 06880
203-226-6983.

SLEEPING GIANT STATE PARK
40

LOCATION - The park is 2 miles north of Hamden off Connecticut 10.

FEATURES - The 2 miles of mountaintops resemble a large man sleeping, giving the region its name.

ACTIVITIES - Hike the 1½-mile trail to the stone observation tower on Mount Carmel to get a great view of Long Island Sound and New Haven. Camp in one of the 6 sites. Go stream fishing, hike the nature trail, and go rock climbing.

In Hamden, tour Eli Whitney Museum at 915 Whitney Avenue. Attend country dances, folk music concerts, and summer theater in the barn built in 1816. Call 203-777-1833 for a schedule.

INFORMATION
Sleeping Giant State Park
Hamden, Connecticut 06517
203-566-2304

SQUANTZ POND STATE PARK
41

LOCATION - The park is 4 miles north of New Fairfield on Connecticut 39.

ACTIVITIES - Enjoy a picnic, take a hike, go boating from the boat launch, swimming, scuba diving, and fishing in the pond. Photographers come here in the fall to film the fall foliage reflected in the water. During the winter, go ice skating and cross-country skiing.

Ogden House and gardens are at 1520 Bronson Road in Fairfield. From I-95, take Exit 20. Its eighteenth-century saltbox farmhouse has Revolutionary era furnishings plus wildflower and kitchen gardens. It's open mid-May through mid-October, Thursday and Sunday from 1:00–4:00. For information, call 203-259-1598.

Attend a play at the American Premier Theater at 5151 Park Avenue in Fairfield from November–June. For information, call 203-374-2777. Candlewood Playhouse, at the intersection of Connecticut 37 and 39, offers Broadway productions from April–November. For information, call 203-746-6531.

Tour Connecticut Audubon Society Fairfield Nature Center, 2325 Burr Street in Fairfield. Take Exit 44 from Connecticut 15. Walk 6 miles of trails in the adjacent 160-acre Larsen Sanctuary. For information, call 203-259-6305.

INFORMATION
Squantz Pond State Park
New Fairfield, Connecticut 06430
203-566-2304

STODDARD HILL STATE PARK
See under FORT SHANTOK STATE PARK

STRATTON BROOK STATE PARK
42
TALCOTT MOUNTAIN STATE PARK
43
PENWOOD STATE PARK
44

LOCATION - Stratton Book State Park is 2 miles west of Simsbury on Connecticut 309.

Talcott Mountain State Park is 3 miles south of Simsbury on Connecticut 185.

Penwood State Park is 4 miles west of Bloomfield on Connecticut 185.

ACTIVITIES - At Stratton Book, ride the bicycle trail through the white pines and over scenic brooks. Go swimming, fishing, and hiking. During the winter, enjoy ice skating and cross-country skiing.

At Talcott Mountain, hike a 1½-mile trail up Talcott Mountain to Heublein Tower, 1,000 feet above the Farmington River valley. The tower is open seasonally. Also enjoy hang-gliding and a picnic.

At Penwood, hike along part of the Metacomet Trail that traverses the park. Follow the interpretive nature trail, enjoy a picnic, or bike the bikeway. During the winter, enjoy cross-country skiing.

In Simsbury, visit Massacoh Plantation, 800 Hopmeadow Street, Connecticut 10. The replica 1683 meetinghouse and other buildings are open year-round, but the plantation is only open May–October with guided tours from 1:00–3:30. For information, call 203-658-2500.

Incoming pilots can land at Simsbury Airport, located 3 miles northeast of town.

INFORMATION

Stratton Brook
Talcott Mountain
Simsbury, Connecticut 06070
293-242-1158

Penwood State Park
Bloomfield, Connecticut 06002
203-566-2304

WADSWORTH FALLS STATE PARK
45
DINOSAUR STATE PARK
46

LOCATION - Wadsworth Falls State Park is 2 miles southwest of Middle-town on Connecticut 157.

Dinosaur State Park is north of Wadsworth Falls, one mile east of Exit 23 off I-91.

ACTIVITIES - At Wadsworth Falls, have a picnic, go stream fishing, hiking, swimming, and visit the waterfall visible from an overlook. Come in spring when the laurel are in bloom. During the winter, go cross-country skiing and ice skating.

In Dinosaur State Park, tour the exhibit center that encloses a rock exposure with tracks made by dinosaurs from the Jurassic period. Attend an interpretive program and go hiking.

Take a boat ride from Harbor Park. For information, call 203-526-4954. Attend summer band concerts on Tuesday evenings at South Green, Middle-town. For information, call 203-344-3520.

The annual Head of the Connecticut Regatta is held in mid-October.

General Mansfield House, 151 Main Street in Middletown, was built in 1810 and offers tours. For times, call 203-346-0746.

INFORMATION

Wadsworth Falls State Park
Middletown, Connecticut 06457
203-566-2304

Dinosaur State Park
Middletown, Connecticut 06457
203-529-8423

WEST ROCK RIDGE STATE PARK
47

LOCATION - The park is northwest of New Haven. Follow Connecticut 10, Dixwell Avenue. Turn west onto Benham. From Benham, go south onto Main Street, and then west onto Wintergreen.

ACTIVITIES - West Rock Ridge rises 627 feet above sea level, providing scenic views of New Haven harbor and Long Island Sound. The park offers walk-in access only.

While in New Haven, stop by Yale University's campus, where guided one-hour tours are offered year-round, Monday–Friday at 10:30 and 1:00, and Saturday and Sunday at 1:30. Begin at Phelps Gateway across from New Haven Green. Attend performances at the Yale Repertory Theater, at Long Wharf Theater, or Shubert Performing Arts Center. Take a walk on the historic New

Haven Green which is bordered by three churches, providing good examples of Gothic, Federalist, and Georgian architecture.

Tour Pardee-Morris House, 325 Lighthouse Road in New Haven. From I-95, take Exit 50. The eighteenth-century Colonial home has furnishings from the seventeenth through nineteenth centuries. It's open June–August on Saturday and Sunday from 11:00–4:00. For information, call 203-562-4183.

In East Haven, tour Shore Line Trolley Museum at 17 River Street. It's a National Register Historic Site with almost 100 classic trolleys. Go for a trolley ride. For details, call 203-467-6927.

Lighthouse Point Park, 2 Lighthouse Road, is an 82-acre park on Long Island Sound. Here you can go swimming, walk nature trails, and ride an antique carousel from Memorial Day through Labor Day.

INFORMATION
West Rock Ridge State Park
New Haven, Connecticut 06820
203-566-2304

WHARTON BROOK STATE PARK
48

LOCATION - The park is 2 miles south of Wallingford on U.S. 5.

ACTIVITIES - Come to go fishing, swimming, hiking, ride the bicycle trails, or have a picnic in the 96-acre woodland.

INFORMATION
Wharton Brook State Park
Wallingford, Connecticut 06492
203-269-5308

DELAWARE

Tiny Delaware was the first state to ratify the U.S. Constitution. Three state parks are located along its shoreline: Cape Henlopen, Delaware Seashore, and Fenwick Island state parks. Shell fishing is popular from May–November. The shores of Indian River and Rehoboth Bay are excellent for clamming and crabbing. Fish for sea trout, blue fish, and flounder from early spring through late fall. For fishing information from May–September, call 302-645-4246. Non-residents need a trout stamp for stream fishing and a freshwater fishing license for all non-tidal fishing areas.

Delaware's state parks operate year-round nature centers at Brandywine Creek State Park and at Cape Henlopen State Park. Cape Henlopen is the eastern terminus of the American Discovery Trail. Seasonal naturalists offer interpretive programs at most of Delaware's 12 state parks from May 1–September 30. Hikers can explore 10 interpretive trails and accept a "Trail Challenge" for hiking in 15 of the state parks.

BELLEVUE STATE PARK
1

LOCATION - The park is 4 miles northeast of Wilmington off I-95 on Carr Road. Take Exit 9, Marsh Road.

FEATURES - Bellevue is the former estate of William du Pont.

ACTIVITIES - Visitors can go bicycling and fishing for bass, catfish, and sunfish. Stroll along the Delaware River or on the estate grounds. Runners have access to a 1⅛-mile fitness track circling a pond where anglers come to fish. Food service is available.

Tennis players have 2 indoor and 8 outdoor clay courts. Golfers play a nine-hole course and equestrians ride equestrian trails. Go for a hayride, attend a concert in the bandshell. During the winter, enjoy cross-country skiing.

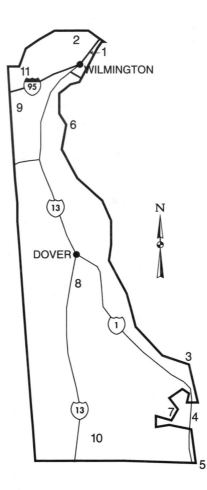

In Wilmington, tour the Delaware Art Museum at 2301 Kentmere Parkway. For information, call 302-571-9590. The Delaware Museum of Natural History is on Delaware 52 between Greenville and Centreville and features a walk across Australia's Great Barrier Reef and an undersea world. For information, call 302-658-9111.

The Wilmington Maritime Center is at Three Christina Centre across from the Amtrak Station. Take a cruise on the Delaware River. For information, call 301-984-0472.

Flower lovers can visit Nemours Mansion and formal French gardens on Alfred I. du Pont's estate, open from May–November. It's on Rockland Road between Delaware 141 and U.S. 202. Arrange a mansion tour by calling 302-651-6912.

Take a tour of Winterthur Museum and Gardens located on Delaware 52, 6 miles northwest of Wilmington. The museum sponsors annual Point-to-Point races in May, featuring steeplechases, pony races, and a parade of horse-drawn antique coaches and carriages. For information, call 302-888-6800 or 1-800-448-3883.

Rockwood Museum is on 610 Shipley Road in Wilmington. Guided tours of the mansion are given Tuesday–Saturday from 11:00–3:00 except on holidays. Special events here include a mid-July Old Fashioned Ice Cream Festival and a Victorian Christmas. For information, call 302-571-7776.

Take a ride aboard an authentic turn-of-the-century steam train through historic Red Clay Valley. It departs from Greenbank Station on Delaware 41. For information, call 302-998-1930.

Kalmar Nyckel Shipyard and Museum is at 823 East 7th in Wilmington. Tour the heritage park's museum and shipyard. For information, call 302-429-SHIP.

In nearby Pennsylvania, visit Brandywine Battlefield in Chadds Ford, site of a Revolutionary War battle. For information, call 215-459-3342.

Longwood Gardens on U.S. 1 north of Kennett Square has year-round displays in 20 indoor conservatories and on 1,050 acres of outdoor gardens and woodlands. It features evening fountain displays and theatrical performances from June–August, year-round concerts, and a chrysanthemum festival in November. For details, call 215-388-6741.

While in Chadds Ford, visit Brandywine River Museum, one block southwest of Delaware 100 on U.S. 1. Request a guided tour Monday–Friday. Call 215-388-7601.

INFORMATION
Bellevue State Park
800 Car Road
Wilmington, Delaware 19809
302-577-3390

BRANDYWINE CREEK STATE PARK
2

LOCATION - The park is 3 miles northwest of Wilmington at the intersection of Delaware 100 and Delaware 92. The park entrance is on Adams Dam Road.

ACTIVITIES - Hikers have 12 miles of trails, including Tulip Tree Trail with 190-year-old tulip poplars. Canoe down the Brandywine River or play disc golf on the eighteen-hole course. Equestrians can ride the equestrian trails. Anglers come to Wilson's Run to fish for trout in early spring. A trout stamp is required.

Tour the nature center open year-round and attend a naturalist program. Freshwater Marsh is Delaware's first dedicated nature preserve and is home to an elusive bog turtle.

INFORMATION
Brandywine Creek State Park
P.O. Box 3782
Wilmington, Delaware 19807
302-577-3534
302-655-5740 (nature center)

CAPE HENLOPEN STATE PARK
3

LOCATION - The park is one mile east of Lewes on Delaware 9 along a sandy peninsula called Delaware's "hook" that divides Delaware Bay and Atlantic Ocean. It's near the boarding station for the Cape May-Lewes ferry.

FEATURES - Cape Henlopen has the highest sand dune between Cape Hatteras and Cape Cod. Called the Great Dune, it rises 80 feet above the shore.

ACTIVITIES - The park is the state's largest, covering 3,270 acres and boasting 4 miles of beach along the Atlantic Ocean. Go swimming, crabbing, and surf fishing. Swim from the guarded beach and purchase a snack from the concession stand. Camp in the 159-site campground from April–October with water hookups and a dumping station.

Hike nature trails, including Pinelands Nature Trail, a designated national recreation trail, and Seaside Nature Trail. Stroll along the park's famous "walking dunes." Go fishing in Delaware Bay from the pier, play disc golf on the nine-hole course, and play tennis, basketball, softball, and hockey. Enjoy a scenic view from the observation platform near the picnic pavilion.

Attend a program at Seaside Nature Center's aquarium, which is open year-round. For details, call 302-645-6852. Camp in the campground and climb the restored tower used during World War II to locate enemy ships. It's open from April–October.

Each May, peaking with the full moon/high tide, thousands of horseshoe crabs come to the shores of Delaware Bay to breed. This attracts countless migratory shorebirds who come to feast on the hatchlings as they trek towards the water.

Visit Lewes Historic Complex on Shipcarpenter Street and West Third. Walking tours begin from the Thompson Store. The complex is open mid-June through Labor Day, Tuesday–Saturday. For information and tours, call Lewes Historical Society, 302-645-7670.

Queen Anne's Railroad has an authentic steam engine that operates from its station in Lewes west of Stango Park. Regular 50-minute trips run from mid-June through Labor Day and a dinner train goes on weekend evenings from May until New Year's. For information, call 302-644-1720.

Take a cruise aboard the tall ship *Jolly Rover*, operating from Lewes 1812 Memorial Park. For details, call 302-645-8073. Sunset cruises also depart from Fisherman's Wharf every day during July through Labor Day and weekends in the spring and fall. For information, call 302-645-8862. Dolphin and whale watching expeditions also leave from the wharf.

Canoeists have over 7 miles of canoe trails in Prime Hook National Wildlife Refuge, 8 miles north of Lewes on Delaware 1. Fish the streams and designated ponds for bass and pickerel. For information, call 302-684-8419.

INFORMATION
Cape Henlopen State Park
42 Cape Henlopen Drive
Lewes, Delaware 19958
302-645-8983
302-645-2103 (campground)
302-645-6852 (nature center)

DELAWARE SEASHORE STATE PARK
4

LOCATION - The park begins 2 miles south of Rehoboth Beach on Delaware 1.

ACTIVITIES - Delaware Seashore State Park covers 1,851 acres. Visitors have access to over 5 miles of ocean beach and access to calm inland bay waters. Go swimming from lifeguarded areas, surfing on the north side of the Indian River Inlet, and surf fishing for sea trout, bluefish, and flounder. Enjoy crabbing and clamming. Purchase a snack at the snack bars.

Go sailboarding, windsurfing, and sailing in Rehoboth Bay and Indian River. Boaters have full services at the Indian River Marina north of the inlet. Boats have year-round access to the Atlantic Ocean, Indian River Inlet, and Inland Bays.

Camp in the 434-site campground south of Indian River Inlet from mid-March through mid-November with 145 sites offering full hookups and a dumping station. Watch for American bald eagles.

Annual events in Rehoboth Beach include the Rehoboth Beach Easter Promenade on Easter Sunday, Rehoboth Beach Kids Convention and Parade of Wheels the second Saturday in May, and Rehoboth Beach's Sandcastle Contest the second weekend in July.

Bethany Beach's bandstand at Garfield Parkway and Pennsylvania Avenue has summer musical programs and theater productions. For details, call 302-539-8011. Outdoor concerts are also presented at Rehoboth Beach Memorial Bandstand on the Boardwalk on Rehoboth Avenue summer weekend nights. For details, call 302-227-6181.

Take a sea kayak tour of Rehoboth Bay, Indian River Bay, Assawoman Bay, Assateague Island, Trap Pond, or Trussom Pond. Tours leave from Millville, 3½ miles west of Bethany on Delaware 26. For information, call 302-539-2339.

INFORMATION
Delaware Seashore State Park
Inlet 850
Rehoboth Beach, Delaware 19971
302-227-2800
302-539-7202 (campground)
302-227-3071 (Indian River Marina)

FENWICK ISLAND STATE PARK
5

LOCATION - The park is near Fenwick Island, 3½ miles south of South Bethany Beach on Delaware 1, close to Ocean City, Maryland.

ACTIVITIES - Visitors have access to 3 miles of Atlantic seashore. Go swimming from the guarded beach, surf from the beach north of the swimming area, and surf fish for bluefish, sea trout, kingfish, and flounder. Each fall, anglers compete in a local fishing tournament. Go boating in Little Assawoman Bay. Purchase snacks from the concession stand.

Fenwick Island Lighthouse is off Delaware 54 on Fenwick Island. The historic lighthouse began operations in 1859. It's open two Wednesdays a month. For information, call 301-250-1098. Look for the Transpeninsular Marker erected on April 26, 1751, on the south side of the lighthouse. The stone marks the east end of the 70-mile-long Transpeninsular Line that connects the Atlantic Ocean and the Chesapeake Bay.

INFORMATION
Fenwick Island State Park
c/o Holts Landing State Park
P.O. Box 76
Millville, Delaware 19970
302-539-9060
302-539-1055 (summers only)

FORT DELAWARE STATE PARK
6

LOCATION - The park is on Pea Patch Island in the Delaware River and is only accessible by boat. Boats depart weekends from 11:00–6:00 every 30 minutes from the foot of Clinton Street in Delaware City, north of the Chesapeake and Delaware Canal.

ACTIVITIES - Fort Delaware, used as a federal prison during the Civil War, is open weekends and holidays from the last weekend in April through the last weekend in September from 11:00–6:00. In July and August, the fort is open Wednesday–Friday from 11:00–4:00. Tour the museum to see Civil War memorabilia and watch an audio-visual presentation. Attend summer performances on the parade grounds. Refreshments are available.

Take a nature walk north of the fort and watch for egrets, herons, and ibis in the island's nature preserve, the largest wading bird nesting area found on the East Coast. Go fishing or take a chartered cruise on the *Delafort* passenger ferry on the Chesapeake and Delaware Canal from April–October. For information, call 302-834-7941.

Polish Day is celebrated at the fort on the second Sunday in June.

In Port Penn, visit the Port Penn Interpretive Center at Market and Liberty, 5 miles south of Fort Delaware. It's open May–September, Wednesday–Friday from 9:00–5:00.

INFORMATION
Fort Delaware State Park
P.O. Box 170
Delaware City, Delaware 19706
302-834-7941

HOLTS LANDING STATE PARK
7

LOCATION - The park is 9 miles northeast of Dagsboro on the south shore of Indian River Bay. If coming from Delaware 1, go west on Delaware 26. Follow signs to Delaware 346.

ACTIVITIES - Go boating in the shallow bay from the small boat-launching ramp. Enjoy windsurfing, fishing, clamming, and crabbing.

INFORMATION
Holts Landing State Park
P.O. Box 76
Millville, Delaware 19970
302-539-9060

KILLENS POND STATE PARK
8

LOCATION - The park is 13 miles south of Dover off U.S. 13.

ACTIVITIES - Tour the mill pond in a pontoon boat and go bass fishing and non-motorized boating with rentals available. Swim in the guarded pool and hike Pondside Nature Trail.

Play golf on the eighteen-hole disc golf course. Camp in the 59-site campground with water and electrical hookups, open year-round. You can also stay in one of the 6 camping cabins. Tour the visitor center and attend an interpretive program.

Attend Killens Pond State Park Country Jamboree held the last Saturday in September.

INFORMATION
Killens Pond State Park
R.D. 1, Box 858
Felton, Delaware 19943
302-284-4526
302-284-3412 (campground)

LUMS POND STATE PARK
9

LOCATION - The pond is 10 miles south of Newark off Delaware 896.

ACTIVITIES - Lums Pond covers 1,757 acres and has the state's largest freshwater pond. Anglers come to fish for bass, bluegill, crappie, catfish, and pickerel. Go boating from the ramp or pier. Swim from the guarded beach. Rent a boat from the full-service Summit North Marina on the Chesapeake and Delaware Canal.

Take a hike or horseback ride on trails through the fields and forest. Work out on the fitness trail. Play horseshoes, basketball, tennis, volleyball, badminton, and shuffleboard. Golfers can play on the eighteen-hole disc golf course. Food service is available.

Stop by the nature center to see their "wall of bees" and take a naturalist-guided hike. Camp in the 68-site campground with a dumping station from April–October. During the winter, go cross-country skiing or snowmobiling.

INFORMATION
Lums Pond State Park
1068 Howell School Road
Bear, Delaware 19701
302-368-6989
302-836-1800 (Summit North Marina)

TRAP POND STATE PARK
10

LOCATION - The pond is 5 miles southeast of Laurel off Delaware 24 and one mile southwest on Delaware 449.

FEATURES - The park contains the Great Cypress Swamp.

ACTIVITIES - Hike nature and pond trails and go horseback riding along the equestrian trails. Go camping in the 132-site campground with water and electrical hookups and a dumping station from April–November. Take a pontoon boat ride or rent a boat to go boating and canoeing along the wilderness trail in Trap Pond.

Anglers can fish for bass, crappie, bluegill, perch, and pickerel. Take a pontoon boat ride or rent a boat. Go swimming from the guarded beach. Vending machines provide snacks.

INFORMATION
Trap Pond State Park
R.D. 2, Box 331
Laurel, Delaware 19956
302-875-5153
302-875-2392 (campground)

WALTER S. CARPENTER JR. STATE PARK
11

LOCATION - The park is 3 miles north of Newark on Delaware 896.

ACTIVITIES - The park covers 1,164 acres. Play golf on the nine-hole disc course, work out on the physical fitness trail, hike the nature trail, or go horseback riding along equestrian trails. White Clay Creek Preserve and visitor center is adjacent to the park. Fish in either the state park pond or in White Clay Creek, which is stocked annually with trout. Hike to a granite marker on the Delaware-Pennsylvania line. Tour the visitor center and attend an interpretive program. During the winter, go cross-country skiing and sledding.

INFORMATION
Walter S. Carpenter Jr. State Park
425 Wedgewood Road
Newark, Delaware 19711
302-731-1310
302-368-6900

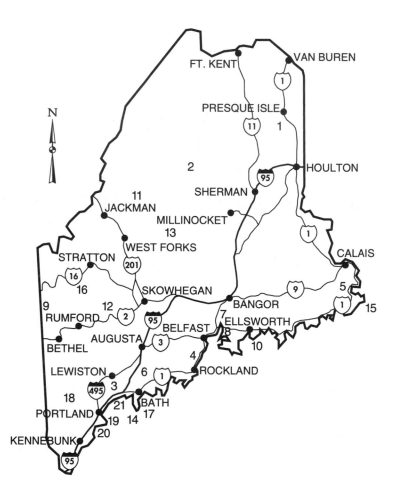

MAINE

Maine has one of the most comfortable summer climates in the continental U.S. with highs generally around 70 degrees. It is almost as big as all of the other five New England states combined. Mount Katahdin in Baxter State Park rises 5,268 feet above sea level and is the end point for hikers completing the entire Appalachian Trail.

The state has 6,000 lakes and ponds, 32,000 miles of rivers and streams, 17 million acres of forests, 3,478 miles of coastline, and 2,000 islands. The Rangeley Lakes region boasts 111 small lakes and ponds. To make reservations for state park campgrounds, except for Warren Island State Park, call 1-800-332-1501 (in-state) or 207-287-3824.

The Kennebec River runs through the center of the state and is a popular recreational area. The Forks, located in the Upper Kennebec Valley, is a major whitewater rafting center and is known among rafters for its exciting rapids and consistent water flow throughout the year. The Penobscot River flows through Ripogenus Gorge, falling 70 feet per minute to create tremendous whitewater rapids. Moosehead Lake is the largest single body of fresh water within any northeastern state and is a popular spot for fishing, water sports, and spectacular fall foliage.

Maine has 63 lighthouses, including the Portland Head Light commissioned by George Washington.

AROOSTOOK STATE PARK
1

LOCATION - The park is on Echo Lake, 8 miles south of Presque Isle off U.S. 1.

FEATURES - Aroostook was the starting point for the successful transatlantic balloon launch of Double Eagle II.

ACTIVITIES - Enjoy camping in one of the 29 campsites, trout fishing, boating from the ramp with rentals available, swimming from the guarded beach, and water skiing on Echo Lake. Bring along a picnic and go hiking up nearby Quaggy Jo Mountain. The mountain's North Peak Trail is 1¼ miles long and the South Peak is ¾ of a mile, but steep and rugged. For a longer hike, follow the 4-mile cross-country trail or climb Haystack Mountain.

During the winter, come to go cross-country skiing on 12 miles of marked, groomed trails and go snowmobiling. A ski shelter and park lodge are open during the day on weekends.

Tour nearby James School, a fully restored one-room schoolhouse. For information, call 207-768-8341.

Ninety-two-mile-long Allagash Wilderness Waterway has some very fast sections of white water for rafting and canoeing. Also enjoy water skiing, sailing, kayaking, and fishing. Go horseback riding, hiking, and golfing. For information on Allagash, contact the Bureau of Parks and Recreation in Augusta at 207-289-3821.

In Presque Isle, attend the Pioneer Playhouse Theater in June and July. Attend June Jubilee in mid-June, Northern Maine Fair in mid-August, or Fall Fest in mid-October. Snowmobile races are held in Presque Isle in January and February.

Attend the Crown of Maine's Hot Air Balloon Fest in nearby Caribou in July. For details, contact the Caribou Chamber of Commerce at 207-498-6156.

Incoming pilots can land at Northern Maine Regional on Presque Isle, located one mile northwest of town. Rental cars are available.

INFORMATION
Aroostook State Park
81 State Park Road
Presque Isle, Maine 04769
207-768-8341

BAXTER STATE PARK
2

LOCATION - The park has 9 separate areas and is north of Millinocket and west of Patten in north central Maine. Take I-95 to Medway and head west to Millinocket on Maine 11 to reach park headquarters.

FEATURES - Technically, Baxter State Park is not part of the state park system, but was named Baxter State Park when Governor Percival P. Baxter donated the land for the park in 1930.

The park is considered the fourth largest "state" park in the U.S. and covers over 314 square miles. It has 46 mountain peaks, 18 rising over 3,000 feet in elevation, many waterfalls, trout streams, plus 64 ponds and lakes. Its highest peak, Mount Katahdin, rises 5,267 feet and one of its ridges, Knife Edge, features a sheer drop of 2,000 feet. Many hikers finish trekking the length of the Appalachian Trail here.

ACTIVITIES - Baxter State Park has 8 campgrounds—7 accessible by car— with space for 700 campers and 30 remote campsites. Two campgrounds, Matagamon Lake and South Branch Pond, are only accessible by canoe. Eleven cabins are available at Daicey Pond and 12 are located at Kidney Pond. Russell Pond and Chimney Pond campgrounds are only accessible by foot trail. Because of the narrow roads, large trailers are prohibited.

Beginning with the 1992 camping season, no public water source will be available in the park because of increased federal water quality regulations. Campers should plan to bring their own water or treat park water prior to drinking it.

Enjoy pond fishing and rent a canoe at South Branch Pond, Russell Pond, and Daicey Pond. The use of motor boats and outboard motors is prohibited except on Matagamon and Webster lakes.

Hike up 3,122-foot South Turner Mountain. The 4-mile round trip begins from Roaring Brook Campground and passes Sandy Stream Pond where moose can often be seen feeding at dawn and dusk. In addition, the park is criss-crossed by approximately 175 miles of trails.

During the winter, cross-country ski and stay in a chain of four huts. Go snowmobiling on Matagamon and Webster lakes and on unplowed portions of the park roads.

Lumberman's Museum in Patten has nine buildings, including a working model of a saw mill, blacksmith shop, and 3,000 lumbering artifacts. It's located at the northern entrance to Baxter State Park and is open Memorial Day through September and weekends from October 1 through Columbus Day.

Incoming pilots can land at Millinocket Municipal Airport, located one mile southeast of town. No rental cars are available.

INFORMATION
Baxter State Park
64 Balsam Drive
Millinocket, Maine 04462
207-723-5140

BRADBURY MOUNTAIN STATE PARK
3

LOCATION - The park is 6 miles west from Freeport-Durham Exit 20 off I-95.

ACTIVITIES - A .3-mile-long trail leads up a gradual incline from the north-west corner of the park's picnic area to the top of 484-foot Bradbury Mountain. From the south summit, you get great views of the ocean and Casco Bay. Another trail goes to the north summit.

Camp in the 41-site campground. Cross-country ski in the winter.

INFORMATION
Bradbury Mountain State Park
Pownal, Maine 04069
207-688-4712

CAMDEN HILLS STATE PARK
4

LOCATION - The park is 2 miles north of Camden on U.S. 1 on the shore of Penobscot Bay in the Megunticook Mountains.

FEATURES - Rockland's lighthouse and 7/8-mile native granite breakwater were constructed in 1888.

ACTIVITIES - A 14-mile paved road leads to the summit of 900-foot Mount Battie, providing panoramic views of Penobscot Bay and Camden Harbor. The park has 30 miles of hiking trails. Hike up Mount Battie or 1,385-foot Mount Megunticook, highest of the Camden Hills. Hike to Maiden Cliff, a rock outcrop rising 800 feet above Megunticook Lake. Ridge Trail's 2.5-mile-long hike provides great views of the ocean, mountains, and lake.

Visitors also have access to both salt- and freshwater beaches. Enjoy a picnic and go camping in one of the 112 campsites with a dump station from May 15–October 15.

During the winter, go snowmobiling along 10 miles of trails. The park has no groomed cross-country ski trails.

Curtis Island Lighthouse is at the end of a mile-long breakwater where you can walk in calm weather. Take a schooner boat ride given daily or for a week-long cruise from Rockland Harbor. State-run ferries make regular runs from the Rockland Public Landing to two islands in Penobscot Bay.

In Rockland, visit Shore Village Museum at 104 Limerock Street to see the largest collection of lighthouse and Coast Guard artifacts in the U.S. It's open daily from June–October. For information, call 207-594-4950.

Rockland's main street is listed in the National Register of Historic Places. Sea captains and famous celebrities have shopped here for over 150 years. Pick up a map from the Chamber of Commerce, located on the boat landing on Commercial Street, to take a self-guided tour.

Tour Merryspring Garden from May–November from 9:00–6:00. It's at the end of Conway Road off Maine 1. For information, call 207-236-4885.

Watch the annual Great Schooner Race in Rockland over July 4th. For accompanying activities, contact the Chamber of Commerce at 207-596-0376. Rockland is known as the Lobster Capital of the World and holds a Maine Lobster Festival in early August featuring a parade, road races, a lobster eating contest, and a lobster crate race. For details, call 207-594-5199.

Many come to Camden to go sailing, windsurfing, and water skiing both on the ocean and on nearby lakes. Windjammer cruises are available during the summer from Sharp's Wharf next to Camden Town landing.

Attend performances by the Camden Shakespeare Company in July. For information, call 207-236-7595. Attend the fall festival in early October and Christmas by the Sea in early December.

Incoming pilots can land at County Regional Airport in Rockland, 12 miles south of Camden. Car rentals are available.

INFORMATION
Camden Hills State Park
SCR 60, Box 3110
Belfast Road
Camden, Maine 04843
207-236-3109

COBSCOOK BAY STATE PARK
5

LOCATION - The park is 6 miles south of Dennysville on U.S. 1 and is surrounded on three sides by Cobscook Bay.

FEATURES - Cobscook is an Indian name meaning "boiling tide." Here you can observe the highest tides in the U.S. with 24-foot tidal currents.

ACTIVITIES - Many of the 107 campsites with a trailer dump station are located beside the water. The campground is open from mid-May through mid-October.

Visitors can go deep sea fishing, sailing, boating, kayaking, scuba diving, golfing, hiking, and bicycle riding around the island. During the winter, cross-country ski on unplowed park roads and along the shore of Cobscook Bay. Adjacent Moosehead National Wildlife Refuge also has cross-country skiing along the refuge roads. Call 207-454-3521 for information.

Witness the power of the Old Sow, the second largest whirlpool in the world. It's visible from Dog Island, Harris Cove, and Deer Island or from on board a commercial boat.

Franklin D. Roosevelt International Park contains Franklin and Eleanor Roosevelt's summer cottage. It's on Campobello Island in New Brunswick. Stop by Pleasant Point Indian Reservation of the Passamaquoddy Tribe to see their arts and crafts. Visit Reversing Falls Park, located northeast of the park.

Watch for bald eagles and osprey in Edmund's Unit of Moosehorn National Wildlife Refuge, bordering the park on the west. Dig for clams in the flats and kayak the bay and its channels. Because of high tides, kayakers should be experienced and prepared for surf running like a river.

Fish for mackerel in the Atlantic. Drive 18 miles southeast to the cliffs at Quoddy Head, the easternmost point on the mainland. Observe the sea creatures at Quoddy Tides Aquarium.

Stroll along the red granite seawall in Eastport's historic district where many buildings are listed on the National Register of Historic Places. Canoe the Dennys and Pennamaquam rivers or hike the Shackford Head State Trail.

Incoming pilots can land at Eastport Municipal Airport. No fuel is available and some local motels provide courtesy ground transportation.

INFORMATION
Cobscook Bay State Park
Dennysville, Maine 04628
207-726-4412

CRESCENT BEACH STATE PARK
See under TWO LIGHTS STATE PARK

FORT EDGECOMB STATE PARK
6

LOCATION - The park overlooks the Sheepscot River on the south end of Davis Island. Take U.S. 1 south to the Edgecomb end of Wiscasset Bridge and turn right.

FEATURES - The park features a timbered fort constructed in 1809 to protect Wiscasset, once the most important shipping center north of Boston.

ACTIVITIES - Enjoy a picnic and tour the restored fort and octagonal blockhouse open May 30 through Labor Day. Attend an interpretive program and bring along a picnic. Watch for harbor seals along the Sheepscot River.

In nearby Boothbay, visit the historic Railway Village on Maine 27 from mid-June through mid-October. Take a ride on the steam train and see an antique auto and truck exhibit. The village has 28 display buildings, including the 1847 Town Hall and 1911 vintage Railroad Station. For details, call 207-633-4727.

Visit the Kenneth E. Stoddard Shell Museum on Hardwick Road, Boothbay, to see one of the world's largest private collections. It's housed inside the covered bridge behind Dolphin Mini-Golf. For information, call 207-633-4828.

Tour the Musical Wonder House at 18 High Street to see antique musical instruments. Guided tours are offered daily 10:00–5:00 from Memorial Day through Labor Day and by appointment only after Labor Day through October 15. To make a reservation to hear a summer concert, call 207-882-7163.

Go whitewater rafting on the Kennebec, Dead, and Penobscot rivers from April–October. For details, call 1-800-766-7238. Go on an ocean kayak tour or rent a mountain bike from the Tidal Transit Company in the Granary Way Building near the footbridge. For details, call 207-633-7140.

Additional boating options are available on the New Meadows River, Sheepscot River, Merrymeeting Bay, or in Casco Bay. Boat rentals are available in Boothbay Harbor. Boat cruises leave from Shore Road in Edgecomb. For information, call 702-882-7909.

From Boothbay Harbor, you can go out on an excursion boat, ride aboard a working lobster boat and assist in harvesting, or go out in a windjammer. Rent a kayak, go saltwater fishing, and go canoeing or sailboarding. Stay overnight on your own private yacht, a floating B & B. Attend the annual four-day Windjammer Days festival in late June or Friendship Sloop Days in late July.

Several lighthouses in the Boothbay Harbor region date back to the 1800s. Visit Owls Head Transportation Museum where many special events are held throughout the summer months. For schedules, call 207-594-4418.

Visit Dodge Point Preserve State Park on River Road near Newcastle on the Damariscotta River. The park features 500 acres of forest, deep-water access, three beaches, and hiking trails.

Arriving pilots can land at Wiscasset Airport, 3 miles southwest of Wiscasset, where you can take a scenic coastal plane ride. Rental cars are available.

INFORMATION

Fort Edgecomb State Park
Edgecomb, Maine 04556
207-882-7777

Chamber of Commerce
P.O. Box 356
Boothbay Harbor, Maine 04538
207-633-2353

FORT KNOX STATE PARK
7

LOCATION - The park is on Maine 174 across the Penobscot River from the town of Bucksport and one mile north from U.S. 1, west of the Waldo-Hancock Bridge.

FEATURES - The fort, high on a bluff overlooking the river, was built in the 1840s with granite from Mount Waldo, in anticipation of war with Great Britain. It was manned during the Civil War and Spanish-American War.

ACTIVITIES - Bring along a flashlight to walk through its subterranean network of tunnels and fortifications. Either take a self-guided tour or a scheduled guided tour and attend interpretive programs.

INFORMATION

Fort Knox State Park
Prospect, Maine 04669
207-469-7719

FORT POINT STATE PARK
8

LOCATION - The park is off U.S. 1, east of Stockton Springs on the tip of a peninsula in Penobscot Bay.

FEATURES - The park is adjacent to historic Fort Pownall, constructed in 1759. To prevent its being taken intact by American patriots, the British burned the fort twice, so that today only earthworks remain. The fort has displays, a lighthouse, and picnicking spots.

Square-towered Fort Point Lighthouse, a state historic site, overlooks Penobscot Bay. Follow Squaw Point Road next to Fort Point State Park to reach the lighthouse.

ACTIVITIES - Come to tour the fort, go fishing from the 200-foot pier, and enjoy a picnic.

INFORMATION
Fort Point State Park
Stockton Springs, Maine 04981
207-236-4617

GRAFTON NOTCH STATE PARK
9

LOCATION - Grafton Notch is on Maine 36 between Upton and Newry.

FEATURES - The park, located at the base of the Mahoosuc Mountains, features Mother Walker Falls, Moose Cave, Step Falls, and the famed Screw Auger Falls where the swirling water of Bear River has worn holes up to 25 feet deep. Old Speck, fourth highest mountain in Maine, and the Baldpate Mountains are separated by Grafton Notch.

ACTIVITIES - The park is well known for its challenging hiking trails, including the Appalachian Trail that enters the state here en route for a 276-mile trek to the summit of Mount Katahdin. Step Falls, located in a preserve of the Nature Conservancy next to the park, is reached by a trail that leaves from Maine 26. Hike to granite ledges overlooking Old Speck Mountain.

Other hiking trails include Moose Cave, Table Rock Trail with a steep one-mile climb up Baldpate Mountain, and Eye Brow Loop that passes Cascade Falls, Old Speck, and Baldpate Mountains. A 4-mile trail up Old Speck Mountain is on Maine 26 north of Bethel and 3 miles north of Screw Auger Falls.

Go fishing or enjoy a picnic at Screw Auger Falls where you can go deep pool swimming in Bear River. At Mother Walker Falls Gorge, a short distance north from Screw Auger, you can cross natural stone bridges and hike easy trails following the 900-foot gorge.

Mountain bicyclists can take a lift up to Sunday River's ski trails from mid-June through Columbus Day weekend. For information, call Sunday River at 207-824-3000. Mountain bike rentals are available in town. Hikers can also ride up the lift, but should be prepared to hike back down the mountain.

Take a scenic auto tour loop through the state park to Errol, New Hampshire, and back to Bethel through Berlin. You pass two spectacular waterfalls, the Cataracts and Dunn falls. Pick up a map at the Bethel Chamber of Commerce.

Photographers come to shoot Artists Bridge, Sunday River's covered bridge located a short distance beyond Sunday River's access road. Constructed in 1870, it's also accessible from the Sunday River cross-country ski trails.

During the winter, downhill skiers have access to Sunday River near Bethel and Mount Abram, which is 5 miles south of Bethel on Maine 26 in Locke Mills. Cross-country skiers can go to Sunday River Inn, Bethel Inn and Country Club, or to Carter's Cross-Country Ski Center, all located in Bethel. Snowmobiles have access to many miles of trails in the Bethel area.

Annual events include many cross-country ski races, Mollyockett Day held the third Saturday in July, Sudbury Canada Days held the second weekend in August, and a blueberry festival also held in August. In April, attend Pole, Paddle and Paw, an April Fool's Day race using skis, canoes, and snowshoes, held at Sunday River Cross-Country Ski Center. For information, call 207-824-2410.

Small plane pilots can land at Col Dyke Field 2 miles northwest of Bethel. Taxis are available.

INFORMATION
Grafton Notch State Park
Bethel, Maine 04217
207-824-2912

LAMOINE STATE PARK
10

LOCATION - The park is 8 miles southeast of Ellsworth on Maine 184 on Frenchman's Bay.

FEATURES - The park has frontage along Frenchman Bay providing stunning views of Cadillac Mountain in Acadia National Park.

ACTIVITIES - Go camping in one of 61 campsites and fishing, boating, and swimming in the bay.

Visit Acadia National Park, located on the Schoodic Peninsula on Mount Desert Island, which is accessible via Maine 186. Take Park Loop Road, a 20-mile scenic drive that takes you past the park's lakes, seashore, and to the summit of 1,530-foot Cadillac Mountain.

Hikers have access to over 120 miles of hiking trails or 50 miles of graded carriage roads shared with equestrians. Tour the visitor center or camp in one of the campgrounds. Go swimming from Sand Beach. For park information, call 207-288-3338.

Take a boat cruise from Bar Harbor. To go on a whale watching trip, call 207-288-9776. Cruise to Nova Scotia aboard the M/V *Bluenose*. For information, call 1-800-432-7344 in Maine or 1-800-341-7981 outside Maine. Working lobster boat excursions are also available from the harbor.

Attend Bar Harbor Music Festival held in July and August. Tour Jackson Laboratory, 1½ miles south of Bar Harbor on Maine 3. The nationally known cancer research institute offers a lecture and audiovisual presentation from mid-June through late August. For details, call 207-288-3371. Go soaring over the area from the Bar Harbor/Trenton Airport.

Winter Harbor on Schoodic Point hosts an annual lobster festival the second weekend in August. Prospect Harbor Light, built in 1891, is nearby.

In Ellsworth, tour the Black House located on West Main off U.S. 1. It was constructed in the 1820s and was occupied by the Black family for three generations. Its carriage house has nineteenth-century carriages and sleighs. For information, call 207-667-8671.

You can also tour the Stanwood Homestead Museum and Birdsacre Sanctuary located in Ellsworth, south of Maine 3 and U.S. 1. The homestead was constructed in 1850 and the sanctuary's 100 acres has nature trails to explore. For information, call 207-667-8460.

The Franciscan Monastery, located off Maine 9, has beautifully landscaped grounds and a woodland walk down to the river. It's open daily from sunrise to sunset.

Incoming pilots can land at Hancock County/Bar Harbor Airport.

INFORMATION
Lamoine State Park
Ellsworth, Maine 04605
207-667-4778

LILY BAY STATE PARK
11

LOCATION - The park is 8 miles north of Greenville on the east shore of 40-mile-long Moosehead Lake.

FEATURES - Moosehead Lake is the largest lake completely contained within one state. Much of Moosehead Lake's 400 miles of shoreline are inaccessible except by boat, canoe, or floatplane. Greenville is the largest seaplane base on the East Coast.

Moosehead is listed among the best freshwater fishing areas in the U.S. and has trout and landlocked salmon. Many moose inhabit the area, and it's not uncommon to see as many as 30 of these magnificent animals in a single day.

ACTIVITIES - Lily Bay State Park offers boating, swimming, picnicking, and bicycling. Camp in one of 89 campsites or rent a houseboat in Rockwood. For information, call 207-534-7711. Enjoy fishing in Lily Bay Lake or in the Moose River for spring salmon. Kennebec and Moose rivers are considered two great brook trout and salmon fishing spots in mid-summer.

Watch for moose along the shoreline. Moosehead Lake's Chamber of Commerce in Greenville has an annual "Moosemania" from mid-May through mid-June when visitors attend informative forums, moose safaris, and cruises. Be sure to check the chamber office's map for the latest moose sightings. For information, call 207-695-2702.

Canoeists come to Moosehead Lake and to the Allagash, St. John, Moose, Penobscot, and Kennebec rivers. The famous 46-mile "Bow Trip" on the Moose River is a favorite wilderness canoe trip. Go whitewater rafting on the Penobscot and Kennebec rivers. Whitewater expeditions leave from town May 15–October 15. For information, call 207-534-7709 or 1-800-346-4666.

Enjoy hiking in the mountains and along cross-country ski trails. Climb Mount Kineo and its fire tower where Indians once collected flint for their arrows. Climb Little Squaw Mountain beginning from the Greenwood Motel on Maine 15. Ride the chair lift up Squaw Mountain.

Golfers can play a nine-hole course at Squaw Mountain Village. For a tee-off time, call 207-695-3609.

Take a flying tour with bush pilots on their routine fire patrols or over the Allagash Wilderness and Mount Katahdin. The International Seaplane Fly-In on Moosehead Lake features the largest gathering of seaplanes in the Northeast. It's on the weekend after Labor Day. Call 207-695-2778 for information.

Photographers, hunters, and anglers can hire guides in Rockwood. For information, call 207-534-7709 or 1-800-346-4666. Walk through the Moosehead Marine Museum. Take a sightseeing tour on Moosehead Lake on the SS *Katahdin*, a restored steam vessel. For information, call 207-695-2716.

During the winter, go ice fishing for trout and salmon. Several ice fishing derbies occur in Greenville and Rockwood. March brings their annual Sled Dog Races. Go downhill and cross-country skiing on 25 miles of maintained trails at Squaw Mountain. Cross-country skiing is also available at the Birches Cross-Country Ski Center or at Moosehead Nordic Ski Center. Snowmobiles have access to 200 miles of groomed trails in the Jackman region, plus connecting trails into Canada or other parts of Maine.

Incoming pilots can land at Greenville Municipal Airport 2 miles east of town. No rental cars are available.

INFORMATION
Lily Bay State Park
Greenville, Maine 04441
207-695-2700

MOUNT BLUE STATE PARK
12

LOCATION - The park is 10 miles northwest of Wilton off Maine 156. From Weld, follow signs on Center Hill Road to reach the park.

FEATURES - Mount Blue State Park is divided into two areas. Center Hill is east of Maine 156 and the camping area is west of Maine 156 on Webb Lake.

ACTIVITIES - Part of the park lies in the town of Avon and has boat rentals and a launching ramp. The campground has 136 campsites, 75 with full hook-ups. Adirondack shelters are available for large groups.

Anglers can fish in Lake Webb for black bass, perch, trout, and landlocked salmon. Attend interpretive programs in the amphitheater and participate in activities in the recreation hall. Guided hikes along the shoreline leave from the camping area. Swim from the beach and picnic at Center Hill for scenic lake views.

Park headquarters are north of town where you can hike 1½ miles to a fire tower located on the summit of 3,187-foot Mount Blue. A multiple-use trail system covers 24 miles in the park's Center Hill and is open to hikers, equestrians, mountain bikes, and ATVs. For trail information, call 207-585-2261.

The park has 15 miles of groomed cross-country ski trails through the woods and along unplowed roads. The main network leaves from the Center Hill parking area. Park snowmobile trails are groomed regularly and provide access to 55 miles of trails winding through Maine's rugged western mountains that connect Mount Blue State Park and Rangeley Lake State Park.

Rangeley Municipal Airport is 2 miles northwest of town and rental cars are available.

INFORMATION
Mount Blue State Park
Weld, Maine 04285
207-585-2347

PEAKS–KENNY STATE PARK
13

LOCATION - The park is on the south shore of 10-mile-long Sebec Lake, 6 miles north of Dover–Foxcroft on Maine 153.

ACTIVITIES - Camp in the wooded 56-site campground with a trailer dump station from mid-May through mid-September. Go swimming in Lake Sebec from the guarded beach. Hike and fish for trout, salmon, and bass. Go boating with rentals available and attend amphitheater programs.

In Dover–Foxcroft, tour Blacksmith Shop Museum to see original tools of the trade.

Incoming pilots can land at Dover–Foxcroft's Charles A. Chase Jr. Memorial Field, located one mile southwest of the city. No rental cars are available.

INFORMATION
Peaks–Kenny State Park
RFD 1, Box 48K
Dover–Foxcroft, Maine 04926
207-564-2003

POPHAM BEACH STATE PARK
14

LOCATION - Follow Maine 209 south for 14 miles from Bath to Phippsburg and then follow park signs.

FEATURES - Popham Beach is considered to be among the top ten beaches in the Northeast.

ACTIVITIES - Take a coastal hike and climb Morse Mountain. Get views of an estuary, Seguin, Fox, and Heron islands, and Mount Washington in New Hampshire. Enjoy a picnic, go deep sea and shore fishing, or swimming in the ocean.

On Wednesday evenings during July, attend outdoor family concerts on the Brunswick Town mall. Maine State Music Theater presents musicals in Pickard Theater on Bowdoin College campus in Brunswick from mid-June through late August. For details, call 207-725-8769. For information on the Bowdoin Summer Music Festival held on campus, call 207-725-3321.

Harriet Beecher Stowe's house, where the author wrote *Uncle Tom's Cabin*, is nearby. Thomas Point Beach hosts an annual Thomas Point Beach Bluegrass Festival over Labor Day weekend.

Between 1862–92, Bath was the nation's fifth largest seaport and almost half of the United States' wooden sailing vessels were built here. Stroll through the Maine Maritime Museum at 243 Washington, along the banks of the Kennebec, to learn more about the area's shipbuilding. For information, call 207-443-1316. Attend Bath's Heritage Days over the July 4th weekend. For details, contact the Chamber of Commerce at 207-443-9751.

Fort Popham is 15 miles from Bath on Maine 209. It was begun in 1861 for use during the Civil War, but never completed. Climb the circular staircase in the unfinished granite fortification to the towers. From the fort, you can see Seguin Island and Lighthouse. The lighthouse was erected in 1795 and is Maine's second oldest. Squirrel Point Lighthouse is visible across the Kennebec River off Maine 209 at Phippsburg.

Take a walking tour of historic Wiscasset. A scenic tourist train leaves Wiscasset daily in the summer. Stroll through Sunken Garden on Main Street. On the banks of the Sheepscot you can see two decaying, four-masted schooners beached here in 1932.

Incoming pilots can land at Wiscasset Airport, located 3 miles southwest of town. Rental cars are available.

INFORMATION
Popham Beach State Park
Route 209
Phippsburg, Maine 04562
207-389-1335

QUODDY HEAD STATE PARK
15

LOCATION - The park is south of Lubec, 4 miles off Maine 189.

FEATURES - Quoddy is located at the easternmost point in the U.S. Its prominent rock cliffs rise almost 100 feet above the ocean, where 28-foot tides ebb and flow every six hours.

ACTIVITIES - The park is open daily from the end of May through Labor Day and weekends until the end of October. Enjoy a picnic by West Quoddy Head Lighthouse above the entrance to Passamaquoddy Bay. Constructed in 1808, it's Maine's only red and white candy-striped tower and the easternmost lighthouse in the U.S. Hike the trail along rock cliffs 80 feet above the ocean or follow a boardwalk over a peat bog. Watch for whales offshore during their summer migration season.

West Quoddy Marine Research has a visitor center open all summer with whale exhibits, nature walks, and tours.

The Roosevelt International Bridge connects Lubec to Campobello Island, site of Franklin Delano Roosevelt's summer home. The 34-room "cottage" was occupied from 1905–21 and is open daily 9:00–5:00 from Memorial Day weekend through mid-October. The surrounding park land has over 8 miles of hiking trails. For information, call 506-752-2997.

Visit Reversing Falls Park's tidal channel at Pembroke, between Lubec and Eastport. At Eastport, attend the Salmon Festival and St. Elmo's Festival in Lubec.

Comb the beaches at Roque Bluffs State Park with both a freshwater swimming pond and beach by the Atlantic Ocean. Go salmon fishing and canoeing in the East Machias River. Cobscook Bay State Park offers camping and hiking. Take a charter boat to Machias Seal Island where puffin nest. Tour Maine Wild Blueberry Company in Machias. For information, call 207-255-8364. Attend the annual Machias Blueberry Festival the third weekend in August. Chamber concerts are presented at Centre Street Church in Machias Tuesday evenings in July through early August.

Incoming pilots can land at Lubec Municipal, located 2 miles west of town. However, no rental cars are available.

INFORMATION
Quoddy Head State Park
Lubec, Maine 04652
207-764-2041

RANGELEY LAKE STATE PARK
16

LOCATION - The park is north of Rumford via Maine 17 and northwest of Farmington via Maine 4 on the south shore of Rangeley Lake.

FEATURES - Rangeley Lake State Park has 1.2 miles of shoreline along Rangeley Lake and encompasses 111 small lakes and ponds.

ACTIVITIES - Rangeley Lake is famous for its trout and landlocked salmon fishing. In addition, over forty trout and salmon lakes and ponds are located within 10 miles of the park.

Enjoy a picnic and camping in one of 50 campsites with a trailer dump station. Go swimming and boating from the ramp. No boat rentals are available in the park, but are nearby.

Annual activities include a Fourth of July picnic and fireworks display, sidewalk art show, blueberry and logging festivals, plus auctions and concerts. In late July, attend Logging Museum Field Days. For details, contact the Chamber of Commerce at 207-864-5364.

Maine's second largest ski area, Saddleback Ski Resort, is 8 miles east of Rangeley and has both alpine and cross-country skiing.

Snowmobiles have access to 150 miles of groomed trails winding through Maine's rugged western mountains that link Mount Blue and Rangeley Lake state parks.

Many hiking trails, including the Appalachian Trail, leave from the Rangeley area. Hike trails in Saddleback Ski Area and Summer Lake Preserve.

Nearby attractions include historic Fort Halifax and Katahdin Iron Works. Play eighteen holes of golf in Mingo Springs. Ride aboard the Sandy River and Rangeley Lakes narrow gauge railroad on the first and third Sundays from May–October.

Incoming pilots can land at Rangeley Municipal Airport, located 2 miles northwest of town. Rental cars are available. Take a scenic flight from here until ice-out, when you can lift off from Rangeley Lake.

INFORMATION
Rangeley Lake State Park
HC 32, Box 5000
Rangeley, Maine 04970
207-864-3858

REID STATE PARK
17

LOCATION - Follow Maine 127 south from Woolwich for 14 miles to Georgetown. Continue east from here to reach the park entrance.

ACTIVITIES - Enjoy a picnic, go hiking along 1½ miles of sand beach along the ocean, or climb the sand dunes. Explore the marshes and go canoeing in Griffith's Head area. Go swimming either in a warm impounded saltwater lagoon or in the ocean. Snacks are available. Newman Wildlife Reserve has wooded and shoreline trails to hike.

INFORMATION
Reid State Park
Route 127
Georgetown, Maine 04548
207-371-2303

SEBAGO LAKE STATE PARK
18

LOCATION - The park is 3 miles south of Naples off U.S. 302.

FEATURES - Sebago Lake, 400 feet deep in places, is Maine's second largest lake and has 1,300 lakefront acres on both sides of the Songo River. Historic Songo Lock, built in 1830, links the north end of Long Lake, Sebago Lake, and Portland Harbor and was part of the Cumberland-Oxford Canal. Songo Lock still provides passage between Sebago Lake and Long Lake for recreational boaters.

ACTIVITIES - Enjoy picnicking, boating from the ramp, hiking, fishing for salmon, and swimming from the guarded beach in the Casco section's day-use area. The Naples section has a 250-site campground with a trailer dump station.

Take a ride aboard the *Songo River Queen II*, a replica of the early Mississippi River paddlewheelers. For information, call 207-693-6861. Visitors to Naples can also enjoy float plane and parasail rides.

Naples Historical Society Museum has a slide presentation on the C&O Canal and old Sebago-Long Lake steamboats.

INFORMATION
Sebago Lake State Park
Naples, Maine 04055
207-693-6231

TWO LIGHTS STATE PARK
19
CRESCENT BEACH STATE PARK
20

LOCATION - Two Lights State Park is off Maine 77 in Cape Elizabeth.

Crescent Beach is 9 miles south of Portland off Maine 77 in Cape Elizabeth.

ACTIVITIES - Two Lights State Park is open from mid-April through November. Enjoy a picnic, go saltwater fishing, and stroll along the network of walkways constructed along the rocky headland. Look for the twin towers of Cape Elizabeth Lights, circa 1827, located on the southern extremity of Cape Elizabeth. From nearby ledges, watch lobster men hauling in their traps.

Come to Crescent Beach to go swimming in the ocean from the 4,000-foot beach and enjoy a picnic or purchase a snack.

Portland Head Light, built in 1791, is off Cape Elizabeth's shore road and is Maine's oldest lighthouse.

In Portland, tour Portland Museum of Art at 7 Congress Square. It has an extensive glass collection and contemporary works of art. For a schedule of events and exhibitions, call 207-775-6148.

Two beautiful historic homes to tour in Portland include Victoria Mansion, 109 Danfort, and Wadsworth-Longfellow House, 487 Congress.

INFORMATION

Crescent Beach State Park`
Cape Elizabeth, Maine 04107
207-767-3625

Two Lights State Park
Cape Elizabeth, Maine 04107
207-799-5871

WOLF'S NECK WOODS STATE PARK
21

LOCATION - Follow Bow Street south off Maine 1 in Freeport.

ACTIVITIES - Attend nature programs and hike trails along Casco Bay and the Harraseeket River. Guided walks are conducted year-round.

Freeport is home of L.L. Bean, the "sportsman's outfitter," which is located on Main Street. The Desert of Maine is in Freeport off U.S. 1 and 95. Because of early farming practices, the top soil eroded and blew away, leaving almost 40 acres of fine sand that built huge sand dunes surrounded by a forest. Visitors can take narrated coach tours, hike nature trails, see the world's largest sand painting, and study 30 to 50 different kinds of mushrooms along a nature trail in the fall. For information, call 207-865-6962.

Bay cruises, seasonal trips to Eagle Island, and deep sea charters are available in South Freeport.

INFORMATION
Wolf's Neck Woods State Park
Freeport, Maine 04032
207-865-4465

MARYLAND

A *National Geographic* writer once referred to Maryland as "America in Miniature" because of its diverse geography. It boasts mountains, rolling farmlands, marshes, swamps, cliffs along Chesapeake Bay, and sandy beaches along the Atlantic Coast.

Southern Maryland is nestled between the Potomac River and the western shore of Chesapeake Bay. The area has many restored historic sites, scenic waterways for excellent boating, and wonderful seafood specialties. Here you can go crabbing and fishing for white perch, pike, bass, and flounder.

Ocean City is famous for its 3-mile-long boardwalk, charter boats, and bountiful sport fishing. It has long been called the "White Marlin Capital of the World." Joggers and hikers have access to a 10-mile stretch of sandy beach.

Maryland has an 8,000-mile-long shoreline, making it the ninth longest in the U.S. Over 500 sheltered harbors provide a haven for fishermen and recreational boats. The Chesapeake and Ohio Canal parallels the Potomac River and has locks, lockhouses, dams, aqueducts, mule barns, and remnants from earlier communities when the canal was active from 1828–1924. Today visitors come to hike and bicycle along the towpath, go canoeing, horseback riding, and fishing. The towpath is most accessible from Hancock, Williamsport, near the Shepherdstown bridge at Antietam Village and off Harper's Ferry Road.

For a unique experience, take a canal barge ride on board a replica nineteenth-century mule-drawn boat. You can board at Great Falls Tavern near Potomac, Maryland, at the C&O Canal National Historical Park. For information, call 301-299-2026.

Deep Creek Lake is the state's largest with 65 miles of shoreline. Lake Habeeb in Rocky Gap State Park has an extensive trail system, sailing, canoeing, and fishing.

Maryland is located along the Atlantic Flyway which extends from Alaska to Mexico. As a result, 5 percent of all America's continental waterfowl winter along the Chesapeake Bay shoreline and adjoining tidal marshes.

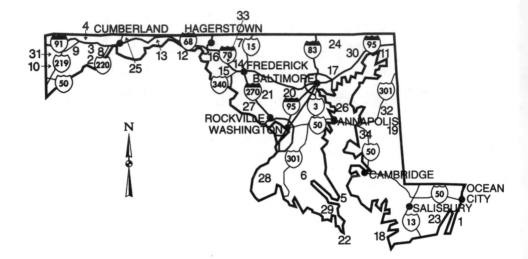

CUMBERLAND
HAGERSTOWN
FREDERICK
BALTIMORE
ROCKVILLE
WASHINGTON
ANNAPOLIS
CAMBRIDGE
OCEAN CITY
SALISBURY

N

Thirty-seven scenic miles of the Appalachian Trail, stretching from Maine to Georgia, pass through two state parks: Washington Monument and Gathland state parks. For complete information on the trail, call 304-535-6331.

ASSATEAGUE ISLAND STATE PARK
1

LOCATION - The park is 8 miles south of Ocean City. Take U.S. 50 east to Maryland 611 and continue south across the Verrazano Bridge.

FEATURES - Visitor facilities are located on the north end of the island near Ocean City and on the south end opposite Chincoteague, Virginia. Over 35 kilometers of roadless barrier island beaches and marshes are located between these points.

ACTIVITIES - The state park occupies a 2-mile segment of Assateague Island National Seashore opposite the island's access bridge. Camp in the state park's 311-site campground or in one of the national park's campgrounds. Both parks have trailer dumping stations. A concessionaire operates a small camp store and restaurant during the summer. Both the national and state parks' campgrounds are extremely popular and maintain continuous and separate waiting lists. Weekends and summer holidays are particularly busy. Sometimes campers have to spend a night or more in a mainland campground before obtaining a campsite on the island. The park's flat terrain often leads to strong winds, especially during thunderstorms, so bring along long tent stakes.

The national park maintains a system of backpack oceanside campsites. For information, call 301-641-1441.

Chincoteague Bay's calm, shallow water has 3 canoe-in campsites. Reservations are necessary and campers should bring plenty of insect repellent. A canoe launch area is at the end of Ferry Landing Road.

Attend a campfire program. Go pan fishing in the ocean and swimming and boating from the ramp. Take a nature walk, go for a bike ride, and hike the trails. Some hiking trails lead to great bird-watching points. Hikers should watch for Assateague's wild ponies that roam freely over the island. Because they are wild, you're advised not to get too close or try to feed them.

Parking along the ocean can be a problem on summer weekends. Parking is usually available at the visitor center for the National Wildlife Refuge and in the Maryland section of the island. If possible, bring along a bicycle to get around from an outlying point.

Toms Cove is open for clamming between high and low tides. Boaters can launch from the public ramp at Chincoteague Memorial Park with rental boats available in Chincoteague. Large and heavily motored boats may use public launch facilities on the mainland at South Point or in Ocean City.

Tour the visitor centers on Assateague Island National Seashore. One is located on the north end of the island near Ocean City and another is on the south end of the island opposite Chincoteague. In order to get from one end of the island to the other, visitors have to return to the mainland. The national seashore offers surf fishing, clamming, crabbing, canoeing, hiking, camping, swimming, and shell collecting. The annual pony round-up and auction is held the last Wednesday and Thursday in July. For information, call 301-641-1441.

Tour Frontier Town, 4 miles south of Ocean City on Maryland 611 off U.S. 50, to see Wild West shows and rodeos from mid-June through Labor Day. For information, call 301-289-7877.

Annual events held in Ocean City include a White Marlin Festival in May, additional white marlin tournaments in August, a Saltwater Festival on Labor Day weekend, and a four-day Sunfest held in late September.

Incoming pilots can land at Ocean City Municipal 2 miles southwest of town. Rental cars are available.

INFORMATION

Assateague Island State Park	Assateague Island National Seashore
7307 Stephen Decatur Road	Route 2, Box 294
Route 2, Box 293	Berlin, Maryland 21811
Berlin, Maryland 21811	301-641-1441
301-641-2120	301-641-3030 (summers)

BIG RUN STATE PARK
2
NEW GERMANY STATE PARK
3
CASSELMAN RIVER BRIDGE STATE PARK
4

LOCATION - Big Run State Park is 11 miles northwest of Luke on Savage River Road near the Savage River Dam. Take Exit 24 off U.S. 48 to New Germany Road.

To reach New Germany State Park from Grantsville, take Exit 24 off U.S. 48 and follow Chestnut Ridge Road to Lower New Germany Road. Go south 5 miles.

To reach Casselman River Bridge State Park, take Exit 24 off U.S. 40 and go west for 2 miles. The bridge is ½ mile east of Grantsville on U.S. 40.

FEATURES - Casselman Bridge, built in 1813, was the longest single-span stone arch bridge in the U.S. when built along U.S. 40, called the National Road. This road was the first major highway to pass through famed Cumberland Narrows in the Allegheny Mountains, thus opening the west for settlement.

ACTIVITIES - In Big Run State Park, go boating and flatwater canoeing from the boat launch. Camp in one of 30 campsites and go freshwater fishing and hiking. During the winter, go ice fishing.

New Germany State Park is in the Savage River State Forest. Go boating from the boat launch and flatwater canoeing. Overnight in one of the cabins or in one of 37 campsites with a dumping station.

Go freshwater fishing for bass and swimming and boating from the ramp with rentals available in New Germany Lake. Tour the nature center, take a nature walk, attend campfire programs, and go hiking. During the winter, go cross-country skiing and ice fishing.

At Casselman River, visit the historic bridge, enjoy freshwater fishing, and bring along a picnic.

Tour Penn Alps/Spruce Forest Artisan Village located ½ mile east of Grantsville on alternate U.S. 40. Observe demonstrations of colonial American arts and crafts and stroll through the Spruce Forest Artisan Village with five restored log houses. For information, call 301-895-5985.

Overnight in the Casselman Hotel on Main Street in Grantsville. This mid-nineteenth-century hostelry was constructed to provide accommodations for travelers along the National Road. For information, call 301-895-5055.

INFORMATION

Big Run State Park
Route 2
Grantsville, Maryland 21536
301-895-5453

New Germany State Park
Route 2
Grantsville, Maryland 21536
301-895-5453

Casselman River Bridge State Park
Grantsville, Maryland 21536
301-895-5453

CALVERT CLIFFS STATE PARK
5

LOCATION - The park is off Maryland 2/4, 14 miles south of Prince Frederick.

FEATURES - Calvert Cliffs State Park has 30 miles of fossil-embedded cliffs with over 600 fossil species. Geologists determined that the area was once a calving ground for whales, thus attracting many sharks. Since sharks can replace lost teeth in as little as a week, many millions of their teeth are found along the 30-mile shoreline.

ACTIVITIES - Hike down Red Trail to the beach where fossils and shark teeth may be found. Collect fossils along the beach. No digging is permitted, but scavenging is. Camp, go freshwater and saltwater fishing, or enjoy a picnic. Take a nature walk along the self-guided nature trail.

Visit Calvert Cliffs Nuclear Power Plant Visitor Center in Lusby on Maryland 2/4, south of Prince Frederick. The converted tobacco barn has dioramas and animated exhibits of Calvert Cliffs and the power plant. For information, call 301-586-2200.

Tour Calvert Marine Museum south of Solomons off Maryland 2/4 at Solomon's Island Road to see their fossil exhibits and maritime history exhibits. Board the *William B. Tennison*, a converted 1899 bugeye, to cruise around Solomons Harbor and the Patuxent River from May–October. For information, call 301-326-2042.

Visit the restored Drum Point Lighthouse, originally commissioned in 1883 and one of the last of its kind on the Chesapeake. Nearby you can tour Lore and Sons Oyster House Annex with its boat-building exhibit and artifacts from the local seafood industry. For details, call 301-326-2042.

Cove Point Lighthouse is the oldest brick tower lighthouse on the Chesa-peake. It has been in continuous service since 1828 and is staffed by the Coast Guard. It's on Cove Point Road, Maryland 497, off Maryland 2/4, north of Solomons. For information on whether it's open, call 301-234-7848.

Explore the northernmost naturally occurring Cypress Swamp in America at Battle Creek Cypress Swamp Sanctuary. The swamp is south of Prince Frederick on Sixes Road off Maryland 231 or Maryland 2/4. Hike along a self-guided ¼-mile boardwalk trail through the swamp and tour the nature center. For details on special programs offered throughout the year, call 410-535-5327.

Jefferson Patterson Park and Museum is listed on the National Register of Historic Places and is off Maryland 2/4, south of Prince Frederick to Maryland 264 and then left on Maryland 265. Tour the museum and see agricultural and archaeological exhibits plus a hands-on exhibit on energy and nuclear power. Power plant tours must be pre-arranged. Call 410-260-4673 or 410-586-2200, ext. 4673. From June–August, watch the excavation of artifacts from 7500 BC through the nineteenth century. The park overlooks the 1814 site of the largest U.S. naval battle in Maryland history during the War of 1812. For park information, call 410-586-0050.

Go out on a charter boat from Chesapeake Beach or Solomons to fish for blues, trout, drum, and flounder.

The end of August, attend the annual North Beach Bay Festival to enjoy music, games, exhibits, and good eating. For information, call 1-800-331-9771.

On the last Saturday in April in Prince Frederick, join the Southern Maryland Celtic Festival and Highland Gathering. For details, call 301-535-3274.

The Waterside Music Festival is held in Solomons the last Saturday in May. For information, call 301-326-2042. The Tenth Century Tidewater Fair is on Solomons in mid-September. Call 326-2042 for information.

INFORMATION
Calvert Cliffs State Park
Route 4, Box 106A
Brandywine, Maryland 20613
301-888-1622

CASSELMAN RIVER BRIDGE STATE PARK
See under BIG RUN STATE PARK

CEDARVILLE STATE PARK
6

LOCATION - The park is 4 miles east of Townshend off U.S. 301 on Cedarville Road and 25 miles south of Washington, D.C.

ACTIVITIES - Camp in the campground with 130 sites and a dumping station. Go freshwater fishing, take a nature walk along the self-guided nature trail, attend a campfire program, hike the trails, and go horseback riding.

Cedarville Natural Resources Management Area is on Cedarville Road off U.S. 301 at the headwaters of Zehiah Swamp. Visitors can camp in a primitive wood setting and go fishing in the swamp or in a pond stocked with bass, blue gill, pickerel, and catfish.

INFORMATION
Cedarville State Park
Route 4, Box 106A
Cedarville, Maryland 20613
301-888-1622

CUNNINGHAM FALLS STATE PARK
7

LOCATION - Cunningham Falls State Park's Houck Area is 3 miles west of Thurmont on Maryland 77. Cunningham Falls Manor Area is south of the state park.

ACTIVITIES - From the Falls' Houck Area, go swimming, launch your boat from the boat launch, or rent a canoe and go flatwater canoeing. Camp in one of 148 campsites with a dumping station. Attend a campfire program in the evening. Concessions and a camp store are available.

Go freshwater fishing, take a nature walk along the self-guided trail, or hike along a section of the Appalachian Trail. The area is especially colorful in the spring when the wildflowers bloom. During the winter, go cross-country skiing and sledding.

In the Manor area, camp in one of 31 campsites and go fishing.

Catoctin Mountain Park, administered by the National Park Service, adjoins Cunningham Falls State Park. Here you can go hiking along 25 miles of trails, camping in Owens Creek Campground with 50 campsites, trout fishing in the stream, and horseback riding along 12 miles of equestrian trails. Go rock climbing and watch a demonstration of whiskey-making at Blue Blazes Still, operated by the National Park Service on weekends from Memorial Day through October. Tour the visitor center off Maryland 77. For information, call 301-663-9388.

Loy's Station Bridge, circa 1850–60, is on Old Frederick Road off U.S. 77, 3 miles from Thurmont. This 90-foot covered bridge spans Owen's Creek. Roddy Road Covered Bridge, circa 1856, is a 40-foot span over Owen's Creek.

Stroll through Frederick's National Historic District. Pick up a self-guided brochure. For information, call 301-663-8703. Tour the Barbara Fritchie House at 154 West Patrick. For admission information, call 301-663-3833. Rose Hill Manor Children's Museum at 1611 North Market was constructed in 1790 and has been restored to depict life in the nineteenth century. Many historical festivals are presented throughout the year. For information, call 301-694-1648.

To do additional hiking, drive to Sugarloaf Mountain, approximately 13 miles south of town on I-270 and Maryland 109. Take the Comas Exit.

Incoming pilots can land at Frederick Municipal Airport, located east of town. Rental cars are available.

INFORMATION
Cunningham Falls State Park
14039 Catoctin Hollow Road
Thurmont, Maryland 21788
301-271-7574

DANS MOUNTAIN STATE PARK
8

LOCATION - The park is 9 miles south of Frostburg.

ACTIVITIES - Open for day-use, visitors can purchase a snack, go freshwater fishing, take a nature walk along the self-guided trail, have a picnic, and swim in the pool. Come to go sledding during the winter.

Frostburg is an historic district. For a self-guided tour, pick up a map at City Hall, 37 Broadway, or call 301-689-6000.

INFORMATION
Dans Mountain State Park
Frostburg, Maryland 21532
301-463-5564

DEEP CREEK LAKE STATE PARK
9
HERRINGTON MANOR STATE PARK
10

LOCATION - Deep Creek Lake State Park is 10 miles south of Oakland and 2 miles east of U.S. 219 at Thayerville.

Herrington Manor State Park is 5 miles northwest of Oakland on Maryland 20.

FEATURES - Deep Creek Lake is Maryland's largest mountain lake and is 12 miles long with 65 miles of shoreline.

ACTIVITIES - At Deep Creek, go boating from the boat launch, flatwater canoeing, and freshwater fishing. Stay in one of their 112 campsites with dumping stations, concessions, campfire programs, and a camp store available. Go water-skiing, swimming, sailing, and hiking. During the winter, go ice fishing, snowmobiling, ice skating, and downhill and cross-country skiing.

Savage River, northeast of Deep Creek Lake, is named for a whitewater route along a 5.5-mile run. The river was the site of 1989 World Championship Whitewater Races and has good fishing available in the reservoir, plus river expeditions.

At Herrington Manor, hike the nature trail, go bicycling with bike rentals available, and boating from the launch with rental boats available. Gas motors are not permitted. You can stay in a rental cabin. During the winter, go cross-country skiing and sledding.

Incoming pilots can land at Garrett County Airport, located 13 miles northeast of Oakland. Rental cars are available.

INFORMATION

Deep Creek Lake State Park
Route 2, Box 70
Swanton, Maryland 21561
301-387-5563

Herrington Manor State Park
RFD 5, Box 122
Oakland, Maryland 21550
301-334-9180

ELK NECK STATE PARK
11

LOCATION - The park is off Irishtown Road, south of North East. From the intersection of U.S. 40 and Maryland 272, go south 10.2 miles on Maryland 272.

ACTIVITIES - Elk Neck State Park has camping in 112 sites, a disposal station, and groceries. Bring along a picnic, hike nature trails, go horseback riding, swimming, fishing, and boating from the ramp with rental boats available. During the winter, go cross-country skiing and winter camping.

Elk Neck Demonstration Forest, north of the park, has boating from the launch, with rowboats and canoes for rent. Go fishing for catfish and flatwater canoeing in Elk River or saltwater fishing in Chesapeake Bay. Rent a cabin or camp in the 304-site campground with dumping stations available. Purchase concessions or camping supplies from the camp store. Tour the nature center, take a nature walk, attend a campfire program, swim in the river, go hiking, and cross-country skiing in the winter.

INFORMATION
Elk Neck State Park
4395 Turkey Point Road
North East, Maryland 21901
301-285-5777
301-287-5333 (campground)

FORT FREDERICK STATE PARK
12
GREEN RIDGE STATE FOREST
13

LOCATION - To reach Fort Frederick State Park from Big Pool and the intersection of I-70 and Maryland 56, go south one mile on Maryland 56.

Green Ridge State Forest is 20 miles east of Cumberland. Take Exit 65 from U.S. 40/48.

FEATURES - Fort Frederick, constructed in 1756, has the best preserved original stone fort in America. It was constructed to protect settlers during the French and Indian War. It was named for Frederick Calvert, Lord Baltimore, who was the last descendant of the original chartered proprietor of Maryland. Remnants of the historic C&O Canal are on the park grounds.

ACTIVITIES - At Fort Frederick you can camp in the 28-site campground where limited camping supplies are available. Attend a campfire program. Go pan fishing in Big Pool and boating or flatwater canoeing on the Potomac River with rentals available. Rent a bicycle to go cycling.

Tour the museum to learn about the fort's restoration and stroll through two restored barracks and the garrison garden, looking as they did in 1756. Costumed guides offer tours during the summer. The museum is open from early April through early November and the fort is open from 8:30 to sunset. During the winter, go cross-country skiing, ice fishing, sledding, and ice skating.

A section of the Chesapeake and Ohio Canal National Historical Park is located 8 miles south of Cumberland off Maryland 51. The national park encompasses part of the 184-mile canal constructed along the Potomac River between Washington D.C. and Cumberland, Maryland. The canal was built between 1828 and 1850 and stopped operating in 1924. Now visitors can go hiking, biking, camping, horseback riding, canoeing, boating, and fishing. Explore the canal museum at Great Falls, Maryland, and take a mule-drawn barge ride from mid-April through October. For reservations, call 301-299-2613.

At Green Ridge State Forest, camp in one of 118 campsites and purchase groceries. Go bass fishing in the Potomac River and boating from the ramp.

In Cumberland, attend Heritage Days in early June and the C&O Canal Boat Festival in late August. Take a self-guided tour of the Washington Street Historic District. Brochures are available. For information, call 301-777-5905.

Incoming pilots can land at Cumberland Regional Airport located 2 miles south of the city. Rental cars are available.

INFORMATION

Green Ridge State Forest
Cumberland, Maryland 21502
301-777-2345

Fort Frederick State Park
Route 1, P.O. Box 177
Big Pool, Maryland 21711
301-842-2155

GAMBRILL STATE PARK
14

LOCATION - Go northwest 6 miles from Frederick on Maryland 40 to Gambrill Park Road and then north ½ mile to Rock Run.

ACTIVITIES - Camp in one of 35 campsites with a trailer dump station available. Go pan fishing in the pond. Tour the nature center, enjoy nature walks, campfire programs, picnicking, and hike a section of the Appalachian Trail. During the winter, go cross-country skiing and ice skating.

Frederick was founded in 1745 and played an important role in the Colonial, Revolutionary, and Civil wars. Pick up a map from the Tourism Council on 19 East Church and explore the 33-block area located within the historic district. Highlights of your tour include Rose Hill Manor, circa 1790, Ross/Mathias Mansion, circa 1815–17, and the law offices of Roger B. Taney and Francis Scott Key, author of our national anthem. This map also shows the location of three covered bridges close to town.

Incoming pilots can land at Frederick Municipal Airport, located east of the city. Rental cars are available.

INFORMATION

Gambrill State Park
Route 8
Frederick, Maryland 21701
301-791-4767 or 473-8360

GATHLAND STATE PARK
15

LOCATION - The state park is one mile west of Burkittsville off Maryland 17.

FEATURES - Originally the estate of Civil War correspondent George Alfred Townsend, the park has the first and only monument in the world erected in memory of the journalists and photographers who covered the Civil War.

ACTIVITIES - Tour the visitor center to see artifacts from the Civil War plus a collection of Townsend's mementos. Take a nature walk, enjoy a picnic, and hike along a section of the Appalachian Trail passing through the park. During the winter, go cross-country skiing and sledding.

INFORMATION
Gathland State Park
Burkitttsville, Maryland 21718
301-293-2420

GREEN RIDGE STATE FOREST
See under FORT FREDERICK STATE PARK

GREENBRIER STATE PARK
16

LOCATION - The park is 10 miles east of Hagerstown. From the intersection of I-70 and Exit 32, go east 3 miles on U.S. 40.

ACTIVITIES - Camp in one of 165 campsites, 28 with electrical hookups, and a trailer dump station. Concessions and a camp store are available. Go fishing for bass in Greenbrier Lake, swimming, flatwater canoeing, and boating from the ramp with rentals available. Tour the visitor center, attend campfire programs, picnic, and hike on a portion of the Appalachian Trail. During the winter, go cross-country skiing, ice fishing, sledding, and ice skating.

Antietam National Battlefield is south of Hagerstown and west of Frederick. Routes I-70 and U.S. 40 or 40-A connect with Maryland 34 and 65. The visitor center is one mile north of Sharpsburg. The Civil War Battle of Antietam was the bloodiest single-day battle fought in American history. Take a self-guided 8-mile driving tour and hike the historic trails. For information, call 301-432-5124.

Miller House, 135 West Washington in Hagerstown, is a nineteenth-century town house museum featuring clock, doll, and crafts exhibits. For information, call 301-797-8782.

Incoming pilots can land at Washington County Regional Airport located 4 miles north of Hagerstown. Rental cars are available.

INFORMATION
Greenbrier State Park
Boonsboro Maryland 21713
301-791-4767

GUNPOWDER FALLS STATE PARK
17

LOCATION - The falls are in the Gunpowder River Valley along the Little and Big Gunpowder rivers west of Kingsville.

ACTIVITIES - Go boating from the launch, go flatwater and whitewater canoeing, swimming, and tubing. Camp in the campground and attend a campfire program, purchase a snack from the concession stand and enjoy freshwater and saltwater fishing. Tour the museum, take a nature walk along the self-guided nature trail, go for a bike ride, horseback ride, or hike the trails. During the winter, go cross-country skiing.

INFORMATION
Gunpowder Falls State Park
Kingsville, Maryland 21207
301-592-2897

HERRINGTON MANOR STATE PARK
See under DEEP CREEK LAKE STATE PARK

JANES ISLAND STATE PARK
18

LOCATION - The park is 1½ miles north of Crisfield. You can reach it via U.S. 13 to Westover, then Maryland 413 south to Crisfield, and Maryland 358 to reach the park. The mainland part of the park is accessible by car, but the island portion is accessible only by boat.

ACTIVITIES - Go camping in Hodson Area on the mainland from April 1–October 31 in one of 104 campsites, with 40 sites offering electrical hookups plus a dump station. Four log cabins are available year-round by reservation only. Hike the one-mile self-guided nature trail in the Hodson area and watch for poison ivy if walking undeveloped sections of the park. Attend naturalist programs or enjoy one of their woodland or seashore walks. Pick up a bird watcher's checklist from the park office and watch for the various species who pass through. Pontoon boat service to Jane's Island is available.

Go crabbing for blue crab and tidal fishing in Chesapeake Bay. A tidal fishing license is required for finfish, but none is for crabbing. Go boating with 25 boat slips available to campers and cabin renters. Boat rentals are available from April–October. Canoe one of the four canoe trails.

Go swimming from one of the island beaches while watching for seasonal jellyfish. The island has miles of isolated shoreline and sandy beaches to explore.

Smith and Tangier Island cruises and charter fishing vessels leave from Crisfield at Somers Cove from mid-May through October.

If you're here the second weekend in October, enjoy Olde Princess Anne Days and tour historic homes and country estates. In mid-July in Crisfield, attend J. Millard Tawes Crab and Clam Bake and enjoy a buffet of local seafood.

In Crisfield over Labor Day weekend, attend National Hard Crab Derby and Fair and watch crab races with crabs from as far away as Hawaii competing for the Governor's Cup. Skipjack races feature commercial sailboats that race in Tangier Sound off Deal Island on Labor Day. For area information, contact the Somerset County Tourist Organization at 1-800-521-9189 or 410-651-2968.

Historic homes to visit in Crisfield include Makepeace, built in 1663, Crockett House, circa 1888, or walk through the city watching for one of the few remaining "smithies," where oyster tongs, clam rakes, and marine equipment are produced.

Incoming pilots can land at Crisfield Municipal Airport located 3 miles northeast of the city. Taxis are available.

INFORMATION
Janes Island State Park
26280 Alfred Lawson Drive
Route 2
Crisfield, Maryland 21817
301-968-1565 or 1-800-492-5062

MARTINAK STATE PARK
19

LOCATION - The park is 2 miles south of Denton off Maryland 404 on Deep Shore Road.

FEATURES - Martinak State Park's two boundaries are along the Choptank River and Watts Creek.

ACTIVITIES - Camp in one of 60 sites with a trailer dump station or in the cabin available year-round overlooking the Choptank River. Go fishing for bass, perch, sunfish, and catfish or boating from the ramp in the Choptank River and Watts Creek. A Chesapeake Bay sport fishing license is required for fishing in the tidal waters of the river and creek. Rent a canoe and go flatwater canoeing.

Tour the log cabin converted into a visitor center with a museum containing Indian artifacts and the remains of a pungy, an extinct fishing and sailing vessel. Hike along the nature trail.

INFORMATION
Martinak State Park
Route 2, Box 12
Deep Shore Road
Denton, Maryland 21629
301-479-1619

NEW GERMANY STATE PARK
See under BIG RUN STATE PARK

PATAPSCO STATE PARK
20

LOCATION - The park is located along the Patapsco River from Baltimore to Liberty Dam near Reistertown. From I-695 and Frederick Road near Catonsville, go west 1.5 miles on Frederick Road to Rolling Road, then south one block to Hilton Avenue. Continue south another 1.5 miles to reach the park. From Ellicott City and the intersection of I-695 and U.S. 40, go west 3 miles on U.S. 40 to reach another section of the park.

ACTIVITIES - In the Hilton area, enjoy camping in one of 24 sites with a dumping station available. The Ellicott City/Hollofield area has 75 additional campsites. Have a picnic, go hiking, and tour the visitor center. Go flatwater and whitewater canoeing, tubing, and bass fishing in the Patapsco River. Take a nature walk along the self-guided nature trail, attend a campfire program, and go for a horseback ride. During the winter, enjoy cross-country skiing.

In Ellicott City, visit the B&O Railroad Station Museum on Maryland Avenue and Main Street. Here you'll see the first passenger terminal for the railroad and can watch their sight and sound show in the visitor center. For information, call 301-461-1944. Pick up a self-guided walking tour brochure to walk through the historic city begun in 1772. For details, call 301-992-2344.

Off U.S. 1 with easy access from I-95 near Savage Mill is the Bollmana Truss Bridge, circa 1869. The bridge was constructed of wrought iron and is an open railroad bridge, the only one of its type in the world. It was restored in 1974. Call 301-992-2323 for details. Savage Mill is on Gorman Road off U.S. 1 at Savage. It specialized in manufacturing cotton duck in the early 1800s. Call 301-792-2820 for details.

INFORMATION
Patapsco State Park
8020 Baltimore National Pike
Ellicott City, Maryland 21043
301-461-5005

PATUXENT RIVER STATE PARK
21

LOCATION - The park is south of Cooksville and 2 miles south of I-70 between Maryland 27 and 97.

ACTIVITIES - Go freshwater fishing, canoeing, and tour the nature center. Take a horseback ride and hike the self-guided hiking trail. During the winter, go cross-country skiing and sledding. Attend Patuxent River Discovery Day the first Saturday in May. Call 301-535-4583 or 301-535-5327 for information.

INFORMATION
Patuxent State Park
11950 Clopper Road
Gaithersburg, Maryland 21227
301-924-2127

POINT LOOKOUT STATE PARK
22

LOCATION - The park is on a peninsula at the confluence of Chesapeake Bay and the Potomac River. It's 4.7 miles south of Scotland on Maryland 5.

FEATURES - Point Lookout was the site of Fort Lincoln, an earthen fort built by Confederate prisoners under Union supervision. Two monuments in the cemetery honor Confederate dead from the prison camp.

ACTIVITIES - Tour the park museum to see Civil War exhibits. It's open Wednesday–Sunday from 10:00–5:00 from Memorial Day through Labor Day, and weekends in May from 10:00–5:00. Civil War living history demonstrations are presented on special occasions. Contact the park for dates.

Camp in one of 147 campsites, 26 with full hookups. The campground has a dump station, laundry, and camp store. Rent a boat and go boating from ramps that provide access to the Potomac River via Lake Conoy. Go flatwater canoeing, swimming in the river or bay, saltwater fishing, and have a picnic. Take a nature walk along the self-guided nature trail, attend a campfire program, and go for a hike or bicycle ride.

Take a boat cruise from the park to Smith Island. For information, call 301-425-2271.

Confederate Days Celebration is held in the park in mid-June. Take their ghost walk at the end of October or a lighthouse tour in early November.

Nearby attractions include Sotterley Plantation on Maryland 245, 3 miles east of Hollywood. Constructed in 1717, the working colonial plantation offers tours of the formal gardens, north and south gate houses, slave cabin, and farm museum. Tours run from 11:00–4:00 daily from June–October except on Mondays and by appointment in April, May, and November. Call 410-373-2280.

INFORMATION
Point Lookout State Park
Star Route, Box 48
Scotland, Maryland 20687
301-872-5688

POCOMOKE RIVER STATE FOREST AND PARK
23

LOCATION - The park has two areas: Milburn Landing and Shad Landing. Milburn Landing is 8 miles west of Snow Hill on Maryland 12. Milburn Landing is also accessible 7 miles northeast of Pocomoke City off Maryland 364. Shad Landing is 4 miles southwest of Snow Hill on U.S. 113.

FEATURES - Open year-round, the river park is located within the state forest, once an ideal hiding place for contraband vessels and slaves fleeing to the north.

ACTIVITIES - Swim in the large pool, go boating from the launch, rent a canoe to go flatwater canoeing, and enjoy bass fishing in the Pocomoke River. Both Milburn Landing and Shad Landing are located along the river, providing easy put-ins and take-outs for canoers. The best canoeing seasons are in the spring and fall. Summers tend to be hot, humid, and buggy.

Camp in one of the campgrounds with a total of 250 campsites, with 30 offering electrical hookups, in the Shad Landing area. Attend an evening campfire program. Walk the self-guided Pusey Branch Nature Trail. Purchase a snack at the concession stand, camping supplies in the camp store, and tour the visitor center.

Pocomoke Cypress Swamps, one of the northernmost stands of bald cypress in the U.S., is located nearby along the Pocomoke River.

Snow Hill has more than 100 homes over a century old, including All Hallows Episcopal Church, Makemie Memorial Presbyterian Church, Mount Zion Schoolhouse, plus many homes along Federal Street. Pick up a self-guided walking tour brochure. For information, call 301-632-0515.

Furnace Town, site of a nineteenth-century industrial village, is 5 miles north of Snow Hill on Maryland 12, then one mile south on Iron Furnace Road. It features the Nassawango Iron Furnace, Maryland's only bog-ore furnace, a broom house, blacksmith shop, and museum. Tour the town from the first weekend in April through the last weekend in October. Park festivals feature art, music, and living history. In early April, attend the Revolutionary War reenactment. In late September, attend Fallfest to participate in nineteenth-century games and auction and listen to bluegrass. For information, call 301-632-2032.

INFORMATION
Pocomoke River State Forest and Park
Route 3, Box 237
Snow Hill, Maryland 21863
301-632-2566

ROCKS STATE PARK
24

LOCATION - The park is on Maryland 24, 8 miles north of Bel Air.

ACTIVITIES - Go flatwater canoeing, tubing, and freshwater fishing. Attend a campfire program, picnic, and go hiking. During the winter, go sledding.

INFORMATION
Rocks State Park
Bel Air, Maryland 21014
301-557-7994

ROCKY GAP STATE PARK
25

LOCATION - The park is 6 miles east of Cumberland on U.S. 40. Take Exit 50 off I-68 heading east.

ACTIVITIES - Rocky Gap State Park has an extensive trail system, bike rentals, sailing, canoeing, boating from the ramp using electric motors with a 10 horsepower limit, and bass fishing in Lake Habeeb. The park is open from April–December. Camp in the campground with 278 campsites, 30 with electrical hookups, dumping stations, concessions, and a camp store available.

Tour the visitor center and attend campfire programs. During the winter, go ice fishing, sledding, and ice skating.

In Cumberland, attend Heritage Days in early June, the C&O Canal Boat Festival in August, and take a walking tour of the Washington Street Historic District. For information, call 301-777-5905.

Incoming pilots can land at Cumberland Regional Airport 2 miles south of the city. Rental cars are available.

INFORMATION
Rocky Gap State Park
Route 40 East
Cumberland, Maryland 21502
301-777-2138

SANDY POINT STATE PARK
26

LOCATION - The park is northeast of Annapolis off U.S. 50/301 at the western end of Bay Bridge.

ACTIVITIES - Go boating, camping, and purchase food and drink from the concession stand. Go saltwater fishing, swim in the bay, and go for a hike or horseback ride. During the winter, go cross-country skiing.

In Annapolis, tour the U.S. Naval Academy, begun in 1845 and bordered by King George Street and the Severn River. Explore the museum in Preble Hall to see ship models, swords, and uniforms. Guided walking tours leave from Ricketts Hall on Monday–Saturday from 9:30–4:00 and on Sundays from noon–5:00. Full dress parades are held three times each semester. For information, call 301-263-6933.

Historic homes to visit include Hammond-Harwood House on 19 Maryland Avenue, William Paca House at 186 Prince George Street, and Chase-Lloyd House at 22 Maryland Avenue. Cornhill Street has several examples of individual restoration being done of old homes in the historic district.

Stroll through the Helen Avalynn Tawes Garden at 580 Taylor Avenue. Access is through Tawes State Office Building weekdays and weekends between the Court of Appeals and District Court. Historic William Paca Garden is at 1 Martin Street off East Street.

Many boat cruises leave from the harbor in Annapolis. To take a walking tour of Annapolis, call 301-263-5401 or 301-267-8149. In August, attend the annual Clam Festival.

INFORMATION
Sandy Point State Park
800 Revell Highway
Annapolis, Maryland 21401
301-757-1841

SENECA CREEK STATE PARK
27

LOCATION - The park is 1.5 miles west of Gaithersburg off I-270 on Maryland 117.

ACTIVITIES - Go boating from the ramp with rentals available. Go fishing, tour the visitor center museum, attend a campfire program, purchase a snack, and hike or bike the C&O towpath. For bike trips, you can ride 14 miles from Great Falls Tavern to Georgetown, 15 miles from Fifteen Mile Creek to Paw Paw Tunnel, or 24 miles from Dam 4 to Lock 33. Primitive camping for hikers and bikers is available approximately every 5 miles from Seneca to Cumberland. Hikers have access to a section of the Appalachian Trail that passes through the park. During the winter, go cross-country skiing, ice fishing, sledding, and ice skating.

At Great Falls, board a replica nineteenth-century mule-drawn boat and "lock through" one of the locks on the Potomac along the C&O Canal. National park naturalists present living history demonstrations. For a schedule, contact the C&O Canal National Historical Park at 301-299-2026. While in Great Falls, tour the Great Falls Museum and watch their film, *The C&O Canal.*

Incoming pilots can land at Montgomery County Airpark, located 3 miles northeast of Gaithersburg. Rental cars are available.

INFORMATION
Seneca Creek State Park
Gaithersburg, Maryland 20877
301-924-2127

SMALLWOOD STATE PARK
28

LOCATION - Smallwood is off Maryland 224, 4 miles southwest of Mason Springs and 4 miles west of Pisgah.

FEATURES - The park has the restored colonial tidewater plantation home of eighteenth-century planter and Revolutionary War patriot, General William Smallwood.

ACTIVITIES - The home is open from early March–December. Bring along a picnic to enjoy and go fishing and hiking. Sweden Point Marina has a boat-launching facility. Concessions are available. During the winter, go cross-country skiing.

INFORMATION
Smallwood State Park
Route 1, Box 64
Marbury, Maryland 20658
301-743-7613

ST. MARY'S RIVER STATE PARK
29

LOCATION - The park is on Camp Cosoma Road off Maryland 5, 3 miles north of Great Mills.

ACTIVITIES - Go freshwater fishing and flatwater canoeing and boating in the 2,250-acre lake. The boat ramp is suitable for small boats, and only electric motors up to one horsepower are permitted. Go hiking through the wetlands.

Tour an 800-acre outdoor living history museum with four major exhibit areas. Governor's Field features the *Maryland Dove*, a square-rigged replica of one of the ships that brought the first settlers from England. Special events are presented year-round. The museum is on Maryland 5, south of Leonardtown. For information, call 301-862-0990.

Tour Tudor Hall, an old Georgian mansion built in 1756, and once owned by the family of Francis Scott Key, author of the "Star Spangled Banner." For details, contact St. Mary's Historical Society, 301-475-2467.

Sotterley Mansion, constructed in 1717, is in Hollywood, east of Leonardtown. This working colonial plantation along the Patuxent River offers tours of the formal gardens, gate houses, slave cabins, and a farm museum. Tours run from 11:00–4:00 daily from June–October except on Mondays and by appointment in April, May, and November. Call 410-373-2280.

INFORMATION
St. Mary's River State Park
Leonardtown, Maryland 20650
301-872-5688

SUSQUEHANNA STATE PARK
30

LOCATION - The park is in Gunpowder River Valley, 3 miles northwest of Havre de Grace on Maryland 155.

ACTIVITIES - Launch your boat from the boat launch, go flatwater canoeing, tubing, and camp in the 70-site campground. Go freshwater fishing in the Susquehanna River and saltwater fishing in the bay. Tour the visitor center, attend campfire programs, picnic, hike the trails, and go horseback riding. During the winter, go cross-country skiing, sledding, and ice skating.

Tour the Carter Mansion to see antique furnishings and the Steppingstone Museum to see their antique doll collection. It's open from Memorial Day through Labor Day. For information, call 301-939-0643. Jersey Toll House, circa 1818, was once the residence of the toll keeper for Rock Run. It's open Memorial Day through Labor Day on weekends from 10:00–6:00. For information, call 301-939-0643.

Rock Run Mill, circa 1794, has a stone mill with a 12-ton water wheel that runs on a limited basis on weekends from Memorial Day through Labor Day. Call 301-939-0643 for details.

Concord Point Lighthouse on Lafayette Street in Havre de Grace was constructed in 1829 and provides a spectacular view of Chesapeake Bay. It's the oldest continually used lighthouse on the East Coast. For information, call 301-939-1800.

Susquehanna Lockhouse Museum, circa 1848, is on Erie Street in Havre de Grace. It's open Sundays in June–August from 1:00–5:00. For details, call 301-939-1800.

Havre de Grace Decoy Museum, 3 miles from Havre de Grace off I-95, Exit 92, has a large collection of carved wooden waterfowl decoys. It's open Tuesday–Sunday from 11:00–4:00. For information, call 301-939-3739.

INFORMATION
Susquehanna State Park
801 Stafford Road
Havre de Grace, Maryland 21078
301-939-0643
301-836-6735 (campground)

SWALLOW FALLS STATE PARK
31

LOCATION - The park is 9 miles northwest of Oakland on Maryland 20.

FEATURES - Muddy Creek Falls tumble down 64 feet of rocks. The scenic waterfall is near the site of the 1918 camp of Henry Ford, Thomas Edison, and Harvey Firestone.

ACTIVITIES - Camp in the 64-site campground. Go trout fishing in the Youghioheny River, hike the nature trails, tour the visitor center, and attend interpretive programs. In the winter, go cross-country skiing and sledding.

Incoming pilots can land at Garrett County Airport, located 13 miles northeast of Oakland. Rental cars are available.

INFORMATION
Swallow Falls State Park
RFD 5, Box 122
Oakland, Maryland 21550
301-334-9180

TUCKAHOE STATE PARK
32

LOCATION - Tuckahoe is 7 miles northwest of Denton, 6 miles north of Queen Anne, and 3 miles north of Hillsboro.

FEATURES - Tuckahoe has a 500-acre arboretum.

ACTIVITIES - Camp in one of 71 campsites with a dumping station and attend a campfire program. Go fishing and boating from the launch in the 60-acre lake. A tidal fishing license is required in the creek south of the dam and a non-tidal license is required in the lake to the north. No gasoline motors are permitted. Canoeists come to canoe in both the lake and creek, with canoe rentals available.

Hike Piney Branch Trail, Lake Trail, or Overcup's self-guided nature trail. Equestrians can ride the horse trail off Maryland 404 on Cemetery Road. Tour the visitor center where naturalists are available from spring through the fall.

During the winter, go cross-country skiing, ice fishing, and sledding.

INFORMATION
Tuckahoe State Park
13070 Crouse Mill Road
Route 1, Box 23
Queen Anne, Maryland 21657
301-634-2810

WASHINGTON MONUMENT STATE PARK
33

LOCATION - The state park is 3 miles southeast of Boonsboro off U.S. 40A and 1½ miles north on Monument Road.

FEATURES - The 34-foot stone monument was erected in 1827 to honor George Washington.

ACTIVITIES - Hike the short trail to the monument along part of the Appalachian Trail. Tour the museum and attend campfire programs. Camp in one of 15 unimproved campsites.

During the winter, go cross-country skiing and sledding.

Dine in the Old South Mountain Inn, circa 1730, across from the park on Alternate U.S. 40, the former National Road. For reservations, call 301-432-6155.

In Boonsboro, tour the Museum of History on 113 North Main to see a collection of historical objects spanning 5,000 years. It's open from May–September on Sundays from 1:00–5:00. For information, call 301-432-6969 or 301-432-5151.

Crystal Grottoes Caverns are 1½ miles southwest of town on Maryland 34. This limestone cavern has jeweled stalactites and stalagmites. For guided tour information, call 301-432-6336.

INFORMATION
Washington Monument
Route 1, Box 147
Middletown, Maryland 21658
301-432-8065

WYE OAK STATE PARK
34

LOCATION - The park is on Maryland 662 off U.S. 50 at Wye Mills.

ACTIVITIES - The park features the largest white oak in the U.S., which is estimated to be over 400 years old and is 95 feet tall. An early Americana schoolroom is located in the small brick building next to the oak. Wye Mills ground flour for Washington's Revolutionary army at Valley Forge in 1779 and still grinds cornmeal, whole wheat, and buckwheat flour. It's open for touring from March–December on weekends from 11:00–4:00. For information, call 301-827-6909 or 301-438-3747.

Wye Church in Wye Mills is one of the United States' oldest Episcopal churches, constructed in 1721.

INFORMATION
Wye Oak State Park
Deep Shore Road
Denton, Maryland 21629
301-479-1619

MASSACHUSETTS

Massachusetts was named for the Massachusett Indians, meaning "place of the great hill." The state's nickname is the Bay State. Massachusetts supplies one-half of all the cranberries and scallops for the U.S.

Four U.S. presidents came from here: John Adams, John Quincy Adams, John F. Kennedy, and George Bush. Other natives include Horace Mann, educator; Daniel Webster, orator; Benjamin Franklin, statesman and investor; and Daniel Chester French, sculptor.

Massachusetts Heritage State Parks are a national model of urban environmental design, historic preservation, and economic revitalization. Historic parks are located at Fall River, Holyoke, Lowell, North Adams, Gardner, Lawrence, Lynn, and Springfield.

Travel the Mohawk Trail, Massachusetts 2, a 63-mile road that follows a legendary Indian trail through 50,000 acres of state forests, parks, and reservations. It's especially popular with fall foliage viewers. The northern east-west route goes from Gardner through Greenfield, then to Williamstown in the Northern Berkshires.

Notch Road takes you to the summit of 3,491-foot Mount Greylock, the state's highest mountain.

The 200-mile Metacomet-Monadnock Trail provides a continuous route through the Connecticut River valley to its terminus at Mount Monadnock in New Hampshire. It passes through Robinson and Holyoke Range state parks plus Wendell State Forest. For details, contact M-M Trail, Berkshire Chapter-AM, P.O. Box 9369, North Amherst, Massachusetts 01059, or call the Appalachian Mountain Club at 1-800-262-4455.

Visit Salem to get a feel of a 1600s Puritan settlement and explore the Salem Heritage Trail, which is dedicated to the memory of the Salem witch trials. Martha's Vineyard features the Flying Horses Carousel, the oldest working carousel in the country. In Shelburne Falls, you can cross the 400-foot Bridge of Flowers. Visit Paper House off Massachusetts 127 at Pigeon Cove. Cycle or hike the 20-mile Cape Cod Rail Trail, going from Dennis to Orleans. Cross-country skiers ski the path during the winter.

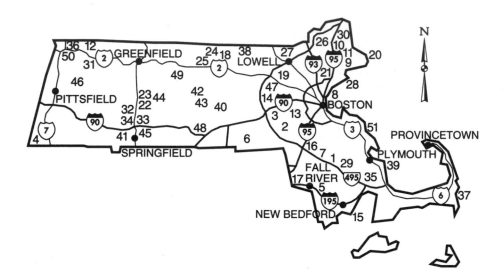

36 12
50 31   2 GREENFIELD   24 18   38   27   26 30
46   25   2   LOWELL   10
PITTSFIELD   23 44   49   19   11 93 95 20
                                                    9
         32 22   42   47   21   28
         34 33   43   40   14 90   8   BOSTON
    90   48   3   13
7 41 45   6   2   95   3   51
4   16   PROVINCETOWN
      SPRINGFIELD   7 1   29   PLYMOUTH
                                     FALL   495 35   39
                                     17 RIVER
                                        5
                                     NEW BEDFORD 195   6 37
                                                    15

N

AMES NOWELL STATE PARK
1

LOCATION - The park is northwest of Abington via Massachusetts 123.

ACTIVITIES - Open year-round for day use only, go canoeing, sailing, and fishing. Hike the trails, ride the bike paths, and go for a horseback ride. Rentals are available. Attend summer visitor interpretive programs. Only motor boats with 10 horsepower are allowed because of shallow lake water. During the winter, go cross-country skiing.

INFORMATION
Ames Nowell State Park
RFD Linwood Street
Abington, Massachusetts 02351
617-857-1336

ASHLAND STATE PARK
2
HOPKINTON STATE PARK
3

LOCATION - Ashland State Park is 2 miles southwest of Ashland on Massachusetts 135. Take I-95 to Main Street in Hopkinton. Go through Hopkinton Center, watching for signs.

Hopkinton State Park is in Hopkinton on Cedar Street. Take I-495 to Massachusetts 85 and follow signs.

ACTIVITIES - At Ashland, hike the paved trail to the reservoir and go swimming, fishing, and non-motorized boating.

At Hopkinton, go canoeing, sailing, fishing, and swimming. During the winter, go cross-country skiing on 10 miles of trails.

INFORMATION

Ashland State Park
71 Cedar Street
Hopkinton, Massachusetts 01748
508-435-4303

Hopkinton State Park
71 Cedar Street
Hopkinton, Massachusetts 01748
508-435-4303

BASH BISH FALLS STATE PARK and
MOUNT WASHINGTON STATE FOREST
4

LOCATION - Bash Bish Falls is 14 miles from Great Barrington via Massachusetts 23 and 41. Take Massachusetts 23 to South Egremont. Turn onto

Massachusetts 41 south and take an immediate right onto Mount Washington Road and follow signs. It's also 4 miles from Copake Falls, New York on Massachusetts 344.

FEATURES - Bash Bish Falls in Mount Washington State Forest is considered the state's most dramatic waterfall, tumbling through a series of gorges to drop 80 feet into a sparkling pool.

ACTIVITIES - Go fishing and hike park trails. Backpacking camping is available year-round in 10 sites.

Mount Washington State Forest has 30 miles of hiking trails. Go wilderness camping, canoeing, fishing, hunting, and horseback riding with rentals available. During the winter, enjoy cross-country skiing and snowmobiling on 21 miles of trails.

Nearby Mount Everett State Forest offers picnicking at Guilder Pond. Drive the auto road to the top of Mount Everett for a view of Massachusetts, New York, and Connecticut.

INFORMATION
Bash Bish Falls State Park
c/o Mount Washington State Forest
RFD 3
Mount Washington, Massachusetts 01258
413-528-0330

BATTLESHIP COVE HERITAGE STATE PARK
5

LOCATION - The park is off I-95 in Fall River.

FEATURES - Battleship Cove is the site of the world's leading textile manufacturer.

ACTIVITIES - Watch the multimedia presentation, "The Fabric of Fall River." Go on board the World War II battleship USS *Massachusetts*, attack submarine USS *Lionfish*, destroyer *Joseph P. Kennedy, Jr.*, and a wooden PT boat.

Tour the Marine Museum at 70 Water and learn about the Old Fall River line that ferried wealthy New York City passengers 70 years ago. View the *Titanic* exhibit.

The Old Colony and Fall River Railroad Museum at Battleship Cove at the corner of Central and Water streets traces the development of both the railroad industry and trolley service. Watch daily railroad movies. For information, call 508-674-9340. Special events include an annual train show the third weekend in January and in mid-summer the Fall River Celebrates America where tall ships and fireworks are featured.

The Fall River Historical Society offers tours of an old mansion at 451 Rock Street. Its 16 Victorian period rooms include exhibits on the mills and mill workers' lives and contain artifacts from the Lizzie Borden ax-murder case. It's closed Mondays, holidays, and January–February. For information, call 508-679-1071.

Take a ride aboard the Fall River Carousel in Battleship Cove, one of the few authentic merry-go-rounds still in existence.

INFORMATION
Battleship Cove Heritage State Park
Fall River, Massachusetts 02720
508-678-1100

BLACKSTONE RIVER AND CANAL HERITAGE STATE PARK
6

LOCATION - The state park is on East Hartford Avenue in Uxbridge.

FEATURES - The park is part of the Blackstone River Valley National Heritage Corridor, birthplace of the American Industrial Revolution.

ACTIVITIES - Stop at Slater Mill Historic Site in Pawtucket, Rhode Island. Slater Mill was built on the banks of the Blackstone River where it could utilize water power to run its spinning operation.

Walk along sections of the Blackstone Canal and towpath located in Uxbridge and in Lincoln, Rhode Island. Hike park trails up Goad Hill and to King Philip's Rock. Go fishing, enjoy a picnic, and go canoeing along the canal. Raft white water in the Blackstone River Gorge. In the winter, go cross-country skiing along the towpath.

Additional hiking is available along trails in Sutton at Purgatory Chasm State Reservation on Purgatory Road. Obtain a permit to go climbing on the chasm walls. For information, call 508-234-3733.

INFORMATION
Blackstone River and Canal Heritage State Park
Uxbridge, Massachusetts 01569
508-278-6486

BORDERLAND STATE PARK
7

LOCATION - Take I-495 to Exit 10. Go north on Massachusetts 123 towards Easton and merge with Massachusetts 106 heading east. One-half mile from here, watch for the park sign onto Poquanticut Avenue. At the next intersection, go left onto Massapoag Avenue and continue another 2 miles to the park.

FEATURES - This country estate, circa 1910, was originally owned by Oakes Ames, a Harvard botanist, and his artist wife, Blanche.

The park is considered to be a "borderland" because it lies between gradually rising hills to the north and flatter land to the south.

Borderland's six ponds have fragrant water lilies and are home to freshwater fish, including perch and bass. The glaciated cliffs and outcroppings on the north contain several glacial erratics, granite boulders torn loose from the bedrock and carried here by the glaciers.

ACTIVITIES - Go canoeing, sailing, and fishing in the ponds. Hike and horseback ride the woodland trails. During spring, summer, and fall, the family's home is open for guided tours Sunday afternoons. During the winter, enjoy cross-country skiing, ice skating, and sledding.

INFORMATION
Borderland State Park
Massapoag Avenue
North Easton, Massachusetts 02356
508-238-6566

BOSTON HARBOR ISLANDS STATE PARK
8

LOCATION - The islands are 45 minutes from downtown Boston and are accessible from three points. Boston's Long Wharf is at the harbor end of State Street and is easily reached from the MBTA Blue Line Aquarium stop. Hewitt's Cove, in Hingham, is located off Massachusetts 3A. Lynn's Seaport Landing Marina is adjacent to Lynn Heritage State Park on Massachusetts 1A.

Ferries from three departure points run from May–October. Once you arrive at Georges Island, you can board a free water taxi to Lovells, Peddocks, Gallops, Grape, and Bumpkin islands. For ferry fare and schedule information, call Bay State Cruise Lines: 617-723-7800; Boston Harbor Cruises: 617-227-4321; or Massachusetts Bay Lines: 617-749-4500. Water taxi information is available at the park office or by calling 617-727-5290 and 617-740-1605.

FEATURES - Seven of the 30 Boston Harbor islands are operated as state parks. Georges Island is dominated by Fort Warren, a National Historic Landmark. Constructed between 1833–69, it was used as a prison for captured Confederates during the Civil War. The island now serves as the entrance to the state park.

ACTIVITIES - Campers need camping reservations. Call DEM at 617-740-1605 or MDC at 617-727-5290 or write to the MDC Reservations and Historic Sites, 98 Taylor Street, Dorchester, Massachusetts. Bring along fresh water unless headed for Georges and Thompson islands.

Take a narrated Bay State Cruise to Georges Island daily from May–October. Limited docking space is available for private boats. Take a guided tour of the island and attend special programs offered six months of the year. Bring along a picnic or pick up a snack from the snack bar. Camp in the 24-site campground with water available.

Enjoy boating and fishing. Hike marked trails, get a good overlook from the observation tower, and attend interpretive programs.

Gallops Island has picnic grounds and hiking paths and once housed a maritime radio school during World War II.

Peddocks Island is one of the largest islands. East Head contains the remains of Fort Andrews, dating back to the turn of the century. It was active in harbor defense from 1904 until the end of World War II. A freshwater pond, campground, and wildlife sanctuary are on West Head.

Bumpkin Island has trails leading to an old children's hospital and stone farmhouse. Reserved camping is available.

Lovells Island has long beaches and the only designated island swimming beach. The remains of Fort Standish, a turn-of-the-century military installation, is in the island's center. Go camping without electricity or running water. Special events and daily programs provide military history and information about the island wildlife. Hike along trails through the dunes, salt marsh, and woods or go fishing.

Grape Island is a wildlife haven and has picnic sites, campsites, and grassy trails.

Thompson Island offers guided tours, hiking, and picnicking. For ferry service, call 617-328-3900.

Little Brewster Island is owned by the U.S. Coast Guard and is the site of the famous Boston Light, the oldest continuous navigational aid in the U.S. For a tour schedule, call 617-740-4290.

While in Boston, tour Boston National Historical Park with naturalists stationed at Faneuil Hall, Charlestown Navy Yard, Bunker Hill Monument, and the visitor center at 15 State Street. For information, call 617-242-5642.

Take a self-guided tour of the Freedom Trail. Pick up a brochure at the information booth on the Tremont Street side of Boston Common and follow the red line painted on the sidewalk. The route covers 2.5 miles, passing 16 sites and winding through the city's historic sections.

One of the sites includes the Old South Meeting House with a special audio system that re-creates the Boston Tea Party. Visitors can see rare colonial artifacts and a scale model of early Boston. The building's most famous meeting occurred here on December 16, 1773, when Bostonians met to discuss the new British tax on tea, resulting in the Boston Tea Party.

Other sites you pass include Faneuil Hall—known as the Cradle of Liberty—built in 1742. Paul Revere's house is Boston's oldest structure. The Old North Church, circa 1723, is Boston's oldest church still in use. Here two lanterns were hung to warn Charlestown that the British were crossing the harbor en route to Concord. Tour the USS *Constitution*, nicknamed *Old Ironsides*, and learn about 1800s shipboard life.

Bunker Hill Monument, site of the June 17, 1775, battle, has daily historical talks.

Take a harbor cruise aboard the *Spirit of Boston* from Rowes Wharf. For information, call 617-569-4449.

Black Heritage Trail winds along Beacon Hill's north slope where nineteenth-century black Bostonians lived. Pick up a trail brochure at the Boston Common Visitor Information Center or at Abiel Smith School, the first public school for black children in the U.S. You'll also see the 1806 African Meeting House, the oldest black church building still standing in the U.S. For information, call 617-742-1854.

INFORMATION
Boston Harbor Island State Park
349 Lincoln Street, Building 45
Hingham, Massachusetts 02043
617-740-1605

BRADLEY PALMER STATE PARK
9
GEORGETOWN–ROWLEY STATE FOREST
10
WILLOWDALE STATE FOREST
11

LOCATION - To reach Bradley Palmer State Park from Boston, follow I-95 north to Massachusetts 1, Topsfield exit. After four miles, turn right onto Ipswich Road and follow signs. Georgetown–Rowley and Willowdale state forests are northwest of the state park.

FEATURES - Bradley Palmer made his fortune in the sugar industry and, after enjoying this area himself, willed it to the state to be shared by others.

ACTIVITIES - Enjoy a picnic, hike, or horseback ride along the park trails, including self-guided Bradley Palmer Nature Trail.

For additional hiking, go to nearby Willowdale State Forest or to Georgetown-Rowley State Forest. Georgetown–Rowley also has a motorized bicycle/ATV trail. During the winter, all three areas provide cross-country ski trails. Bradley Palmer and Georgetown–Rowley both have snowmobile trails.

Attend the annual sculpture exhibition in Bradley Palmer State Park in early September through the end of October.

INFORMATION
Bradley Palmer State Park
Willowdale State Forest
Georgetown–Rowley State Forest
Asbury Street
Topsfield, Massachusetts 01983
508-887-5931

CALLAHAN STATE PARK
See under COCHITUATE STATE PARK

CLARKSBURG STATE PARK AND FOREST
12

LOCATION - Clarksburg is 3 miles north of Clarksburg on Massachusetts 8. Take Middle Road and follow signs to the park.

FEATURES - The forest offers views of both the Berkshire Hills and Green Mountains.

ACTIVITIES - Go camping in one of 47 campsites near the lake. Also enjoy fishing, canoeing, non-motorized boating, or swimming from the beach by Mauserts Pond. Go bicycling or hike around the pond or along part of the Appalachian Trail. Enjoy cross-country skiing during the winter.

INFORMATION
Clarksburg State Park
Middle Road, Route A
Clarksburg, Massachusetts 01225
413-664-8345 or 663-8469

COCHITUATE STATE PARK
13
CALLAHAN STATE PARK
14

LOCATION - Both parks are near Boston. Callahan is reached via Massachusetts 9, Edgell Road. Turn left on Belknap Road, then right on Millwood Street.

Cochituate State Park is 3 miles east of Framingham off I-90 and is reached by taking Exit 13 onto Massachusetts 30.

ACTIVITIES - At Cochituate, go swimming, enjoy a picnic at over 100 pine-shaded tables, and fishing in one of the lakes for stocked trout, bass, pickerel, and sunfish.

Go freshwater boating in one of three lakes: North, Middle, and South lakes. A small boat-launch area for non-motorized craft, including canoes and sail-boats, is located on North Lake with access from Massachusetts 30.

Hikers and equestrians can go to nearby Callahan State Park, which is laced with trails. Go cross-country skiing in the winter.

INFORMATION

Cochituate State Park	Callahan State Park
93 Commonwealth Road	P.O. Box 5485
Cochituate, Massachusetts 01778	Marlborough, Massachusetts 01752
508-653-9641	508-653-9641

DEMAREST LLOYD STATE PARK
15

LOCATION - Demarest Lloyd State Park is on Slocum Neck, 3 miles south of Dartmouth off U.S. 6 on Chase Road. From I-195 heading east, take Exit 12.

ACTIVITIES - Enjoy picnicking, swimming in the calm waters by the beach, fishing, and boating from the ramp.

INFORMATION
Demarest Lloyd State Park
c/o Horseneck Beach State Recreation Area
Route 88
Westport, Massachusetts 02790
508-636-8816

F. GILBERT HILLS STATE PARK
16

LOCATION - Take I-95 south to Massachusetts 140 and head north. Go three-fourths of the way around the Foxboro's common, bearing right onto South Street. Turn right onto Mill Street and follow signs.

ACTIVITIES - The 980-acre park offers picnicking, hiking trails, and horse-back riding. Enjoy cross-country skiing during the winter.

INFORMATION
F. Gilbert Hills State Park
Mill Street
Foxboro, Massachusetts 02035
508-746-0005

FALL RIVER HERITAGE STATE PARK
17

LOCATION - The park is off I-195, Exit 5, at 200 Davol Street in Fall River. It's next to Battleship Cove. To reach the park from Massachusetts 75 South, take the Davol Street Exit.

FEATURES - At its peak, Fall River's mills produced more cloth than any other city in the world.

ACTIVITIES - The park is open year-round, but is closed Monday. Tour the visitor center to learn about Fall River's textile and nautical history and watch the multimedia presentation, "The Fabric of Fall River."

Walk the boardwalk along the waterfront where the Taunton and Quequechan rivers merge and take a guided tour of the old commercial district on Main Street. Climb to the top of the bell tower for an overlook of the skyline and harbor where the USS *Massachusetts* is moored.

In late August attend Fall River Celebrates America, featuring fireworks, boat races, concerts, and a parade.

Battleship Cove State Park at 70 Water Street has several twentieth-century vessels, including the battleship *Massachusetts*, a PT boat, destroyer, and submarine. Tour the Marine Museum. For information, call 508-678-1100.

Tour Old Colony and Fall River Railroad Museum at Battleship Cove, located on the corner of Central and Water streets. An annual train show is held the third weekend in January. For information, call 508-674-9340.

Fall River Historical Society offers tours of the historic mansion, circa 1843, at 451 Rock Street. Besides Victorian displays, you'll see exhibits from the famous Lizzie Borden ax-murder case. The mansion is closed Mondays, holidays, and January–February. For information, call 508-679-1071.

Take a ride on the Fall River Carousel at Battleship Cove, one of the few authentic merry-go-rounds left in the U.S.

INFORMATION
Fall River Heritage State Park
200 Davol Street West
Fall River, Massachusetts 02720
508-675-5759

GARDNER HERITAGE STATE PARK
18

LOCATION - The visitor center is one mile north of Gardner. To reach the park, take Massachusetts 2 to the Massachusetts 68 Hubbardston/Baldwinville Exit. Follow Massachusetts 68, Main Street, north for .3 mile to the center of

Gardner. At the five-way intersection, take an immediate right and follow Lynde Street to the municipal parking lot.

FEATURES - Gardner was known as the Chair City of the World. It has earned an international reputation for its high quality of wicker and wooden furniture.

ACTIVITIES - The park is closed Mondays, but you can attend year-round recreational programs and community events, including a summer outdoor concert series. For a recorded message of the week's events, call 508-632-2099. Tour the visitor center in the restored nineteenth-century firehouse. Watch videos on Gardner's chairmaking and silversmithing industry.

Go canoeing, sailing, picnicking, and swimming. Hike the one-mile nature trail and attend a visitor interpretive program. Take a ride aboard the summer excursion boat.

Take a guided walking tour of Gardner's nineteenth-century commercial district. Arrange for a tour at the visitor center.

Dun Pond Park, close to the state park, has a nature trail, or you can go canoeing, swimming, or take an excursion boat ride.

INFORMATION
Gardner Heritage State Park
26 Lake Street
Gardner, Massachusetts 01440
508-630-1497 (park office)
508-632-2099 (upcoming events)

GEORGETOWN–ROWLEY STATE FOREST
See under BRADLEY PALMER STATE PARK

GREAT BROOK FARM STATE PARK
19

LOCATION - The farm is 20 miles northwest of Boston. From Massachusetts 2, follow signs to Concord. Continue north to Carlisle. Turn left at the Carlisle center rotary and continue towards Chelmsford on Lowell Street for 2 miles.

FEATURES - The farm was developed to give the public an opportunity to observe firsthand the workings of a modern New England dairy farm.

ACTIVITIES - Go canoeing, sailing, fishing, horseback riding, and hiking. During the winter, go cross-country skiing on 7 miles of trails, with night skiing available Tuesday and Thursday. Ski rentals are available. Warm up in the rustic lodge. For ski conditions, call 508-369-7486.

INFORMATION
Great Brook Farm State Park
Lowell Road, Box 829
Carlisle, Massachusetts 01741-0720
508-369-6312

HALIBUT POINT STATE PARK and HALIBUT POINT RESERVATION
20

LOCATION - Take Massachusetts 128 to Gloucester. At the traffic circle, follow Massachusetts 127 to Rockport, watching for the park sign. Turn left on Gott Avenue.

ACTIVITIES - The park is open for day-use only. Park headquarters is located in the World War II Tower building. Pick up a trail guide, including one for the Babson Farm Quarry. Guided tours are given Saturday mornings at 10:00 and 11:30 from May–October.

Go hiking on a section of the Metacomet-Monadnock Trail, a 117-mile trail that passes through the park en route from Connecticut to New Hampshire. Have a picnic, attend visitor programs, go fishing and hiking, and tour the visitor center. During the winter, go cross-country skiing on 4 miles of trails.

Tour Paper House off Massachusetts 127 at Pigeon Cove. It's built completely out of newspapers, including all the furniture. The house is open daily 10:00–5:00 from July–August.

In Amherst, attend the annual Teddy Bear Rally held each August on Amherst Common. Emily Dickinson's home is at 280 Main Street. Seasonal tours are offered. For details, call 413-542-8161. To see the world's largest mastadon, tour Pratt Museum of Natural History at Amherst College.

The Sewall-Scripture House at 40 King has early American and Victorian rooms and costumes, paintings, and photographs. Call 508-546-9533 for hours.

Attend concerts performed by Rockport Chamber Music Festival in June. International dory races and the New Fish Festival are held in Gloucester in mid-June. The Gloucester Waterfront Festival is near the end of August, and Gloucester's Schooner Festival is over Labor Day weekend. For details, contact Cape Ann Chamber of Commerce at 508-283-1601 or 1-800-321-0133.

Take a Cape Ann Island cruise, go lobster trap hauling, or enjoy a whale watching cruise from Rose's Wharf in Gloucester.

INFORMATION
Halibut Point State Park
P.O. Box 710
Rockport, Massachusetts 01966
508-546-2997

HAMPTON PONDS STATE PARK
See under MOUNT TOM STATE RESERVATION

HAROLD PARKER STATE FOREST
21

LOCATION - The park is south of North Andover. From I-95, follow Massachusetts 114 west for 10 miles, following signs.

ACTIVITIES - Go camping, sailing, canoeing, and fishing. Take a hike, go swimming, and attend visitor programs.

In North Andover, tour Stevens-Collidge Place and gardens at 139 Andover Street. The Colonial Revival house has been restored and is open seasonally and on Sunday afternoons. For details, call 508-682-3580.

The Museum of American Textile History at 800 Massachusetts Avenue has exhibits on America's clothing-making history. It's open Tuesday–Sunday. For information, call 508-686-0191.

INFORMATION
Harold Parker State Forest
Route 114
North Andover, Massachusetts 01845
508-686-3391

HOLYOKE HERITAGE STATE PARK
22
HOLYOKE RANGE STATE PARK
23

LOCATION - Holyoke Heritage State Park is between Dwight and Appleton streets behind City Hall in Holyoke. Follow Massachusetts Turnpike to Exit 4. Then take Massachusetts 91 north to Massachusetts 202 north, Exit 16. Turn right at the seventh traffic light.

Holyoke Range State Park is on Massachusetts 116, west of Amherst. Follow Massachusetts Pike to Exit 4. Then take Massachusetts 91 north to the second Northampton Exit. Follow Massachusetts 9 east to Massachusetts 47, then go south to Bay Road and Massachusetts 116 south.

FEATURES - The park showcases the lives of nineteenth-century mill workers.

ACTIVITIES - Holyoke Heritage State Park is open from mid-May through late November. Tour the visitor center resembling a railroad roundhouse and watch "Holyoke Is Its People." The visitor center offers performances, films, ethnic festivals, concerts, historic home tours, children's programs, and an annual Celebrate Holyoke weekend. For schedules, call 413-534-0909.

Take a ranger-led walking tour of Holyoke's nineteenth-century canals and mills. Enjoy an hour-long narrated train ride on a 1920s vintage railroad on Saturday and Sunday from mid-May through mid-October.

Take a self-guided or a weekend guided tour during the spring and summer to see Skinner Silk Mills, Whiting Paper Company, and workers' housing. For reservations, call 413-534-1723.

Visit the Volleyball Hall of Fame to see photographs and exhibits tracing the sport's history. For information, call 413-536-0926. Bring along a picnic to enjoy in the adjacent park.

To go hiking, go to Holyoke Range State Park where a section of the 117-mile-long Metacomet-Monadnock Trail passes en route from Connecticut to New Hampshire. Have a picnic, attend visitor programs, go fishing, and tour the visitor center. During the winter, go cross-country skiing on 4 miles of trails.

INFORMATION

Holyoke Heritage State Park	Holyoke Range State Park
221 Appleton Street	Route 11
Holyoke, Massachusetts 01040	Amherst, Massachusetts 01002
413-534-1723	413-253-2883

HOPKINTON STATE PARK
See under ASHLAND STATE PARK

LAKE DENNISON STATE RECREATION AREA
24
OTTER RIVER STATE FOREST
25

LOCATION - Lake Dennison State Recreation Area is southwest of Winchendon. From Massachusetts 2 west, take Exit 20. Turn right onto Baldwinville Road, and then another right onto U.S. 202 north. It's 2 miles beyond Otter River State Forest.

Otter River State Forest is on Winchendon Road, one mile north of Baldwinsville on U.S. 202.

ACTIVITIES - At Lake Dennison, camp in the 151-site campground with a dump station from Memorial Day through Columbus Day. Enjoy a picnic, non-motorized boating from the ramp, fishing, swimming, and canoeing. Ride equestrian trails, go hiking, and attend interpretive programs. During the winter, go cross-country skiing and snowmobiling.

At Otter River, camp in the 100-site campground from Memorial Day through Labor Day. Go trout fishing in the stream, hiking, hunting, swimming, and picnicking. During the winter, go cross-country skiing.

INFORMATION

Lake Dennison State Recreation Area
Route 202
Winchendon, Massachusetts 01475
Mailing address:
Otter River State Park
Baldwinville, Massachusetts 01436
508-939-8962

Otter River State Forest
New Winchendon Road
Baldwinville, Massachusetts 01436
508-939-8962

LAWRENCE HERITAGE STATE PARK
26

LOCATION - The park is at One Jackson Street in Lawrence. Follow I-495 to Exit 45, Marston Street. Go left onto Canal Street and continue 3 blocks to Jackson Street.

FEATURES - Lawrence is referred to as Queen of the Mill Towns when its mills produced 800 miles of cloth daily. Its landmark textile strike in 1912, the Bread and Roses strike, led to national reform of the laws regarding workers' rights.

ACTIVITIES - The park is open from early May through early November. Tour the visitor center located in an 1840s restored workers' boarding house along the canal. Watch the video presentation, "The Great Strike of 1912." Visit a turn-of-the-century kitchen.

Take a walking tour of Lawrence, a mill town settled in 1655. Many beautiful old mansions and mill buildings have been restored. For tour information, call the state park.

Visit Immigrant City Archives at 135 Parker to see old photographs and to hear oral histories from historical Lawrence. It's open Monday–Thursday from 9:00–4:30 and by appointment. Call 508-686-9230.

Enjoy a picnic, fish for shad, and hear a free band concert at Pemberton Park along the banks of the Merrimack. Call 508-685-2591 for recorded events in the park, including River Monster Week, Great Pemberton Pumpkin Hunt, and the Bread and Roses Labor Day Heritage Festival.

Visit one of America's first water towers at the top of Amers Street in Tower Hill's "district of mansions" and enjoy a scenic view of Lawrence and Merrimack Valley. For tours, call 508-685-2951.

INFORMATION

Lawrence Heritage State Park
1 Jackson Street
Lawrence, Massachusetts 01840
508-794-1655

LOWELL NATIONAL HISTORICAL PARK AND HERITAGE STATE PARK

27

LOCATION - To reach Lowell Heritage State Park at 25 Shattuck Street in Lowell, take either I-495 or Massachusetts 3 to the exit for the Lowell Connector. Stay on the Connector to Exit 5N, Thorndike Street, and follow signs.

FEATURES - Lowell, called City of Spindles in the early 1800s because of all its power looms, is the largest of the Heritage State Parks and requires at least two full days to see all its major offerings. It commemorates Lowell's role in the American Labor Movement, and you'll learn about the mills, the "mill girls," and how the innovative canals were developed. Both the state and national park include over 5 miles of canals, operating gatehouses, and nineteenth-century commercial structures.

ACTIVITIES - Take a guided walking tour of historic Lowell or a guided 2.5-hour mill and canal tour offered during the summers.

Take a 2¼-hour barge or reconstructed 1901 trolley car tour offered July–Columbus Day. Tours go every day from Memorial Day through Columbus Day and advance reservations are required. Call 508-459-1000.

Watch the slide show and tour the waterpower exhibit in the Mack Building to learn how transportation locks work. Stroll through the restored 1835 mill boarding house to get a glimpse into the life of early immigrants who worked here.

Stop by the national park visitor center at 246 Market Street to see "Lowell: The Industrial Revelation." Boott Cotton Mills Museum features a re-created weave room with 90 operating power looms.

Stroll along the Merrimack River on the Vandenberg Esplanade's 1.5-mile-long landscaped riverbank park. Go down to the Bellegarde Boathouse to take a boat ride through the newly restored transportation locks on Lowell's historic canal system. Enjoy an evening cruise on the river from June–August. Attend summer concerts at the Sampas Pavilion.

Market Mills on Market Street is a restored mill complex now housing a gift shop, ethnic cuisine, and an art gallery. The New England Quilt Museum located within the complex is the only one of its kind on the East Coast. It's open Tuesday–Sunday from 11:00–5:00 year-round. For information, call 508-459-7819.

Tour Whistler's House and Museum of Art at 243 Worthen Street. They're open Wednesday–Saturday from 11:00–4:00 and Sundays from 1:00–4:00 from March–December. Call 508-452-7641 for guided tour reservations.

Ten minutes from the park is Lowell-Dracut-Tynsboro State Forest where you can hike scenic trails beside quarry sites, glacial boulders, and ponds.

Many visitors come during the spring to enjoy the wildflowers and then in the fall for the colorful fall foliage. Come to cross-country ski during the winter. Call 508-453-1950 for information.

INFORMATION

Lowell National Historical Park
169 Merrimack Street
Lowell, Massachusetts 01852
508-459-1000

Lowell Heritage State Park
25 Shattuck Street
Lowell, Massachusetts 01852
508-453-1950

LYNN HERITAGE STATE PARK
28

LOCATION - The park is on the water opposite the North Shore Community College at 154 Lynnway in Lynn. To reach the park, take Route 1A, the Lynnway. The visitor center is at 590 Washington Street.

FEATURES - Lynn is famous for its shoe manufacturing and for the nineteenth-century reformers who lived here.

ACTIVITIES - Exhibits are open year-round on Wednesdays and Sundays from 10:00–4:00. Tours on other days are available by reservation. Rent paddle boats on weekends and Wednesday evenings in July and August. Visit the Boston Harbor islands by boat or water taxi in July, leaving from Lynn's Waterfront Park. Call 617-740-1605 for information.

Walk along Waterfront Park's boardwalk, watching for the large ceramic and Venetian glass mosaic depicting the city's history. Go fishing and tour the visitor center and watch their slide show. Attend a free summer outdoor concert in the park.

Annual functions at Seaport Landing in Lynn include fishing tournaments, Harbor Monster Day, Blessing of the Fleet, regattas, a mystery rendezvous, and dock parties. For details, call 617-592-5821 or 617-592-6010.

INFORMATION

Lynn Heritage State Park
590 Washington Street
Lynn, Massachusetts 01902
617-598-1974

MASSASOIT STATE PARK
29

LOCATION - Massasoit is 3 miles west of Middleboro off Massachusetts 18. It's also 2 miles south of East Taunton. Take Massachusetts 24 south to U.S. 44 and follow signs.

ACTIVITIES - Camp in the 126-site campground, 96 with electrical hookups and a trailer dump. Go bass fishing in the lake and swimming and boating from the ramp.

In Middleboro, tour Middleboro Historical Museum off Massachusetts 105 and North Main. For information, call 508-947-1969.

INFORMATION
Massasoit State Park
Middleboro Avenue
Taunton, Massachusetts 02780
508-822-7405

MAUDSLAY STATE PARK
30

LOCATION - To reach Maudslay from the north and south, take I-95 to Massachusetts 113 East. Follow 113 East ½ mile to Noble Street. At the stop sign, turn left onto Ferry Road. Follow signs for 3.3 miles.

From the west, off I-495 take Exit 55 to Massachusetts 110 east. Continue one mile to Merrill Street. Turn right at the second street and continue on Merrill Street/Spofford Street for 1.5 miles. Turn right before the stop sign onto Ferry Road. Follow signs for 4 more miles to reach the park.

FEATURES - The park occupies the former Moseley Estate, and features nineteenth-century gardens, including one of the largest stands of mountain laurel in eastern Massachusetts.

ACTIVITIES - Maudslay is open year-round from 8:00 AM until dusk where you can hike scenic trails. Three special walks include the ¾ mile Garden Walk, the 1¼-mile River Trail, and the 3-mile Laurel Trail. Attend an interpretive program. Equestrians and bicyclists also enjoy exploring the trails and cross-country skiers arrive in the winter.

Stroll through Cushing House Museum at 98 High in Newburyport. The Federal mansion, circa 1808, has many paintings, a carriage house, and garden. It's open seasonally Tuesday–Sunday. For details, call 508-462-2681. The Custom House Maritime Museum on 25 Water Street has maritime history exhibits. It's closed winter weekdays. For details, call 508-462-8681.

INFORMATION
Maudslay State Park
Curzon's Mill Road
Newburyport, Massachusetts 01950
617-465-7223

MOHAWK TRAIL STATE FOREST
31

LOCATION - The 6,457-acre forest is 3 miles west of Charlemont off Massachusetts 2.

FEATURES - A 63-mile touring road runs from Orange to North Adams, following a legendary Indian trail.

ACTIVITIES - Go camping in the 56-site campground from May 1 through Columbus Day or stay in one of the 5 cabins available year-round. Most cabins must be reserved in advance. Go fishing, hiking the various trails to lookouts, or climb Clark or Todd mountains. Go picnicking, swimming, and attend visitor interpretive programs. The park is a popular spot for fall foliage viewers. During the winter, go cross-country skiing and snowmobiling.

INFORMATION
Mohawk Trail State Forest
Route 2, P.O. Box 7
Charlemont, Massachusetts 01339
413-339-5504

MOORE STATE PARK
See under RUTLAND STATE PARK

MOUNT TOM STATE RESERVATION
32
MOUNT CHICOPEE MEMORIAL STATE PARK
33
HAMPTON PONDS STATE PARK
34

LOCATION - Chicopee Memorial State Park is on Burnett Road in Chicopee. Follow Massachusetts Pike to Exit 6. Bear right and continue another 1.4-mile. The park is on the left side of the road.

Mount Tom is on Reservation Road north of Holyoke. Follow Massachusetts Pike, I-90, to Exit 4 and take I-91 north to Exit 17A. Follow Massachusetts 5 north for 4 miles.

Hampton Ponds is near Westfield. Follow Massachusetts Pike to Exit 3, Massachusetts 10/202 north. At the traffic light, follow Massachusetts 202. The park is 2 miles further on the left side of the road.

FEATURES - Mount Tom Reservation includes an entire mountain range, wonderful views of the Pioneer Valley, and year-round recreation.

ACTIVITIES - Come to Mount Tom for a picnic, fishing, swimming, hiking on 30 miles of trails, and to climb the lookout tower. Late summer visitors to the Pioneer Valley can enjoy numerous country fairs, ethnic festivals, and other annual events. Nearby Mount Tom Ski Area offers 17 slopes and trails plus a 4,000-foot alpine slide and a wave pool. Go ice skating and skiing in the winter.

At Chicopee Memorial State Park, enjoy a picnic, go swimming, fishing, bicycling, and cross-country skiing during the winter.

At Hampton Ponds, enjoy a picnic and go swimming, fishing, or boating.

INFORMATION

Mount Tom State Reservation
Route 5
Holyoke, Massachusetts 01401
413-527-9858
413-536-0416

Chicopee Memorial State Park
Burnett Road
Chicopee Falls, Massachusetts 01020
413-594-9416

Hampton Ponds State Park
Route 202
Westfield, Massachusetts 01089
508-413-3985

MYLES STANDISH STATE FOREST
35

LOCATION - The forest covers over 14,000 acres in the towns of Plymouth and Carver. From Massachusetts 3 in Plymouth, take either Exit 5 or 6. From Massachusetts 58, take Tremont Street in South Carver and then Cranberry Road. Forest headquarters are on Cranberry Road.

FEATURES - Thirty-five of the park's glacial "kettle ponds" were formed over 10,000 years ago when the last continental glacier receded from North America.

ACTIVITIES - The park has one of Massachusetts's largest camping areas with 470 campsites. Two day-use areas offer picnicking, swimming, fishing, and canoeing. Bicycle along 15 miles of trails. Equestrians have access to 20 miles of trails and recreational vehicles have 35 miles of trails. Three miles of hiking trails take visitors into a pine forest.

Go hunting in season and fishing in stocked ponds for bass, perch, and pickerel. Attend interpretive programs, including pond shore walks, cranberry bog explorations, and fire tower tours.

During the winter, cross-country skiers come to ski 18 miles of trails.

INFORMATION
Myles Standish State Forest
Cranberry Road
South Carver, Massachusetts 02366
508-866-2526

NATURAL BRIDGE STATE PARK
36

LOCATION - From downtown North Adams, follow Massachusetts 8 north for approximately ½ mile.

FEATURES - The 550-year-old natural marble bridge was formed by water erosion as water tumbled through the 45-foot-deep gorge.

In the 1800s, a quarry operated here, producing coarse-grained white marble used for tombstones in Hillside Cemetery and old Phoenix Hotel in North Adams.

ACTIVITIES - The park is open from May 15–October 30. Many walking trails cross the park.

Enjoy a picnic, go fishing, and attend interpretive programs year-round. Bring your camera to photograph the natural bridge.

Mount Greylock, rising 3,491 feet, is Massachusetts's highest peak. Accessible by car, attend interpretive programs given during the summer months on the mountain's summit and at the visitor center at Lanesboro. Camp in one of 35 campsites.

INFORMATION
Natural Bridge State Park
c/o Western Gateway Heritage State Park
Visitors Center, Building 4
North Adams, Massachusetts 01247
413-663-6392 or 663-6312 (summer) and 413-442-8928 (winter)

NICKERSON STATE PARK
37

LOCATION - Take U.S. 6 to Exit 12, Massachusetts 6A west. The park is 4 miles east of Brewster on Massachusetts 6A.

FEATURES - It has 8 inland freshwater "kettle" ponds formed when glaciers retreated from the Cape over 10,000 years ago. Nickerson is one of the largest state parks.

ACTIVITIES - Nickerson has 418 campsites located around the ponds and a dump station. Enjoy motor boating and canoeing on Cliff Pond. Swim, picnic on the beach, and canoe on Flax Pond. Also, go fishing for trout and bass stocked year-round at Higgins Pond.

Bicyclists have access to 8 miles of the 20-mile Cape Cod Rail Trail passing through the park on its way from Dennis to Eastham, as well as cycling an 8-mile park bicycle trail. ATVs are allowed on park trails. Equestrians have a 2-mile marked trail plus access to roads in the woods which are beside the Cape Cod Trail.

Tour the nature center. Bird watchers come to Higgins Pond, a regular stop for many birds on the migratory route. Hikers can explore 3 trails around the park ponds.

During the winter, go ice skating and ice fishing on the frozen ponds and cross-country skiing.

Brewster is in the center of Cape Cod and has many beautiful nineteenth-century homes built by early sea captains. Tour Cape Cod Museum, 3 miles west of town on Massachusetts 6A. For information, call 508-385-9252.

The Cape's oldest windmill, built in 1893, is on U.S. 6, opposite the town hall in Eastham. It's open the last week in June–September 15.

Tour Cape Cod's Museum of Natural History and hike the nature trails. It's 1.5 miles west of town on U.S. 6A. For information, call 508-896-3867.

Hikers can take an 8-mile walk along the seashore from historic Highland Lighthouse to Race Point.

Cape Cod National Seashore has additional hiking trails. Near Marconi Station, the Atlantic White Cedar Swamp Trail takes you via boardwalk to a well-hidden swamp hollow. From the Salt Pond Visitor Center, the Nauset Marsh Trail winds from the meadow to a pine forest.

Bicyclists, walkers, and equestrians have access to several trails within the national seashore. A scenic bike ride follows a series of loops south of Race Point Beach. To obtain a "Bikeways on Cape Cod" brochure, contact the Cape Cod National Seashore at 508-349-3785.

Visitors can also go surfing, board sailing, or fishing in the ocean.

INFORMATION
Nickerson State Park
P.O. Box 787
Brewster, Massachusetts 02631
508-896-3491

OTTER RIVER STATE FOREST
See under LAKE DENNISON STATE RECREATION AREA

PEARL HILL STATE PARK
38

LOCATION - Pearl Hill State Park is near West Townsend on Massachusetts 119. Turn left at the traffic lights onto New Fitchburg Road.

ACTIVITIES - Go canoeing, sailing, fishing, and swimming. Camp in the 51-site campground from Memorial Day through Labor Day. Go hiking and horseback riding on the trails. During the winter, go cross-country skiing and snowmobiling.

INFORMATION
Pearl Hill State Park
Willard Brook State Forest
P.O. Box 111, New Fitchburg Road
West Townsend, Massachusetts 01474
508-597-8802

PILGRIM MEMORIAL STATE PARK (PLYMOUTH ROCK)
39

LOCATION - Pilgrim Memorial is on Water Street in Plymouth Harbor.

FEATURES - Plymouth Rock commemorates the Pilgrim's landing spot in 1620 and is one of the United States' most famous historic sites.

ACTIVITIES - Visit the Plymouth Rock's historic site which is accessible via paved, level walkways. Enjoy fishing and boating.

In Plymouth, visit Cranberry World's Visitor Center at 225 Water Street to learn the various uses for the cranberry. For information, call 508-747-2350. Take a walking tour of historic Plymouth. Pick up a map at the visitor center.

Mayflower II, moored at State Pier, is a reproduction of the ship that brought the Pilgrims to the New World and portrays life on the 66-day voyage. It's open daily from April–November. Purchase a combination ticket that enables you to visit Plimoth Plantation. For information, call 508-746-1622.

Plimoth Plantation is 3 miles south of town on Massachusetts 3A. Here you'll see costumed interpreters presenting life during the seventeenth century. It's open daily from April–November. For information, call 508-746-1622.

During August, go to Burial Hill at the head of Town Square at 5:00 each Friday. Citizens come dressed in Pilgrim garments and reenact the church service performed in 1620 for the 44 survivors of their first winter in Plymouth. To learn more about the early Pilgrims, go to Pilgrim Hall Museum on Court and Chilton. It's open daily 9:30–4:30. For information, call 508-746-1620.

Visit historic buildings, including the Old Court House in the Town Square, the Richard Sparrow House on 42 Summer, and the Spooner House at 27 North Street. Pilgrim Hall Museum at 75 Court has Pilgrim artifacts.

INFORMATION
Pilgrim Memorial State Park
103 Long Pond Road
Plymouth, Massachusetts 02360-2604
508-746-0005

QUINSIGAMOND STATE PARK
40

LOCATION - This urban park is on the western shore of Lake Quinsigamond on North Lake Avenue in Worcester. Take Massachusetts Pike to Millbury Exit. Follow Massachusetts 122 east to Massachusetts 20 and then go east to Sunderland Road. Take the second right onto Lake Avenue, across Massachusetts 9, and follow signs.

ACTIVITIES - Regatta Point is in the northernmost section of the park and offers fishing from a large fishing deck, sailing, and boating. You can also go camping and swimming from the beach.

While in Worcester, visit New England Science Center east of town via Massachusetts 9. You'll see a primate center, natural science exhibits, and the Alden Omnisphere. For information, call 508-791-9211.

The Worcester Art Museum at 55 Salisbury has an outstanding art collection. For details, call 508-799-4406. Tour Salisbury Mansion at 40 Highland Street to see a restored mansion re-creating the life of an 1880s family. It's open Tuesday–Sunday. For details, call 508-753-8278.

Tour Old Sturbridge Village on Massachusetts 20. Open year-round, the living history museum re-creates 1830s New England. Special events, tours, and lectures are available. For information, call 508-347-3362.

INFORMATION
Quinsigamond State Park
10 North Lake Avenue
Worcester, Massachusetts 01605
508-755-6880

ROBINSON STATE PARK
41

LOCATION - Follow Massachusetts Pike to Exit 4. Then follow Massachusetts 91 south to Massachusetts 57 west. Then take Massachusetts 187 north to North Street in Agawam and follow signs.

ACTIVITIES - The park is open from Memorial Day through October 1. Go fishing, hike along a section of the Metacomet-Monadnock Trail that passes through the park from Connecticut en route to New Hampshire, and attend visitor interpretive programs. A recreational field is located in the Provin area. Swimming is available at the Trestle area.

INFORMATION
Robinson State Park
North Street
Agawam, Massachusetts 01001
413-786-2877

RUTLAND STATE PARK
42
MOORE STATE PARK
43

LOCATION - Rutland State Park is 3 miles southwest of Rutland on Massachusetts 122A.

Moore State Park is northwest of Paxton and south of Rutland on Massachusetts 122A.

ACTIVITIES - Rutland State Park has three ponds. From Memorial Day through Labor Day, enjoy canoeing, sailing, motor boating, and swimming in the largest pond. Go fishing for bass, perch, crappie, and bullheads in Long Pond. During the winter, go snowmobiling along summer hiking trails.

Moore State Park offers additional fishing and boating opportunities.

INFORMATION

Rutland State Park
Route 122A
Rutland, Massachusetts 01543
508-886-6333

Moore State Park
Mill Street
Paxton, Massachusetts 01612
508-792-3969

SKINNER STATE PARK
44

LOCATION - The park is 3 miles north of South Hadley. Follow Massachusetts 9 east and then Massachusetts 47 south.

ACTIVITIES - Skinner State Park is for day-use only and covers 390 acres on 954-foot Mount Holyoke. As you drive into the park, watch for Titan's Piazza, a volcanic formation with overhanging rock columns, and Devil's Football, a magnetic boulder that weighs 300 tons.

Drive to the top of Mount Holyoke to get a wonderful view of the Connecticut Valley. Go hiking and tour the visitor center. The Metacomet-Monadnock Trail passes through the park en route from Connecticut to New Hampshire. Go cross-country skiing in the winter.

INFORMATION
Skinner State Park
Route 47
Hadley, Massachusetts 01075
413-477-2880

SPRINGFIELD HERITAGE STATE PARK
45

LOCATION - The park is in Court Square on Main Street in Springfield.

ACTIVITIES - Attend concerts in Symphony Hall and sporting events in Civic Center. A 300-foot campanile is open by reservation Monday–Friday from 8:00–4:30 from May–October weather permitting. For reservations, call 413-787-6080.

In Springfield, basketball fans can tour the Naismith Memorial Basketball Hall of Fame off I-91, using Exits 4 and 7. Watch "Hoopla," shoot baskets from moving walkways, and witness a multi-screen game presentation. For information, call 413-781-5759.

Museum-goers can tour several museums at Chestnut and State streets, including the Connecticut Valley Historical Museum, George Walter Vincent Smith's Art Museum, Museum of Fine Art, and Springfield Science Museum.

Motorcycle buffs can tour Indian Motorcycle Museum off I-291 via St. James Avenue, Exit 4, on Hendee Street. For details, call 413-737-2624.

INFORMATION
Springfield Heritage State Park
Springfield, Massachusetts 01109
413-549-1461

WAHCONAH FALLS STATE PARK
46

LOCATION - The park is 3 miles north of Dalton. Follow Massachusetts 7 north and then Massachusetts 9 east and follow signs.

FEATURES - Come to see Wahconah Falls and enjoy a picnic and hike along several miles of scenic roads.

To learn more about papermaking, stop by the Crane Museum of Papermaking, located one mile west of Dalton on Massachusetts 9. It's open Monday–Friday from 2:00–5:00 from June 1 through mid-October. For information, call 413-684-2600.

In nearby Pittsfield, go hiking and tour Arrowhead at 780 Holmes Road, where Herman Melville wrote Moby Dick. For details, call 413-442-1793. The ski lodge in Pittsfield State Forest accommodates 75 people.

Hancock Shaker Village is on Massachusetts 20 and has nineteenth-century buildings, craft demonstrations, and tours. For information, call 413-443-1088.

INFORMATION
Wahconah Falls State Park
c/o Pittsfield State Forest
Cascade Street
Pittsfield, Massachusetts 01201
413-442-8992

WALDEN POND STATE RESERVATION
47

LOCATION - The pond is in the greater Boston area. Follow Massachusetts 2 and then Massachusetts 126 south and follow signs.

FEATURES - Walden Pond is a National Register Historic and Literary Landmark. Over a half-million people visit here annually.

ACTIVITIES - Once the park's limit of 1,000 people is reached, it is closed with a reopening time posted at entry points to the park. Parking is restricted to the lot off Massachusetts 126.

Come to go swimming with lifeguards on duty from Memorial Day through Labor Day. Swimming across the pond is prohibited. Visitors can also go canoeing, rowing, picnicking, hiking, and fishing. Park interpreters offer guided walks and educational programs year-round. They also staff a replica of Thoreau's house where he lived from 1845–47.

While in Concord, visit Minute Man National Historical Park on Battle Road, Massachusetts 2A. Tour Battle Road Visitor Center and North Bridge Visitor Center. Walk over the North Bridge west of Monument Street. Continue another mile east of town to tour the Wayside on Friday–Tuesday from mid-April through October.

Other historical homes to visit include Old Manse on Monument Street, Orchard House on Lexington Road, and Thoreau Lyceum at 156 Belknap Street.

INFORMATION
Walden Pond State Reservation
Route 126
Concord, Massachusetts 01742
508-369-3254

WELLS STATE PARK
48

LOCATION - The park is 2 miles north of Sturbridge off Massachusetts 49N.

ACTIVITIES - Camp in the 59-site campground with a trailer dump station. It's open May 1 through mid-October. Go fishing and swimming or canoeing, sailing, and motorboating from the ramp in Walker Pond. Attend visitor interpretive programs and go horseback riding and hiking.

Visit Old Sturbridge Village on Massachusetts 20W, ½ mile west of the intersection of I-84 and I-90. Wander through this re-created New England farming village, circa 1830s, and watch costumed interpreters demonstrate what life was like in the early nineteenth century. For information, call 508-347-5383.

INFORMATION
Wells State Park
Route 49, Mountain Road
Sturbridge, Massachusetts 01566
508-347-9257

WENDELL STATE PARK
49

LOCATION - Follow Massachusetts 2 east to Massachusetts 63. Go south through Miller Falls. Follow Montague Road and park signs.

ACTIVITIES - Go canoeing, fishing, hiking, picnicking, and swimming. Go cross-country skiing on 20 miles of groomed trails and roads during the winter.

Attend their annual Northeast Chevy-GMC truck meet in early August.

INFORMATION
Wendell State Park
Wendell Road
Wendell, Massachusetts 01379
413-659-3797

WESTERN GATEWAY HERITAGE STATE PARK
50

LOCATION - The park is at 9 Furnace Street in North Adams off Massachusetts 8, south of Main Street and Massachusetts 2.

FEATURES - North Adams is the state's smallest city, snuggled in the hills of the Northern Berkshires.

The park occupies a restored freight yard district with shops and restaurants. Exhibits explain the nineteenth-century miracle of the building of the Hoosac Railroad Tunnel.

ACTIVITIES - Enjoy a picnic. Stop by the visitor center housed in the Boston and Maine Freight House to learn about nineteenth-century railroading. Walking tours are offered weekends from Memorial Day through Columbus Day. Attend outdoor concerts on Thursdays in July and August.

Take a free guided tour of the park buildings and old railroad yard. Another tour takes you to see the Victorian architecture of North Adams. For reservations, call 413-663-6312.

Children can take a ride through the freight yard on a miniature train from May–October, weather permitting.

Come in the fall for the annual Fall Foliage Festival.

Visit nearby Natural Bridge State Park, 2 miles away from the visitor center. The park's 30-foot white marble formation is estimated to be 500 million years old.

INFORMATION
Western Gateway Heritage State Park
9 Furnace Street Bypass
North Adams, Massachusetts 01247
413-663-6312

WILLOWDALE STATE FOREST
See under BRADLEY PALMER STATE PARK

WOMPATUCK STATE PARK
51

LOCATION - The park is off Massachusetts 228 and southeast of Hingham. Follow Free Street to Union Street and go south for 1.5 miles to reach the park entrance.

ACTIVITIES - Wompatuck includes 3,500 acres of woods, fields, streams, and ponds. Enjoy hiking and bicycling along 15 miles of paved trails. Camp in the 400-site campground, 120 with electrical hookups and a dump station. Go canoeing, sailing, fishing, hiking, and bicycling. Attend visitor interpretive programs and tour the visitor center. Visit Mount Blue Spring at the bottom of a steep staircase.

During the winter, go snowmobiling or cross-country skiing on 9 miles of trails.

INFORMATION
Wompatuck State Park
Union Street
Hingham, Massachusetts 02043
617-749-7160

NEW HAMPSHIRE

New England has over 60 peaks with summits rising over 4,000 feet with 48 located in New Hampshire's White Mountains. Mount Washington, rising to 6,288 feet, is the highest peak in the Northeast. Mount Monadnock is the single most climbed mountain in North America.

The White Mountain National Forest has over 250 trails, 45 lakes and ponds, 650 miles of fishing streams, and the largest moose population in the state. Moose Mania Weekend in early June kicks off the area's celebrations. Moose tours are featured daily from July 4th through foliage season. For details, call the Chamber of Commerce at 603-752-6060 or 1-800-992-7480.

One of the most spectacular drives in America, especially during "leaf peeping" season is along the Kancamagus Highway. The 34½-mile road stretches from Conway to the Pemigewasset River at Lincoln along New Hampshire 112. It climbs almost 3,000 feet as it crosses the flank of Mount Kancamagus. Stop for a picnic at Lower Falls or Rocky Gorge.

Three good hikes from Kancamagus include the 3¼-mile Boulder Loop Trail from Dugway Road which is next to Covered Bridge Campground, a 4-mile hike to Greely Ponds which starts 9½ miles east of Lincoln, or a 5-minute walk to the gorge at Rocky Gorge Scenic Area.

One of the best places for enjoying the fantastic fall foliage is in the White Mountains in late September–October. For a free copy of *The Leaf Peepers' Guide: Autumn in White Mountains Attractions*, write to P.O. Box 10MG, North Woodstock, New Hampshire 03262.

The Cathedral of the Pines provides one of the most spectacular views of Mount Monadnock. It's located off New Hampshire 119 in Rindge. Altar of the Nation is an outdoor chapel with a 55-foot belltower dedicated as a memorial to American women who died serving their country. Carillonic chimes in the tower play each half hour. Tour the museum to see memorabilia from the American Revolution through the Gulf War. Services are held Sundays May–September.

Hikers seeking information on mountain weather and trail conditions can contact the Appalachian Mountain Club, Route 16, Pinkham Notch, New Hampshire 03581, or call 603-466-2727. One of the best times for hiking in

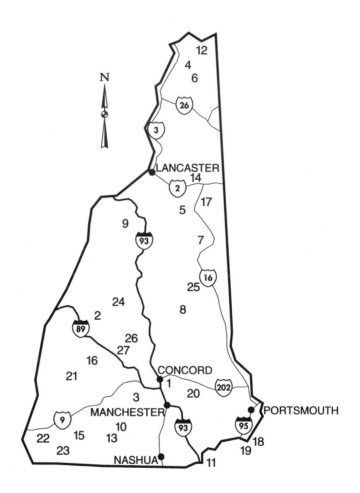

N

12
4
6

26

3

LANCASTER
14
2

5
17

9
93
7

16

25

24

8

2
89

26
27

16
CONCORD

21
1

20
202

3
MANCHESTER
PORTSMOUTH

9
95

10
93

22
15
13
18

23
19

NASHUA
11

the White Mountains is during spring runoff and again in the fall, usually in mid- to late September. Bring plenty of insect repellent and wear waterproof hiking boots, especially in spring and early summer.

AMC operates a shuttle service among major trailheads in the White Mountains so you can leave a car at the destination end of your trip and shuttle to your starting point. For information, call 603-466-2721. AMC also has a series of huts located a day's hike apart along the Appalachian Trail.

Several sections of the New Hampshire Heritage Trail are complete. Eventually, this 230-mile trail will extend the length of the state from Massachusetts to Canada following several major rivers.

New Hampshire has 6 ATV-bike trails, offering over 150 miles of riding. These trails are also utilized by equestrians, mountain and trail bikes, and snowmobiles, and provide access routes to fishing streams and ponds.

Several notches, known as gaps but actually narrow mountain passes, are located in New Hampshire. Seven well-known ones in the White Mountains include Kinsman, Franconia, Crawford, Bear, Pinkham, Dixville, and Evans.

New Hampshire has 11 state parks that offer tent camping, and 3 RV parks that offer full hookups. Campgrounds are generally open mid-May through mid-October. Lafayette campground in Franconia Notch and Monadnock State Park remain open for winter camping, but there is no water.

Visitors planning to participate in winter outdoor activities in the White Mountains should realize that winters are known for their severity. Expect sudden and extreme variations, low temperatures, and high winds. Obtain a current local weather forecast before setting out.

For special events within the state in spring, summer, and fall, including foliage reports and alpine skiing conditions, call 603-224-2525 or 1-800-258-3608. For cross-country ski conditions, call 603-224-6363 or 1-800-262-6660. For snowmobile trail conditions, call 603-224-4666 or 1-800-258-3609 outside New Hampshire.

BEAR BROOK STATE PARK
1

LOCATION - The large state park is 5 miles northeast of Hooksett off New Hampshire 28 and 2 miles east of Allenstown. It's also 8 miles northeast of Suncook off New Hampshire 28.

ACTIVITIES - The 10,000-acre park is open from mid-May through mid-October. Visitors can go swimming from the beach, picnicking, practice archery, work out on a fitness course, and enjoy canoe and rowboat rentals. Hike along 20 miles of hiking trails, mountain bike, and go stream and pond fishing. Camp in the 81-site campground with a dump station and purchase supplies in the camp store.

Tour the museum complex composed of three museums. The CCC Museum, Family Camping Museum, and the historic meeting house are open summer weekends from 10:00–4:00. The Snowmobile Museum, with its impressive collection of snow machines is open weekends, December–March. A nature center is open from May–October.

Go cross-country skiing and snowmobiling in the winter.

INFORMATION
Bear Brook State Park
RFD 1, Box 507
Allenstown, New Hampshire 03275
603-485-9874

CARDIGAN STATE PARK
2

LOCATION - The park is off U.S. 4 and New Hampshire 118, 4½ miles east of Canaan.

ACTIVITIES - A mountain road leads to a picnic spot on Mount Cardigan's western slope. Hike to the 3,121-foot summit via Westwoods Trail. Many hikers use the AMC lodge east of the park as a starting point for their hikes. Visit the solar-powered fire tower, manned from April–November. Cross-country skiers come here during the winter to practice their telemarking.

A nearby attraction is Sculptured Rocks Natural Area, 2 miles west of Groton between New Hampshire 3A and 118. Here you'll see interesting potholes eroded into various shapes by water-borne stones and sediments dating back to the last Ice Age. Bring along a picnic.

INFORMATION
Cardigan State Park
P.O. Box 163
Canaan, New Hampshire 03741
603-523-4562

CLOUGH STATE PARK
3

LOCATION - The park is between New Hampshire 114 and 13, approximately 5 miles east of Weare.

ACTIVITIES - Go swimming in the 140-acre river pool from the 900-foot beach. Go fishing, boating from the launch, and bring along a picnic to enjoy. During the winter, cross-country ski or snowmobile.

INFORMATION
Clough State Park
Weare, New Hampshire 03281
603-529-7112

COLEMAN STATE PARK
4

LOCATION - The park is off New Hampshire 26 via an unnumbered road, 12 miles east of Colebrook on Little Diamond Pond in the Connecticut Lakes region.

ACTIVITIES - Camp in the campground with 30 primitive tent sites and a dump station from mid-May through mid-October. Go hiking and trout fishing in both the lake and stream nearby or in the park pond. Go boating in small boats only. During the winter, enjoy cross-country skiing and snowmobiling.

INFORMATION
Coleman State Park
RFD 1, Box 183
Coleman, New Hampshire 03576
603-237-4560

CRAWFORD NOTCH STATE PARK
5

LOCATION - The park is 12 miles northwest of Bartlett on U.S. 302.

FEATURES - The park features 6 miles of rugged beauty along a scenic mountain pass. A plaque marks the site of Willey House, a stopover for wagons traveling in the late 1700s. In 1826, Samuel Willey, his family, and two hired men died here in a landslide.

ACTIVITIES - The park is open from mid-May through mid-October. Go stream fishing and hiking in the White Mountain National Forest. The park is crossed by trails of the Appalachian system, some leading to incomparable views of the Presidential Range. One 2-mile hike goes to 170-foot Arethusa Falls, the highest in New Hampshire.

You can also take a 2-mile hike beside Flume and Silver Cascade north of U.S. 302. Begin at Willey House on the Kedron Flume Trail.

Climb Mount Willard from Crawford Railroad Station on New Hampshire 302. The trail goes to the ledges above the cliffs overlooking Crawford Notch via a 3-mile trail.

Look for the natural stone profile of Elephant Head, seen from the site of the old Crawford House.

Camp in the 30-tent site Dry River Campground. A snack bar provides food. Tour the visitor center.

Arriving pilots can land at Twin Mountain Airport, located one mile southwest of Twin Mountain. Rental cars are available.

INFORMATION
Crawford Notch State Park
P.O. Box 177
Twin Mountain, New Hampshire 03595
603-374-2272

DIXVILLE NOTCH STATE PARK
6

LOCATION - The park is east of Dixville on New Hampshire 26.

FEATURES - The park, located in the White Mountains, features a scenic gorge and waterfalls and is the state's most northern, smallest mountain notch. Lake Gloriette, the Cathedral Spires, Cascades, and Table Rock are located here.

ACTIVITIES - Follow hiking trails to Table Rock. One begins in the Notch and is a steep, difficult trail. Another trail begins on New Hampshire 26 near the Balsams/Wilderness Ski Area's entrance road. Both involve approximately 2.5 miles round trip.

Hike 3-mile Sanguinari Ridge Trail beginning at Flume Brook picnic area. It stays on the steep north wall of Dixville Notch where you get spectacular views of Lake Gloriette and the Balsams Hotel. Sanguinari Ridge gets its name from the rocks that appear blood red at sunset. Drive the scenic auto road and enjoy a picnic. For additional hiking, pick up a park trail map.

The Balsams Wilderness Ski Area offers winter activities. The cross-country area has 73 kilometers of groomed trails and 27 kilometers of back-country ski trails to explore. Rentals are available at the cross-country center and at the alpine ski center. For snow conditions, call 603-255-3951. Snowmobilers have access to many trails within the wilderness area that connect with a 110-mile system maintained by the state. Pick up a trail map from the ski area. The wilderness also offers miles of private roads and trails for bicycling. Flyfish for trout in Lake Gloriette.

INFORMATION
Dixville Notch State Park
Route 26
Dixville, New Hampshire 03576
603-788-3155

ECHO LAKE STATE PARK
7

LOCATION - The park is 2 miles north of North Conway off New Hampshire 302.

ACTIVITIES - Drive the scenic road to a point near the top of Cathedral Ledge where rock climbers congregate 700 feet above the river valley. Go swimming from the lake beach from which White Horse Ledge is visible. Hike the park trails.

Mount Cranmore Skimobile is ½ mile from the center of North Conway Village. It takes you to the summit of Mount Cranmore. For information, call 613-356-5543.

Conway Scenic Railroad offers one-hour trips in either open-air or enclosed cars. The Victorian 1874 railroad station in North Conway has a museum and snack bar. The train runs from mid-April through pre-Christmas. For dining reservations in the dining car, call 603-356-5251.

Attend concerts in the park or summer repertory theater presentations offered by Mount Washington Valley Theater Company. For information, call 603-356-5776. Arts Jubilee performs in Schouler Park summers. Bring along a picnic and blanket. For a schedule, call 603-356-9393.

To see a covered bridge, go to the Saco River or to the Swift River near Conway.

The World Mud Bowl is held in North Conway in September. For details, call 603-356-5702.

INFORMATION
Echo Lake State Park
Route 302
Conway, New Hampshire 03818
603-356-2672

ELLACOYA STATE BEACH
8

LOCATION - The beach is on the southwest shore of Lake Winnipesaukee.

FEATURES - Lake Winnipesaukee is the state's largest inland lake with a shoreline of 283 miles. It's also the sixth largest natural lake located entirely in the U.S. and has 274 habitable islands. Winnipesaukee is an Indian term meaning "smile of the great spirit" or "beautiful water in high place."

ACTIVITIES - Camp in the 38-site campground with full hookups from May–October. Go swimming from the 600-foot-long beach and bring along a picnic. Go fishing and boating and enjoy good views of the Ossipee/Sandwich Mountains. Take a cruise on the lake aboard M/S *Mount Washington*. For information, call 603-366-5531.

For additional camping, go to Gunstock County Recreation Area on New Hampshire 11A in Gilford. You can also swim in the Olympic-sized swimming pool, go fishing, paddle boating, and horseback riding. Special events offered year-round include an annual March Maple Sugar Festival and Fall Oktoberfest.

Attend Broadway shows in the Inter-Lakes Auditorium at the gateway to the Lakes Region on New Hampshire 25 in Meredith. For reservations and information, call 603-279-9933.

Visit nearby Daniel Webster Birthplace Historic Site off New Hampshire 127, one mile south of Franklin. Restored in 1913, it contains antique furnishings and mementos. For information, call 603-934-5057.

Incoming pilots can land at Laconia Municipal Airport 3 miles north of town. Rental cars are available.

INFORMATION
Ellacoya State Beach
Route 11
Gilford, New Hampshire 03246
603-293-7821

FRANCONIA NOTCH STATE PARK
9

LOCATION - The park is located 8 miles north of North Woodstock via U.S. 3, and 8 miles north of Lincoln via U.S. 3.

FEATURES - The Flume gorge features an 800-foot chasm with sheer walls rising above it as high as 70 feet. It was carved by the Pemigewasset River, a name which means "swift or rapid current" in Abnacki Indian language. The Old Man of the Mountain, a natural rock formation towering 1,200 feet above Profile Lake on the east side of Cannon Mountain, consists of five separate ledges.

The Basin is a glacial granite pothole over 20 feet in diameter and is located at the base of a beautiful waterfall along the river. Boise Rock is an erratic, meaning it is one of the boulders scattered about the park which was left behind by the receding glacier.

ACTIVITIES - The park is open mid-May through mid-October. Take a shuttle from the visitor center to the base of the gorge, beginning in late June. Watch the movie at the information center and pick up something to eat in the cafeteria.

Walk along boardwalks through the gorge to see rare mountain flowers and mosses growing from the moist walls. Hike trails to two historic covered bridges, the pool, and several waterfalls. Hike 1½ miles to Artist's Bluff for a good gorge overlook. Basin-Cascades Trail begins at the Basin and ascends along beautiful Cascade Brook, ending at Cascade Brook Trail in 2 miles. The 3¼-mile-long Lonesome Lake Trail follows an old bridle path.

Falling Waters Trail begins opposite Lafayette Campground and leads past three waterfalls—Stairs, Swiftwater, and Cloudland—as well as to the top of three peaks—Mount Lafayette, Lincoln, and Little Haystack.

Cannon Mountain Tramway, located ½ mile north of the Profile at Parkway Exits 2 and 3 on I-93, takes passengers up 2,022 feet to an observation platform at 4,200 feet for a spectacular view of the surrounding mountains and valleys. Hike additional trails from here and enjoy a summit barbecue in July and August. For information, call 603-823-5563.

Tour the New England Ski Museum beside Cannon Mountain Aerial Tram. It's open daily from noon–5:00, but closed Wednesday. For information, call 603-823-7177.

Go swimming, fishing, wind surfing, and boating in Echo Lake, the park's largest body of water. Visit the interpretive cabin at Lafayette Place.

Camp in the 97-site Lafayette Campground with a camp store open mid-May through mid-October. The campground provides easy access to the Appalachian Trail and to a 9-mile paved bike path that goes from Skoocum-chuck Brook, 3 miles north of the tramway, through the notch, and to the Flume. Bicycle rentals are available at Franconia Sport Shop. Attend summer interpretive programs. A campground by Echo Lake has 10 sites with full hookups, swimming beach, and bathhouse.

Visit Robert Frost's place on Ridge Road in Franconia where he lived from 1901–09. Listed on the National Register of Historic Places, it's open spring weekends from 1:00–5:00 and summer through fall daily from 1:00–5:00, except it's closed Tuesday. The structure is typical of housing in New England in the 1880s and has period furnishings and a nature-poetry interpretive trail. For information, call 603-432-3091.

Golfers can play at Profile Club in Franconia. For a tee-off time, call 603-823-9568. Horseback riding is available at Franconia Inn.

Visit nearby Lost River Gorge, located 6 miles west of North Woodstock. The river winds through a series of glacial caverns and giant potholes. Walk along the boardwalk through the steep-walled gorge. Squeeze through Lemon Squeezer and descend into the glacial caverns to see the Hall of Ships. The area is open from mid-May through mid-October. For information, call 603-745-8031.

Attend Broadway musicals performed in the Eastern Slope Playhouse in North Conway from July 1 through Labor Day. For information, call 603-356-5776.

Loon Mountain Bike Center on the Kancamagus Highway in Lincoln will shuttle you and your bicycle to the top of Franconia Notch State Park to explore the area and fall foliage as you cycle down the paved bike path to Loon Mountain. There you can do more challenging mountain bike riding along Loon's 35 kilometers of ski trails.

From May–October, take Loon Mountain Gondola Skyride to the summit of Loon Mountain. Enjoy the Summit Cave Walk and the view from the four-story observation tower. Hike the self-guided mountain trail. At the mountain's base, take aim at the revolutionary laser trap or traditional archery range.

Go boating or canoeing down the Saco River as well as 7 other nearby rivers. Contact Saco Bound/Downeast River Trips at 603-447-2177.

During the winter, enjoy downhill skiing on Cannon Mountain with 28 trails. For ski conditions, call 603-823-7771. You can also downhill or cross-country ski at Bretton Woods or on Loon Mountain. For conditions, call 603-745-8111.

Nordic skiers will find over 50 kilometers of trails at the Franconia Touring Center. Winter visitors can also go for a sleigh ride, snowshoe, and ice skate in Franconia.

In Sugar Hill, tour Sugar Hill Historic Museum to see a replica of a nineteenth-century tavern kitchen, carriage barn with rare vehicles, and a blacksmith shop. It's open July 1–October. For information, call 603-823-8142.

Sugar Hill also offers summer performances by the North Country Chamber Players at the Sugar Hill Meetinghouse. Additional performances are offered at Loon Mountain.

Incoming pilots can land at Twin Mountain Airport which features scenic airplane rides daily, weather permitting. Rental cars are available. You can also land at Franconia Airport 2 miles south of town. No rental cars are available here.

INFORMATION
Franconia Notch State Park
Route 3
Franconia, New Hampshire 03580
603-745-8391
603-825-5563 (Lafayette Campground)

GREENFIELD STATE PARK
10

LOCATION - The park is one mile west of Greenfield off New Hampshire 136 on the shore of Otter Lake.

ACTIVITIES - Go swimming, hike the nature trails, rent a rowboat, and fish in the pond. Enjoy a picnic and camp in the 252-site campground with a dump station from mid-May through mid-October. Campers have their own swimming beach. Refreshments are available. Go mountain climbing up Mount Monadnock or Crotched Mountain. During the winter, go snowmobiling and cross-country skiing.

Visit Curtiss Dogwood State Reservation at Lyndeborough off New Hampshire 31. Come in the spring to see some of New England's best dogwood displays, which generally peak in early May. Attend summer theater at Peterborough.

INFORMATION
Greenfield State Park
P.O. Box 203
Greenfield, New Hampshire 03047
603-547-3497

HAMPTON BEACH STATE PARK
11

LOCATION - The beach is south of Hampton off New Hampshire 1A.

ACTIVITIES - The park is open Memorial Day through Labor Day. Camp along the Atlantic Ocean in the 24-site campground with full hookups. Purchase supplies at the park store. Attend programs in the amphitheater. Enjoy swimming, saltwater fishing, and picnicking.

North Hampton State Beach, north of Hampton Beach, also has swimming with lifeguards available.

The Seashell is in the heart of the resort section of Hampton Beach and has a band shell and amphitheater.

Attend summer theater in the Hampton Playhouse, a 200-year-old barn located on Winnacunnet Road near the beach.

Tour Fuller Gardens at 10 Willow Avenue in North Hampton from mid-May through October daily from 10:00–6:00. For information, call 603-964-5414.

Incoming pilots can land at Hampton Airfield, located 2 miles north of town. Rental cars are available.

INFORMATION
Hampton Beach State Park
Route 1A
Hampton, New Hampshire 03842
603-926-3784

LAKE FRANCIS STATE PARK
12

LOCATION - The park is 7 miles off U.S. 3, northeast of Pittsburg. It's on River Road by the Connecticut River at the inlet to Lake Francis.

ACTIVITIES - The park is open from early May through early November. Camp in one of 36 campsites. Have a picnic. Go boating from the launch either in Lake Francis or in the Connecticut River. Both are famous for trout and salmon fishing.

INFORMATION
Lake Francis State Park
RFD 1, Box 37B
Pittsburg, New Hampshire 03592
603-538-6965

MILLER STATE PARK
13

LOCATION - The park is located 3 miles east of Peterborough off New Hampshire 101.

FEATURES - Miller State Park is the state's oldest, established in 1891 as a memorial to General James Miller, a hero in the Battle of Lundy's Lane during the War of 1812.

ACTIVITIES - Drive the auto road to the 2,300-foot summit of Pack Monadnock Mountain or hike Wapack Trail, one of the trails leading up the mountain. From the summit, you can enjoy a picnic or explore additional hiking trails.

Wapack National Wildlife Refuge is off New Hampshire 101 on North Pack Monadnock Mountain, northeast of Miller State Park. The area is a popular hawk migration area. Go hiking, ski touring, and snowshoeing.

INFORMATION
Miller State Park
Route 101
Peterborough, New Hampshire 03458
603-547-3497

MOOSE BROOK STATE PARK
14

LOCATION - The park is off U.S. 2 and is 2 miles northwest of Gorham.

ACTIVITIES - Moose Brook is located in the heart of stream fishing country for bass, pickerel, and perch. You can also camp in one of 42 tent sites, go swimming, and have a picnic. The park is also used as a base for hiking the Crescent and Presidential ranges of the White Mountains.

Incoming pilots can land at Berlin Municipal Airport, located 7 miles north of town. Limousine transportation is available.

INFORMATION
Moose Brook State Park
RFD 1, Jimtown Road
Berlin, New Hampshire 03570
603-466-3860

MOUNT MONADNOCK STATE PARK
15

LOCATION - The park is located 4 miles northwest of Jaffrey off New Hampshire 124.

ACTIVITIES - Climb Mount Monadnock, one of the most popular mountains in North America, to view all six New England states from its 3,165-foot summit. Forty miles of mountain trails provide a variety of hiking options. One trail to the top of Mount Monadnock is 2-mile-long White Dot Trail off New Hampshire 124 in Jaffrey.

Tour the visitor center. Camp in the 21-tent site campground open year-round located at the base of the mountain. Purchase snacks in the park store. During the winter, go cross-country skiing and winter hiking.

Take a scenic flight over the Monadnock Mountains from Silver Ranch Airpark at the Jaffrey Airport. For information and flight reservations, call 603-532-8870.

In Jaffrey, attend Jaffrey Jubilee, a weekend of fireworks and a parade. July–August features lectures and speeches with discussions every Friday at 8:00 PM at the Meeting House in Jaffrey Center. For details, contact the Chamber of Commerce at 603-532-7903.

Incoming pilots can land at Jaffrey Municipal-Silver Ranch, located one mile southeast of town. Rental cars are available.

INFORMATION
Mount Monadnock State Park
Jaffrey Center, New Hampshire 03454
603-532-8862

MOUNT SUNAPEE STATE PARK
16

LOCATION - Take Exit 9 off I-89 and follow New Hampshire north to Newbury. The park is 3 miles southwest of Newbury and 3 miles south of Sunapee.

ACTIVITIES - The park is open year-round. Hike the trails, purchase refreshments, and enjoy a picnic. Go swimming from the large beach, boating, canoeing, sailboarding, and fishing for salmon and lake trout in 10-mile-long Lake Sunapee.

During the summer, take a scenic chairlift ride up 2,743-foot Mount Sunapee. On top, get a bite to eat in the cafeteria after you've checked the various views from the observation platform. Visit the exhibition trout pool near the base building where you can also get something to eat. Attend the annual Craftsmen's Fair held each August.

Take a narrated cruise aboard the M/V *Mount Sunapee II*. Cruises go daily from Sunapee Harbor from mid-May to mid-October. To reach the harbor, go to River Road off New Hampshire 91 and 89. Go to the blinking light on New Hampshire 11 on Sunapee Harbor. For information, call 603-763-4030. The M/V *Kearsarge* also has dinner cruises. For information, call 603-763-5477.

Mount Sunapee has the largest alpine ski area between Boston and the White Mountains with 30 trails. For skiing conditions, call 603-763-2356. You can also go cross-country skiing and snowboarding.

Fells Historic Site in the John Hay National Wildlife Refuge is in Newbury on New Hampshire 103A. Hike the trails, take a garden tour, a guided tour of the house, and attend interpretive programs. It's open weekends and holidays from late June–October. For information, call 603-763-5041.

Attend the Annual League of New Hampshire Craftsmen's Fair in Newbury in August.

Sunapee Historical Society's Museum in Sunapee Harbor has artifacts of old Sunapee and its steamboat era. Call for times: 603-763-2101.

For a scenic drive, follow New Hampshire 103A and 103B around Lake Sunapee.

INFORMATION
Mount Sunapee State Park
Route 103
Newbury, New Hampshire 03255
603-763-2356

MOUNT WASHINGTON STATE PARK
17

LOCATION - The park is off New Hampshire 16, north of Pinkham Notch.

FEATURES - Mount Washington, 6,288 feet high, was named for George Washington. It's the highest peak in northeastern North America and is surrounded by the White Mountain National Forest. The mountain is known for its weather extremes with the highest surface wind ever recorded on earth: 231 miles per hour, clocked on April 12, 1934. In fact, winds over the peak exceed 100 mph at least once each month, and from November–April they reach hurricane force of 74 mph almost daily because of the collision of several storm tracks flowing over the mountain. Fog shrouds the mountain summit at least 300 days a year.

ACTIVITIES - Hike to the summit of Mount Washington via 8-mile Tuckerman Ravine Trail. The trail leaves AMC headquarters in Pinkham Notch.

Drive up the 8-mile-long Mount Washington Road, opened as a carriage road in 1861. Visit Tip Top House, the oldest building still standing on the mountain summit. Mount Washington Observatory Museum features exhibits on the history, weather, and natural wonders of the mountain. If you want a guided tour, call 603-466-2988.

Ride up the mountain on the Mount Washington Cog Railway, completed in 1869 as the first rack and pinion railroad in the world. A round-trip ride aboard this authentic coal-fired steam train requires three hours. One trestle, called Jacob's Ladder, climbs an incredible 37-percent grade. The 3-mile route is the second steepest railway in the world. For information, call 1-800-922-8825, ext. 7, or 603-846-5404.

Annual events include the Mount Washington Auto Climb to the Clouds held in June. Other events include the Mount Washington footrace in June, Mount Washington Bicycle Hillclimb in September, and the Autumn Muster in the Mountains. For details, call 603-466-3988 or the Twin Mountain Chamber at 603-846-5407.

Look for the natural stone profile of Lion Head located between Tuckerman and Huntington ravines on Mount Washington, visible from the Glen House at the base of the auto road.

Take a ride on a gondola to the summit of Wildcat Mountain to enjoy views from the observation deck and purchase a snack or hike the nature rails. The gondola is halfway between Jackson and Gorham on New Hampshire 16 and runs Memorial Day through Columbus Day. For details, call 603-466-3326.

The Gorham Historical Society Museum on Railroad Street features a 1907 depot, 1911 steam locomotive, and a Dolly Copps's spinning wheel. It's open summer and fall Monday, Wednesday, and Friday from 1:00–5:00. For information, call 603-486-5570.

Pinkham Notch Camp is at the base of Mount Washington, a few miles by trail from Tuckerman Ravine. Open year-round, the roadside lodge offers access to dayhikes as well as backpacking trips.

Incoming pilots can land at Gorham Airport, located one mile northwest of town. No rental cars are available.

INFORMATION
Mount Washington State Park
Route 16, Box 278
Gorham, New Hampshire 03581
603-466-3988

ODIORNE POINT STATE PARK
18
WENTWORTH–COOLIDGE MANSION STATE HISTORIC SITE
19

LOCATION - Odiorne Point State Park is northeast of Rye on New Hampshire 1A.

The Wentworth–Coolidge Mansion is near Portsmouth at the end of Little Harbor Road off New Hampshire 1A.

FEATURES - New Hampshire's first settlement, called Pannway Plantation, was established at Odiorne's Point in 1632. Fort Dearborn, a U.S. Army military base, was constructed here to protect Portsmouth Harbor from possible attack during World War II.

ACTIVITIES - At Odiorne Point, attend interpretive programs offered by the University of New Hampshire and Audubon Society in the Seacoast Science Center. The museum is open year-round and features an indoor tidal pool touch tank and an interactive aquarium. Call 603-436-8043 for information.

Take an imaginary journey nearly 260 feet below sea level to Seabrook's cooling tunnels and view local marine life in ocean aquariums. Hike the ¾-mile Owascoag Trail through a salt marsh and woodland. For information, call 1-800-338-7482.

Enjoy a picnic or go boating from the launch. The park is open Memorial Day through Labor Day. Along the coast look for stumps of a sunken forest, remains of trees that grew here approximately 4,000 years ago. During the winter, enjoy cross-country skiing.

Sugden House, constructed of native rubble stone, was built in 1920 as a seasonal home for Robert L. Sugden. Today it's part of the visitor center.

Tour Fort Dearborn to see a battery gun emplacement with two 16-inch guns that could fire a 3,400-pound projectile 26 miles. Battery 204 represents a typical World War II intermediate range harbor defense battery. Two other nearby forts, Stark and Constitution, help you learn about the United States' changing military theories and the development of armaments. Fort Constitution Historic Site is on New Hampshire 1B at the U.S. Coast Guard Station in New Castle.

Take a seacoast cruise aboard a steamship relic from Steamship Dock at 315 Market to nine of the Isles of Shoals. For information, call 603-431-5500. Go on a whale watch from Rye Harbor State Marina on New Hampshire 1A, Ocean Boulevard. For information, call 603-964-5545 or 1-800-872-4753.

Go deep sea fishing from April–October for cod, mackerel, or bluefish, with the Atlantic Fishing Fleet docked in Rye Harbor. For information, call 603-964-5220.

Golfers can play on Wentworth by the Sea's golf course. For a tee-off time, call 603-433-5010.

Stop by nearby Rye Harbor State Park. Enjoy a picnic on the breezy, rocky promontory overlooking the harbor and Atlantic Ocean. Go saltwater fishing from the pier or from aboard a charter boat rented at the commercial wharf. For information, call 603-436-6607. Swim from the 700-foot sand beach at Wallis Sands State Beach 2 miles north of Rye Harbor.

Tour Wentworth–Coolidge's 42-room Colonial mansion, home of Benning Wentworth, Royal Governor of New Hampshire from 1741–67. The oldest part of the house is believed to have been built in 1695. The mansion overlooks Little Harbor and is listed as a National Historic Landmark. Guided tours are given from Memorial Day through Columbus Day. An archaeological dig is active during the summer. For information, call 603-436-6607.

Wentworth State Beach is 5 miles east of Wolfeboro. This small park on the shore of Lake Wentworth offers swimming and picnicking.

Plummer Ledge in Wentworth is the site of ten glacial potholes varying in size from 2 feet to over 10 feet across.

To tour a Georgian house, visit Wentworth–Gardner House at 140 Mechanic Street in Portsmouth. Built in 1760, it's open Tuesday–Sunday from 1:00–4:00. For information, call 603-436-4406.

Annual events in Portsmouth include Market Square weekend the second weekend in June, a Jazz Festival in late June, and Prescott Park Arts Festival from July 4 through mid-August.

To see several other historic homes in town, pick up a map at the tourist information booth in Market Square on Monday–Friday from July 1 through Labor Day or at the Greater Portsmouth Chamber of Commerce at 500 Market. For information, call 603-436-1118.

Incoming pilots can land at Portsmouth International Tradeport, located one mile west of town. Rental cars are available.

INFORMATION

Odiorne Point State Park
Route 1A
Rye, New Hampshire 03870
603-436-7406

Wentworth–Coolidge Mansion State Historic Site
Little Harbor Road
Portsmouth, New Hampshire 03801
603-436-6607

PAWTUCKAWAY STATE PARK
20

LOCATION - The park is north of Raymond, 3½ miles north of the intersection of New Hampshire 101 and 156.

ACTIVITIES - Swim from the large beach with a bathhouse and picnic area. Camp in one of the 170 tent sites in either Big Island or Horse Island campgrounds. Purchase supplies in the camp store. Rent a canoe to go canoeing, boating with motors permitted, and fishing. Hike and bike the trails. Tower Trail off New Hampshire 156 provides the easiest route to the summit of South Mountain.

During the winter, cross-country ski and go snowmobiling.

INFORMATION
Pawtuckaway State Park
RFD 1
Raymond, New Hampshire 03077
603-895-3031

PILLSBURY STATE PARK
21

LOCATION - The park is 5 miles north of Washington on New Hampshire 31.

ACTIVITIES - The park is a major link of the Monadnock-Sunapee Greenway, a 52-mile hiking trail that connects Mount Monadnock with Mount Sunapee.

You can also hike park nature trails. Camp in one of 20 primitive tent sites on the shore of May Pond. Go stream and pond fishing and enjoy a picnic. Go boating without motors.

Tour Franklin Pierce Homestead Historic Site, circa 1804, located near Hillsborough near the junction of New Hampshire 9 and 31. Franklin Pierce, our fourteenth U.S. president, lived here. It's open mid-June through Labor Day. For information, call 603-464-5858.

INFORMATION
Pillsbury State Park
Route 31
Washington, New Hampshire 03280
603-863-2860

PISGAH STATE PARK
22

LOCATION - The park is north of Hinsdale with park entrances off New Hampshire 9, 10, 63, and 119.

FEATURES - The park encompasses a 13,500-acre undeveloped wilderness, the largest property in the state park system.

ACTIVITIES - Go hiking, hunting, fishing, bicycling, or ride an ATV through the rough forested terrain. A 4½-mile hike leaves Horseshoe Road off New Hampshire 63 at Chesterfield.

During the winter, enjoy cross-country skiing and snowmobiling.

Chesterfield Gorge Natural Area is on New Hampshire 9. Hike the ¾-mile wilderness loop trail winding along a deep glacial stream. Tour the visitor center on weekends to see their logging tool collection and local mammal display.

INFORMATION
Pisgah State Park
Route 63
Hinsdale, New Hampshire 03451
603-239-8153

RHODODENDRON STATE PARK
23

LOCATION - The park is 2½ miles northwest of Fitzwilliam in the Allegheny Mountains off New Hampshire 12.

FEATURES - Over 16 acres of wild rhododendron burst into bloom annually around mid-July in this area, which is designated a Natural National Landmark.

ACTIVITIES - Explore a one-mile path around the entire glen. For additional hiking, follow the one-mile foot trail up Little Monadnock Mountain. For a floral display, hike Wildflower Trail or Laurel Trail that takes you through the rhododendrons.

Captain Sam Patch's Place is listed on the National Register of Historic Places. He fought in the Battle of Bunker Hill in 1775.

INFORMATION
Rhododendron State Park
Route 12
Fitzwilliam, New Hampshire 03447
603-532-8862

ROLLINS STATE PARK
See under WINSLOW STATE PARK

WELLINGTON STATE BEACH
24

LOCATION - The beach is northwest of Bristol off New Hampshire 3A on the west shore of Newfound Lake.

ACTIVITIES - The park has one of the state's finest inland beaches open from May–September. Go swimming, fishing, stroll the scenic walking trail, enjoy a picnic, and purchase picnic supplies in the beach store. You can also take a walk at Sculptured Rocks.

INFORMATION
Wellington State Beach
Route 3A
Bristol, New Hampshire 03222
603-744-2197

WENTWORTH–COOLIDGE MANSION STATE HISTORIC SITE
See under ODIORNE POINT STATE PARK

WHITE LAKE STATE PARK
25

LOCATION - The park is ½ mile northwest of West Ossipee and southeast of Tamworth on New Hampshire 16.

FEATURES - The park is close to the White Mountain National Forest and has a 72-acre stand of native pitch pine which is listed as a National Natural Landmark.

ACTIVITIES - Camp in the 200-site campground open from mid-May through mid-October. Purchase supplies in the camp store, go hiking, and enjoy a picnic. Enjoy swimming and trout fishing and rent a canoe or rowboat to go boating in White Lake. Boating with motors are permitted, but at trolling speed only.

During the winter, go cross-country skiing.

INFORMATION
White Lake State Park
P.O. Box 273
West Ossipee, New Hampshire 03890
603-323-7350

WINSLOW STATE PARK
26
ROLLINS STATE PARK
27

LOCATION - Winslow State Park is off New Hampshire 11 or Exit 10 of I-89, 3 miles south of Wilmot Flat.

Rollins State Park is 4 miles north of Warner off New Hampshire 103.

ACTIVITIES - Both parks provide access to 2,937-foot Mount Kearsarge. You can either drive up to the summit for a panoramic view of the White and

Green mountains or hike to the bare granite peak summit via a mile-long trail. This is a wonderful place to view sunsets. Come to cross-country ski during the winter.

INFORMATION

Winslow State Park
Route 11
Wilmot, New Hampshire 03287
603-526-6168 or 927-4724

Rollins State Park
Route 103
Warner, New Hampshire 03278
603-239-8153

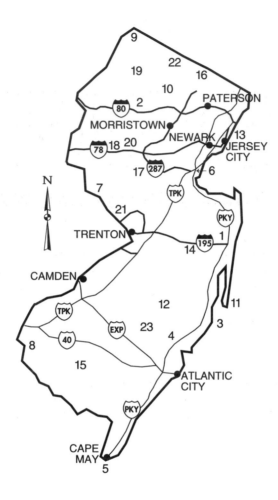

N

9
19   22   16
10
80 2   PATERSON
MORRISTOWN   13
78 18 20   NEWARK   JERSEY
CITY
17 287   6
TPK
7
PKY
21
TRENTON   195   1
14
CAMDEN
11
12
TPK   23   3
EXP   4
40
8
15   ATLANTIC
CITY
PKY
CAPE
MAY
5

NEW JERSEY

New Jersey was one of the thirteen original colonies and served as the crossroads of the American Revolution. George Washington and his army spent over a third of the war years here and many historic sites have been preserved.

New Jersey has over 4,000 freshwater lakes, ponds, and streams, providing good freshwater fishing. Ocean beaches offer excellent surf fishing.

Most inland parks open for swimming on Memorial Day weekend, while oceanfront areas open in mid-June. New Jersey's waterways, canals, rivers, and lakes are perfect for canoeing, boating, and sailing.

Come in October to see the fall foliage. Four spots to visit include Wharton and Stokes state forests and Ringwood and Washington Crossing state parks.

Seventy miles of the 2,100-mile-long Appalachian Trail are located in New Jersey. The trail follows the Kittatinny Ridge from the Delaware Water Gap and exits the state west of Greenwood Lake, passing through High Point and Wawayanda state parks.

ALLAIRE STATE PARK
1

LOCATION - The park is near Allaire, 3 miles west of Garden State Parkway, southbound Exit 98 or via 195, Exit 31B, Monmouth County. It's also 12 miles southeast of Freehold via U.S. 9 and New Jersey 524.

FEATURES - Iron was smelted over a century ago at the historic Howell Works, a bog ore furnace and forge.

ACTIVITIES - The park is open year-round. Tour historic Allaire Village, built in 1822 and listed on the National Register of Historic Places. Historic buildings are open from May–October. Costumed interpreters demonstrate corn husking, militia muster, and nineteenth-century lawn games. For information, call 908-938-2253.

Take a ride on the narrow gauge Pine Creek Railroad from early April through mid-October. For a schedule, call 908-938-5524.

On weekends, enjoy special events like craft and antique shows, square dancing, and decoy carving.

Hike, horseback ride, or bicycle the multi-use trails. Paddle canoe trails on the Manasquan River, tour the visitor center, enjoy a picnic, and go fishing for stocked trout. Camp in the 55-site campground and attend campfire programs.

Play eighteen holes of golf on Spring Meadow Golf Course and purchase a snack. In the winter, go sledding and cross-country skiing.

INFORMATION
Allaire State Park
Box 220, Route 524
Farmingdale, New Jersey 07727
908-938-2371

ALLAMUCHY MOUNTAIN STATE PARK
2

LOCATION - The park is 2 miles north of Hackettstown on Willow Grove-Waterloo Road.

FEATURES - Allamuchy was named for the Delaware Indians whose village was called Allamuchahokkingen, meaning "place within the hills." The name was later shortened to Allamucha.

The park has two sections: Stephens/Saxton Falls and Allamuchy Mountain. Stephens/Saxton Falls is located along the Musconetcong River. At one time, 28 locks were located along the river and the remains of one of them is visible at Saxton Falls.

ACTIVITIES - The park is open from April–October. Camp in the 40-site campground, go trout fishing in the Musconetong River, and hike the trails. Enjoy a picnic in Stephen's section of the park. In the winter, go cross-country skiing and ice fishing.

Take a tour of historic Waterloo Village with many buildings from the 1800s. It's open from April–December, Tuesday–Sunday. The Waterloo Festival for the Arts occurs May–October on weekends when various music and dance programs are presented. For information, call 201-347-4700.

INFORMATION
Allamuchy Mountain State Park
180 Stephens State Park Road
Hackettstown, New Jersey 07840
908-852-3790

BARNEGAT LIGHTHOUSE STATE PARK
3

LOCATION - The lighthouse, known as Old Barney, is located on the north tip of Long Beach Island at the entrance to Barnegat Inlet. It's accessible via Garden State Parkway, Exit 63. Follow New Jersey 72 east onto Long Beach Island Boulevard.

ACTIVITIES - Tour the lighthouse, known as the Grand Old Champion of the Tides, that was built in 1857 to mark Barnegat Shoals, scene of over 200 shipwrecks. Climb its 217 steps for a panoramic view. The lighthouse is open weekends in May, September, and October and every day Memorial Day through Labor Day from 10:00–4:30.

Visitors can also walk the beach, go surfing, scuba diving, and fishing from the south jetty for bass, bluefish, blackfish, and flounder. Purchase a snack, enjoy a picnic, and play tennis. Birders come to observe beach nesting birds.

Tour the Edith Gwin Garden by the Barnegat Light Museum on Central Avenue between Fifth and Sixth Streets. For information, call 609-494-3522.

INFORMATION
Barnegat Lighthouse State Park
P.O. Box 167
Barnegat Light, New Jersey 08006-0167
609-494-2016

BASS RIVER STATE FOREST
4

LOCATION - The park is 25 miles north of Atlantic City and 6 miles west of Tuckerton on New Jersey 592. It's accessible from U.S. 9 and Garden State Parkway. If coming from the south, take Exit 52 or Exit 50 from the north.

ACTIVITIES - The area is open year-round. Camp in the 178-site campground, in one of the 9 closed lean-tos or in one of 6 rustic cabins.

Go boating from the launch in canoes or boats with electric motors. Rentals are available. Go swimming in guarded Lake Absegami, fishing for pickerel, sunfish, and catfish, have a picnic, and purchase a snack.

Batona Trail, 50 miles long, goes from Bass River to Lebanon State Forest. The trail crosses many roads so it can be reached by car at various points. The park also has miles of sand and gravel roads open for year-round hiking and horseback riding.

In the winter, go ice skating, ice fishing, cross-country skiing, and snowmobiling.

Visit historic Batsto Village located in Hammonton. This iron mining village was the principal source of ammunition for the American Revolutionary War, and today traditional crafts are still demonstrated. Interpretive programs are offered Thursday–Sunday. For information, call 609-561-0024.

In Batsto Village, attend the Historic Arts Festival the third weekend in September, a decoy and woodcarvers show the second Sunday in June, an outdoor art show the third Sunday in September, a glass bottle and antique show the first Sunday in October, and a country living fair the third Sunday in October.

Tour the home of financier Joseph Wharton from Memorial Day through Labor Day. For information, call 609-561-3262.

INFORMATION
Bass River State Forest
P.O. Box 118
New Gretna, New Jersey 08224
609-296-1114

CAPE MAY POINT STATE PARK
5

LOCATION - Cape May Point is located on historic Cape May Peninsula at the southern tip of New Jersey, approximately 2 miles west of Cape May. The park may be reached from the Garden State Parkway and U.S. 9.

FEATURES - Historic 157-foot Cape May Point Lighthouse was constructed in 1859. It's still active and is visible up to 24 miles at sea.

ACTIVITIES - Climb the spiral staircase to the watchroom to enjoy a panoramic view of the ocean. Tours are offered daily spring through fall and on a reduced schedule the remainder of the year. Tour the visitor center and museum. Enjoy a picnic and go surf fishing for bluefish, flounder, and striped bass.

The park is located along the Atlantic flyway and is a popular site for bird watching. A raised platform provides some good views of migrating hawks in September and October. The park's natural area has 3 miles of trails and boardwalks.

Take a trolley tour of Cape May's historic district. Tours begin from the station on Beach Drive at Gurney Street during the summer, from the Washington Street Mall information booth during the spring and fall, and from Physick Estate throughout the winter.

Cape May County Historical Society is housed in eighteenth-century John Homes's house with 300 years of local history plus an extensive genealogical library. For information, call 609-465-3535.

Stop by the Cape May Whale Watch and Research Center at 1286 Wilson Drive in Cape May from mid-April through late November for whale watching information. Call them at 609-898-0055.

Join a guided walking tour or carriage tour beginning from the Washington Mall information booth or pick up a map to take a self-guided tour. Purchase a ticket for a special evening house tour at the Physick Estate.

Attend summer afternoon band concerts in Cape May County Park. Tour Leamings Run's 27 gardens and Colonial farm, located 5 miles north of town off New Jersey 9, Exit 13 of the Garden State Parkway.

Ride the ferry from Cape May to Lewes, Delaware. Lewes is Delaware's oldest settlement and has many restored historic buildings and homes. For information, call 609-886-9699. For ferry schedule times, call 1-800-64FERRY.

Annual events include a tulip festival in the Convention Hall the last weekend in April and the Cape May Musical Festival in the Christian Admiral Recital Hall during the last weekend in May through early July. A Victorian Fair is held the third weekend in June at the Emlen Physick Estate.

For additional hiking, camping, fishing, and boating, go to Belleplain State Forest. It's easily accessible from the Garden State Parkway southbound, Exit 17, onto New Jersey 550, or northbound on the parkway from Exit 13 onto New Jersey 9 and 550, Sea Isle Boulevard. Canoe rentals are available at Lake Nummy from Memorial Day through Labor Day.

Campers have 3 campgrounds with 188 campsites. The main 6.5-mile hiking trail connects Lake Nummy and East Creek Pond recreational areas. Additional miles of forest roads are used by bicyclists and equestrians. For information, call 609-861-2404.

INFORMATION
Cape May Point State Park
P.O. Box 107
Cape May Point, New Jersey 08212
609-884-2159

CHEESEQUAKE STATE PARK
6

LOCATION - The park is near Raritan Bay, approximately 6 miles southeast of Perth Amboy. From the junction of Garden State Parkway and Matawan Road, Exit 120, follow signs to the park.

ACTIVITIES - Camp in the 53-site campground with a dumping station. Go canoeing with rentals available and fishing for perch, sunfish, and bass. Enjoy swimming in Hooks Creek Lake and purchase a snack at the snack bar and walk the short boardwalk. Hooks Creek offers excellent blue-claw crabbing in late summer.

Hike three park trails. The longest trail, 3.5 miles, goes through a typical pine barrens forest down to a freshwater swamp with magnolia and red maple. A shorter trail goes to Hooks Creek Lake. Bicyclists bike park roads.

In the winter, go cross-country skiing, sledding, snowmobiling, ice skating, and ice fishing.

Boxwood Hall, Boudinot Mansion State Historic Site, is located in Elizabeth at 1073 Jersey Street. The mansion was built in 1750 and was visited by General George Washington in 1789 while en route to New York for his presidential inauguration. The mansion is open Wednesday–Saturday from 10:00–noon and 1:00–5:00 and Sunday from 1:00–5:00. For information, call 201-648-4540.

INFORMATION
Cheesequake State Park
Matawan, New Jersey 07747
908-566-2161

DELAWARE AND RARITAN CANAL STATE PARK
7

LOCATION - The Delaware and Raritan Canal State Park is on the Delaware River, 7 miles west of New Brunswick on New Jersey 514. The Bull's Island section of the park is 3 miles north of Stockton on New Jersey 29.

FEATURES - Begun in 1834, the original 66-mile-long canal has expanded into an 80-mile-long park stretching from Milford through Trenton to New Brunswick. The site of original outlet locks are still visible beside the Raritan River in New Brunswick.

Along the canal you'll see nineteenth-century bridges, locktender houses, cobblestone spillways, and hand-built culverts. The canal and its structures are listed on the National Register of Historic Places, and its trail system is designated as a National Recreation Trail.

ACTIVITIES - Camp in the 75-site campground in the Bull's Island Natural Area section with a trailer dump station. Fish the canal for catfish, eel, bass, and stocked trout and in the river for catfish, bass, pickerel, and carp. Hike the nature trail beginning near the park office, paralleling the canal to the southernmost point of the island.

Canoes, kayaks, rowboats, and electric-powered boats may be used on both the river and canal, while power boats are permitted only on the Delaware River. Access to the river is available from Kingwood, Bryam, Bull's Island, Lambertville, and Fireman's Eddy.

The canal section has picnicking, a boat launch for electric motorboats, rentals, fishing, and canoe trails. The historic towpath along the main canal from Bakers Basin Road to New Brunswick has a 10-mile section utilized by hikers, joggers, equestrians, and bicyclists. Access is from Weston Canal Road. The path connects Washington Crossing State Park.

During the winter, go cross-country skiing and ice fishing.

Nearby attractions include Flemington Glass Works in New Hope, Pennsylvania, and Peddlers Village, Pennsylvania, historic Trenton, New Jersey, and Washington Crossing State Park, 8 miles northwest of Trenton on New Jersey 29 and then northeast on New Jersey 546. It commemorates the American success at the Battle of Trenton in December 1776. Tour the visitor center and take an historical tour. The annual reenactment of Washington's crossing of the Delaware begins on the Pennsylvania side of the river on December 25 when volunteers maneuver replicas of the Durham boats. For details, call 609-737-9304.

Attend the Festival of Lights the first week in September in Trenton. For information, call 609-393-4143.

In New Brunswick, tour Rutgers Display Gardens and the primeval forest of Helyar Woods. Access is via Ryders Lane east of U.S. 1, south of New Jersey 18.

INFORMATION

Delaware and Raritan Canal Park	Bull's Island Recreation Area
643 Canal Road	R.D. 2, Box 417
Somerset, New Jersey 08773	2185 Daniel Bray Highway
908-873-3050	Stockton, New Jersey 08559
	609-397-2949

FORT MOTT STATE PARK
8

LOCATION - The park is on the Delaware River, 6 miles northwest of Salem and 6 miles south of the Delaware Memorial Bridge off New Jersey 49.

FEATURES - The fort was constructed in 1896 to defend the Delaware River in anticipation of the Spanish-American War. Finn's Point National Cemetery is adjacent to the park where 2,436 Confederate prisoners of war and 300 Union soldiers are buried.

ACTIVITIES - Take a walking tour to see their abandoned fortifications and defense structures. Enjoy a picnic, go boating, tidewater fishing, and crabbing in the Delaware River.

Nearby Salem is one of the oldest English settlements, begun along the Delaware River in 1675. Visitors can see several pre-Revolutionary buildings, including the restored Alexander Grant House, circa 1721, located at 78 Market Street.

Hancock House, circa 1734, is located 5 miles out of Salem in Hancock's Bridge. It was the site of a Revolutionary massacre of Quaker patriots by the British. The house is open Wednesday–Sunday. For information, call 609-935-4373.

To see a 500-year-old oak, visit the entrance to the Friends' Burying Ground on West Broadway.

INFORMATION
Fort Mott State Park
R.D. 3
Salem, New Jersey 08079
609-935-3218

HIGH POINT STATE PARK
9

LOCATION - High Point State Park is 8 miles northwest of Sussex on New Jersey 23 and south of Port Jervis, New York.

FEATURES - High Point boasts the state's highest point of 1,803 feet and includes the state's first natural area with an almost virgin woodland and cedar swamp.

ACTIVITIES - Enjoy hiking one of nine park trails, including the ridge above Kryden Kuser Natural Area and along a section of the Appalachian Trail. Climb to High Point Monument for a panoramic view. Camp in the 50-site campground from April–October or stay in one of the two family cabins.

Tour the visitor center, go fishing for trout and bass, and go swimming in Lake Marcia. Food service is available. Boats with electric motors may be launched at Sawmill Lake and Lake Steenykill.

During the winter, go cross-country skiing, snowmobiling, and ice skating.

Stokes State Forest is southwest of the park. Open year-round, camp in the 77-site campground or stay in one of the 10 cabins. Enjoy boating, fishing, and hiking on 9 miles of Appalachian Trail plus 23 other trails. For information, call 201-948-3820.

INFORMATION
High Point State Park
1480 State Route 23
Sussex, New Jersey 07461
201-875-4800

HOPATCONG STATE PARK
10

LOCATION - The park is at the southwest end of Lake Hopatcong, New Jersey's largest lake. From I-80, Exit 28, go 2 miles north of Landing.

FEATURES - Hopatcong includes a section of the old Morris Canal, once the chief means for conveying coal, iron, and zinc across the state in the 1800s.

ACTIVITIES - The day-use park is open year-round. Go fishing in the lake for stocked trout, bass, pickerel, perch, and catfish. Enjoy boating from the launch ramp Monday–Friday.

Swimmers can swim in the guarded lake and purchase concessions from ~~May-September.~~

During the winter, go snowmobiling, ice skating, ice boating, sledding, and ice fishing.

INFORMATION

Hopatcong State Park

Box M-519, Lakeside Boulevard

Landing, New Jersey 07850-0583

201-398-7010

ISLAND BEACH STATE PARK
11

LOCATION - The beach covers 10 miles from Seaside Park to Barnegat Inlet.

FEATURES - The park is divided into three areas. The northern and southern natural areas contain acres of sand dunes, saltwater marshes, and freshwater bogs.

ACTIVITIES - Island Beach is open year-round. Go hiking and fishing along the northern beach. Nature tours are available. Public access to the southern natural area is limited to the beach for picnicking, sunbathing, fishing, and nature study. Visitors must keep off the sand dunes.

The central part of the park has a guarded beach and concessions from mid-June through Labor Day.

Six miles of open ocean beach in the southern and central portions are open for equestrian use from October 1–April 30. Surfers can go to the southern end of the designated bathing area.

Scuba divers and anglers enjoy 2.5 miles of beach north of Barnegat Inlet. Anglers fish for bass and bluefish, and for blackfish and sea bass from the north jetty. Winter flounder are caught in Barnegat Inlet.

Bicyclists can cycle a 3.3-mile bikepath in the northern natural area.

INFORMATION

Island Beach State Park

P.O. Box 37

Shore Road, Route 35

Seaside Park, New Jersey 08752

908-793-0506

LEBANON STATE FOREST
12

LOCATION - The forest is south of Fort Dix, accessible via New Jersey 70 and 72.

ACTIVITIES - Tour historic Whitesbog Village, circa 1870. Swim in Pakin Pond, developed from a former cranberry reservoir, guarded from Memorial Day through Labor Day. Three rustic cabins, located on the south shore of Pakim Pond, are available or you can camp in the campground.

Hikers have access to many miles of sand roads. Batona Hiking Trail begins at Ong's Hat and passes through Wharton State Forest, ending in Bass River State Forest, 49.5 miles away. Many of these roads are utilized by equestrians.

INFORMATION
Lebanon State Forest
P.O. Box 215
New Libson, New Jersey 08064
609-726-1191

LIBERTY STATE PARK
13

LOCATION - The park is near Jersey City, off Exit 14B of the New Jersey Turnpike.

FEATURES - This urban park faces Liberty Island, site of the Statue of Liberty and Ellis Island.

ACTIVITIES - Come during the summer to attend a free concert while enjoying a view of the New York City skyline. Tour the Interpretive Center located on Freedom Way. Nature trails and observation points are found in the nearby natural area. Go fishing in the Hudson River for bluefish, shad, bass, and blue-claw crabs.

Pool facilities are available with lifeguards and concessions from Memorial Day through Labor Day. A boat-launching ramp provides boaters and anglers access to both the Hudson River and Atlantic Ocean. Bicyclists can cycle 3 miles along park roads.

Take a ride aboard the ferry, *Miss Freedom*, to visit the Statue of Liberty. The statue is the tallest built in modern times and houses the American Museum of Immigration in its base. The ferry leaves hourly from 10:00–4:00 from March–December. For information, call 201-915-3400. Circle Line offers year-round ferry service from Liberty State Park to Ellis Island. Call 201-435-9949 for information.

INFORMATION
Liberty State Park
Morris Pesin Drive
Jersey City, New Jersey 07304-4678
201-915-3400

MONMOUTH BATTLEFIELD STATE PARK
14

LOCATION - The state park is 3 miles west of Freehold on New Jersey 33.

FEATURES - The park is the scene a major Revolutionary battle fought on June 28, 1778. Here General George Washington led his troops from Valley Forge against the British.

ACTIVITIES - Stop by the visitor center to attend their audio-visual program. Tour the park and Craig House constructed in 1710 where the British operated a temporary field hospital.

On Labor Day weekend, attend the Revolutionary War Military Encampment at the Spy House Museum complex.

In the winter, go cross-country skiing, sledding, tobogganing, and snowmobiling.

Tour the nature center in Owl Haven on New Jersey 522 and attend summer concerts.

INFORMATION
Monmouth Battlefield State Park
R.D. 1, Box 258
Freehold, New Jersey 07728
908-462-9616

PARVIN STATE PARK
15

LOCATION - The park is 6 miles west of Vineland on New Jersey 540 and 7 miles northeast of Bridgeton.

ACTIVITIES - Camp in the 56-site campground from March–November or rent one of fifteen cabins located on the northwest shore of Thundergust Lake.

Rent a rowboat or canoe to go boating in Parvin Lake. No outboard motors are permitted. Go swimming and fishing for bass, pickerel, bluegill, carp, catfish, and crappie. Explore the natural area and purchase a snack from the snack bar.

In the winter, go cross-country skiing, ice fishing, snowmobiling, and ice skating.

Nearby attractions include boating and fishing in Delaware Bay. Bridgeton's Historic District has 2,200 homes and buildings from the Colonial, Federalist, and Victorian periods and is the state's largest historic district. Walking, trolley, and escorted motor coach tours are available. For information, call 609-451-4802.

Attend Bridgeton Music and Heritage Festival in Waterworks Park the third week in September. For information, call 609-455-3230.

INFORMATION
Parvin State Park
R.D. 1, Box 374
Elmer, New Jersey 08318
609-358-8616

RINGWOOD STATE PARK
16

LOCATION - The park is 2.5 miles north of Ringwood via Skyland Drive, New Jersey 511, and Sloatsburg Road. Shepherd Lake is 14 miles north of Pompton Lakes.

ACTIVITIES - Tour the twentieth-century, 50-room Skylands Manor and the 78-room Ringwood Manor. For information, call 201-962-7031. Go fishing and hike the trails. Bicyclists have a hilly 10-mile paved park road. During the winter, go ice fishing, snowmobiling, cross-country skiing, and sledding.

Walk the paths at Skylands Botanical Gardens with 300 acres of flowering trees from around the world. During the winter, go snowmobiling and ice fishing.

Shepherd Lake has picnicking facilities, a bathhouse, a boat launch for electric motorboats, boat rentals, fishing, and hiking trails. During the winter, go cross-country skiing, ice skating, ice fishing, and sledding.

INFORMATION
Ringwood State Park
R.D. Box 1304
Ringwood, New Jersey 07456
201-962-7031

ROUND VALLEY STATE RECREATION AREA
17

LOCATION - The area is 13 miles east of Clinton off U.S. 22.

ACTIVITIES - Camp in the 116-site wilderness campground accessible only by hiking, canoe, or small boat. Fish for bass, sunfish, and trout and enjoy hiking and horseback riding. Bring a picnic, purchase refreshments, and swim in the guarded reservoir. Go scuba diving and boating from the launch with motors up to 10 horsepower.

During the winter, go ice boating, ice skating, cross-country skiing, ice fishing, and sledding.

Nearby attractions include Pequest Trout Hatchery, Flemington Glass Works, and Clinton Historical Museum on 56 Main Street in Clinton. Tour the country village with two floors of milling exhibits and see an eighteenth-century restored gristmill. It's open from April–October on Tuesday–Sunday from 10:00–4:00. Outdoor concerts are presented in the summer. For information, call 908-735-4101.

INFORMATION
Round Valley State Recreation Area
Box 45D, Lebanon Stanton Road
Lebanon, New Jersey 08833
908-236-6355

SPRUCE RUN STATE RECREATION AREA
18

LOCATION - From Somerville, take I-78 to Clinton Exit onto New Jersey 31. Go north to Van Syckels Road, then left for another 1.5 miles.

ACTIVITIES - The 70-site campground is open April 1–October 31. Enjoy a picnic or purchase a snack. Go swimming from the 1/4-mile-long beach with lifeguards from Memorial Day through Labor Day and boating in Spruce Run Reservoir where boat rentals are available.

Anglers can fish in Spruce Run Creek and Mulhockaway Creek or in Spruce Run Reservoir. Both the reservoir and the creeks are stocked with trout and hybrid bass.

In the winter, go ice fishing, ice boating, and cross-country skiing.

Nearby attractions include Pequest Trout Hatchery and Flemington Glass Works.

INFORMATION
Spruce Run State Recreation Area
Box 289-A, Van Syckels Road
Clinton, New Jersey 08809
908-638-8572

SWARTSWOOD STATE PARK
19

LOCATION - The park is 5 miles west of Newton off U.S. 206.

ACTIVITIES - Camp in the 70-site campground with a dump station. Enjoy a picnic and boating from the launch with electric motors. Boat rentals are available. Hike and horseback ride on park trails and go fishing. Tour the nature center and purchase a snack at the snack bar.

During the winter, go cross-country skiing, snowmobiling, ice skating, ice fishing, and ice boating.

Visit nearby Delaware Water Gap National Recreation Area to go fishing, swimming, hiking, and canoeing. For information, call 717-588-6637.

INFORMATION
Swartswood State Park
P.O. Box 123
Swartswood, New Jersey 07877-0123
201-383-5230

VOORHEES STATE PARK
20

LOCATION - The park is 2 miles north of High Bridge and 5 miles north of Clinton. From I-78, Exit 17, take New Jersey 31 north to New Jersey 513.

ACTIVITIES - Camp in the 50-site wooded campground with a dumping station. Enjoy a picnic and hike one of the four trails. Enjoy views from the scenic overlooks on Hill Acres Road and Vista Trail Overlook.

Work out on the parcourse fitness circuit and visit the observatory. Tour its visitor center and attend one of the evening programs offered year-round. For information, call 908-638-8500.

Nearby attractions include Pequest Trout Hatchery, boating and fishing at Spruce Run and Valley recreation areas, Flemington Glass Works, and Ken Lockwood Gorge Natural Area.

INFORMATION
Voorhees State Park
R.D. 2, Box 80, Route 513
Glen Gardner, New Jersey 08826
908-638-6969

WASHINGTON CROSSING STATE PARK
21

LOCATION - The park is 8 miles north of Trenton on New Jersey 29 and then northeast on New Jersey 546.

FEATURES - Washington Crossing is where General Washington and his Continental army made their historic crossing of the Delaware River Christmas night, 1776.

ACTIVITIES - Continental Lane is marked with historical memorials. An annual reenactment of Washington's crossing of the Delaware begins on the Pennsylvania side of the park at 2:00 on December 25 when volunteers maneuver replicas of the Durham boats.

Tour the visitor center open Wednesday–Sunday and tour the Revolutionary War museum and nature center. Historic Nelson House, across New Jersey 29 on the Delaware River, is open summers. For information, call 609-737-1783.

The eighteenth-century Ferry House, located at the south end of Continental Lane, is open Wednesday–Sunday and features living history demonstrations. For more information, call 609-737-2515. Stroll through George Washington Memorial Arboretum.

During the summer, attend performances at the Washington Crossing Open Air Theater. For information, call 609-737-1826.

The park has a nature center and picnic sites. Go hiking on 13 miles of trails, mountain biking on the bicycle trail, and horseback riding along 2.5 miles of equestrian trails. Fish in the Delaware River or in the Delaware and Raritan Canal for bass, catfish, and panfish. During the winter, go cross-country skiing, sledding, and ice skating.

Watch a planetarium show and tour the state museum in Trenton at 205 West State Street. For information, call 609-292-6333 or 609-292-6308.

INFORMATION
Washington Crossing State Park
355 Washington Crossing, Pennington Road
Titusville, New Jersey 08560-1517
609-737-0623

WAWAYANDA STATE PARK
22

LOCATION - The park is on Upper Greenwood Lake, 3 miles east of Vernon via the Warwick Turnpike.

ACTIVITIES - Enjoy camping, picnicking, and hiking the trails. The Appalachian Trail enters from the west and climbs Pochuck Mountain. Go boating from the ramp with electric motors. Boat rentals are available. Go fishing, horseback riding, and purchase a snack. In the winter, go snowmobiling on Lake Wawayanda.

INFORMATION
Wawayanda State Park
P.O. Box 198
Highland Lakes, New Jersey 07422
201-853-4462

WHARTON STATE FOREST
23

LOCATION - The park is accessible from the Atlantic City Expressway, Garden State Parkway, and U.S. 30 and U.S. 206.

ACTIVITIES - Camping is available year-round with 50 campsites and a dump station at Atsion and 49 sites at Godfrey Bridge. Seven more primitive areas have over 1,000 sites. These include Buttonwood Hill, Bodine Field, Hawkins Bridge, Batona Campsite, Mullica River Wilderness, Lower Forge, and Goshen Pond. Three campgrounds permit horses in the campsites.

Nine cabins are located on the north shore of Atsion Lake. Atsion has a guarded swimming area.

Almost 500 miles of sand roads are open year-round for hiking and horseback riding. The 50-mile Batona Trail passes through here. Mountain bicyclists cycle along 20 miles of forest trails.

Four rivers, including the Mullica, Batsto, West Branch of the Wading, and Oswego, offer excellent canoeing. Canoes may be rented at Atsion and motorized boats may be launched at Crowley Landing on the Mullica River. Boats are restricted to electric-powered boats under 10 horsepower. The park has four major canoe trails.

Tour Batsto Village, site of a former bog iron and glassmaking industrial center. Guided tours of the mansion depart daily from 10:00–3:30. Stagecoach tours go from Memorial Day through Labor Day. Interpretive programs are offered 9:00–4:30 Thursday–Sunday. For information, call 609-561-3262.

INFORMATION
Wharton State Forest
Batsto R.D. 9
Hammonton, New Jersey 08037
609-561-0024

NEW YORK

New York has over 200 state parks and historic sites. Niagara Reservation State Park is the oldest park in the nation. Reservations for campground or state-operated cabins may be made by calling 1-800-456-CAMP.

Many visitors come to the Thousand Islands region of northern New York to drive across 1,000 Islands International Bridge that links the U.S. with Canada. Visitors can take a cruise through the islands on the St. Lawrence River and stop at historic Boldt Castle, a reproduction of a German castle, located on Heart Island.

Some of the best fishing, power boating, and sailing conditions in the U.S. are located in Thousand Islands. Fishing hotlines include Niagara County, 716-433-5606; Lake Erie Salmon and Trout Association, 716-366-5464; Finger Lakes, 315-536-7480; Lake Erie/Upper Niagara River, 716-366-3743; and Buffalo, 716-885-3474.

Visit the state parks in the Alexandria Bay Area in the fall when the foliage is at its height along the St. Lawrence River or in August when Bill Johnston's Pirate Weekend invades town with buccaneers and tall ships in the harbor. For details, contact the Chamber of Commerce at 315-482-9531 or 1-800-541-2110.

Approximately 10,000 years ago, the last continental glacier receded, leaving behind steep valleys that created 11 deep Finger Lakes with 600 miles of shoreline and spectacular gorges. Gorges are found in Buttermilk Falls, Fillmore Glen, Robert H. Treman, Stony Brook, and Watkins Glen state parks.

The North Country Trail passes through New York, entering in Allegany State Park and continuing east as it follows 300 miles of the Finger Lakes Trail. It passes through several state parks—Letchworth, Watkins Glen, Old Erie Canal—and continues through the Adirondacks, leaving the state at Crown Point State Historic Site on the shore of Lake Champlain.

When you hike in the woods, it's advisable to wear bug repellent and protective clothing of long sleeves and pants. Deer ticks can carry Lyme disease and are tiny and hard to see.

Eighteen state parks have golf courses. Those with championship status include Montauk Downs, James Baird, Rockland Lake North, Hudson Valley,

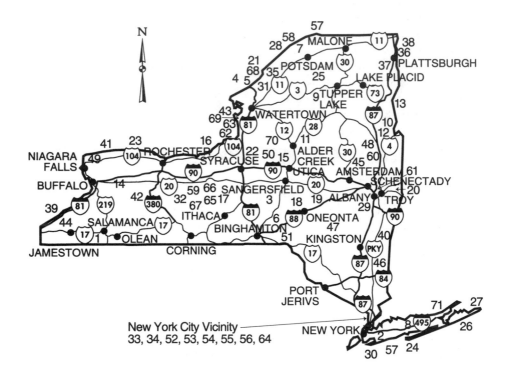

N

57
28 58 MALONE 11 38
21 7 36
68 35 POTSDAM 30 37 PLATTSBURGH
4 31 11 25 LAKE PLACID
5 3 73
9 TUPPER
43 LAKE 13
69 WATERTOWN 87 10
63 81 12 28 12
62 70 11 48 4
16 104 22 50 15 ALDER 30 60
41 23 ROCHESTER CREEK 45
NIAGARA 104 SYRACUSE UTICA AMSTERDAM 61
FALLS 49 90 90 SCHENECTADY
BUFFALO 14 20 20 20
42 20 59 66 SANGERSFIELD 19 ALBANY TROY
39 81 219 32 65 17 3 18 29 90
44 67 ITHACA 81 6 88 ONEONTA
SALAMANCA 17 BINGHAMTON 51 47 KINGSTON 40
17 1 OLEAN CORNING 17 PKY
JAMESTOWN 87 46
84

PORT
JERIVS
New York City Vicinity 87
33, 34, 52, 53, 54, 55, 56, 64 NEW YORK 71 27
8 495 26
2
30 57 24

Saratoga Spa, Battle Island, Fulton, Chenango Valley, Binghamton, Green Lakes, Fayetteville, Bethpage, and Beaver Island on Grand Island.

The Adirondacks cover 6 million acres and feature 46 high peaks rising above thousands of lakes, ponds, rivers, and streams.

Seaway Trail, part of the National Scenic Byway System, extends along the St. Lawrence River and Lake Ontario from Rooseveltown to Niagara Falls. For information, call 315-646-1000.

New York's canal system, the first of its kind in America, follows the course of the original 1825 Erie Canal and has 524 miles of recreational waterways. Canalside bike trails extend eastward from Lockport to Rochester and from Scotia to Albany. For information on events along the canal system from April–December, call 1-800-422-1825.

Palisades Interstate Parkway consists of a chain of state parks and state historic sites along the west side of the Hudson River. The 38-mile-long parkway runs from New York City's George Washington Bridge to Bear Mountain State Park.

ALLEGANY STATE PARK
1

LOCATION - The park is south of Salamanca on State Park Road 1. Quaker Run is 11 miles west of Salamanca, Exit 18 off New York 17. Red House is 7 miles west of Salamanca, Exit 19 off New York 17.

ACTIVITIES - Allegany is New York's largest state park. Quaker Run Campground has 189 sites, 95 with electrical hookups, and a dump station. Red House campground has 134 sites, 67 with electrical hookups, and two dump stations. Attend year-round interpretive programs.

You can also stay in one of over 300 cabins, 100 winterized and available year-round. Three restaurants operate seasonally.

The park has many streams and two large lakes: Red House and Quaker. Trout season runs from April 1–September 30, except on Quaker Lake where it's year-round. Motorized boats are not permitted anywhere except for those with electric motors on Quaker Lake. Boat rentals are available.

Swimming is permitted from Memorial Day through Labor Day at Red House Lake and from mid-June through Labor Day at Quaker Lake.

Hikers have access to 18 trails covering 70 miles. These range in length from .5-mile-long Bear Springs Trail to the 18-mile-long segment of the North Country Trail which passes through the park. Equestrians can explore 55 miles of trails and rent horses in the Summit area. Bring along insect repellent and watch for poison ivy along the trails.

Bicyclists can circle Red House Lake on a 5.5-mile paved trail that crosses a rustic covered bridge. Bicycles and boats are available for rent. Mountain bicyclists get a good workout by cycling in the Art Roscoe Ski Touring Area.

Motorists can pick up a free copy of *Allegany State Park Auto Tour Guide Book* for a self-guided 25-mile tour.

During the winter, go cross-country skiing on 30 miles of trails, including those in the Art Roscoe Ski Touring Area, or snowmobiling along 55 miles of trails.

In nearby Salamanca, tour the Salamanca Rail Museum at 170 Main to see a restored 1912 passenger depot. For information, call 716-945-3133. Seneca Iroquois National Museum on the Allegany Indian Reservation is off U.S. 17, Exit 20. For information, call 716-945-3133.

Visit Chautauqua Institute, located northwest of the park. Purchase a ticket to tour the grounds or attend musical concerts and plays in the amphitheater from late June–August. For event information, call 716-357-6200. To play golf, call 716-357-6211 for a tee-off time.

Incoming pilots can land at Olean Municipal Airport, located 10 miles north of Olean. Rental cars are available.

INFORMATION
Allegany State Park
2373 ASP 1, Ste. 3
Salamanca, New York 14779
General park information: 716-354-9101 or 716-354-4065
Quaker Run rentals: 716-354-2181
Red House rentals: 716-354-9121

BEAR MOUNTAIN STATE PARK
See under PALISADES INTERSTATE PARKS

BETHPAGE STATE PARK
2

LOCATION - The park is one mile north of Farmingdale on Long Island.

ACTIVITIES - Bethpage boasts tennis courts and 5 eighteen-hole golf courses. To reserve a tee-off time, call 516-249-0700. The Long Island Golf Classic is held in August.

Attend Sunday afternoon polo games from May–October. Ride equestrian trails, cycle bicycle trails, or rent a boat to go boating.

From early April through the end of November stay in Battle Row Campground with 64 sites, including 30 with electrical hookups and a trailer dump station. Food service is available.

Tour Old Bethpage Village on Round Swamp Road. From the Long Island Expressway, take Exit 48 onto Northern Parkway or take Exit 31 onto

Southern Parkway. The pre-Civil War farm village has costumed interpreters. For information, call 516-420-5288.

In the winter, go downhill skiing, cross-country skiing, and sledding. A Winter Arts Festival is held January–February.

Incoming pilots can land at Republic Airport one mile east of Farmingdale. Rental cars are available.

INFORMATION
Bethpage State Park
Farmingdale, New York 11735
516-249-0700 (park office)
516-293-7120 (campground)

BOWMAN LAKE STATE PARK
3

LOCATION - The lake is 8 miles northwest of Oxford off New York 220 in New York's central region.

ACTIVITIES - Camp in the 198-site campground with a trailer dump and limited groceries and snacks. Go swimming, trout fishing, and boating in Bowman Lake with rentals available. Also enjoy bicycling and hiking.

INFORMATION
Bowman Lake State Park
Star Route off New York 220
Oxford, New York 13830
607-334-2718

BURNHAM POINT STATE PARK
4

LOCATION - The park is 4 miles east of Cape Vincent on New York 12E, 6 miles northeast of Lake Ontario on the St. Lawrence River.

ACTIVITIES - Camp in the 52-site campground, 16 with electrical hookups and a trailer dump station. Thousand Islands are known for excellent fishing for bass, pike, muskellunge, and walleye. Cape Vincent is called the "home of the gamey black bass" and has the world title for its river muskies. Black bass and muskie season begins in mid-June and lasts until fall. Boaters can go for miles on the St. Lawrence River.

In Cape Vincent, tour the Cape Vincent Historical Museum on Lower James Street near the ferry dock. For hours, call 315-654-3126. Cape Vincent Aquarium is open daily 1:00–5:00, May–October. For information, call 315-654-2147.

INFORMATION
Burnham Point State Park
c/o Cedar Point State Park
R.D. 2, Route 12E
Clayton, New York 13624
315-654-2522

CAYUGA LAKE STATE PARK
See under TAUGHANNOCK FALLS STATE PARK

CEDAR POINT STATE PARK
5

LOCATION - The park is 6 miles west of Clayton on New York 12E.

FEATURES - Cedar Point is in the heart of Thousand Islands. The ruins of Fort Haldimand are located on Carlton Island west of Cedar Point. The fort was constructed by the British prior to the Revolutionary War.

ACTIVITIES - The park season runs from early May through Columbus Day weekend. Visitors can go boating on the St. Lawrence River with rentals and a marina, swimming from a guarded beach, and watch freighters passing by. The St. Lawrence River is known for its excellent fishing for pike, muskellunge, walleye, bass, and panfish.

Camp in the 172-site campground, 85 with electricity and 32 with full hookups. Summers bring folk singers, puppet shows, and other performers to the park.

In the winter, go ice fishing and cross-country skiing.

Nearby attractions include the Sackets Harbor Battlefield State Historic Site, overlooking the only natural harbor at the east end of Lake Ontario. It's one mile from New York 3 on the west side of Sackets Harbor village. Two battles were fought here during the War of 1812.

Take a guided tour of the visitor center housed in the 1817 Union Hotel. The center is open Wednesday–Saturday from 10:00–5:00, and Sundays in late May through late September from 1:00–5:00. The site has a nineteenth-century village center. Each July, attend the annual Can-Am Festival when muskets are fired and tall ships arrive in the harbor. For information, call 315-646-3634.

Sackets Harbor is one of the deepest harbors in Lake Ontario where anglers fish for bass and salmon. Compete in their annual fishing derby. For area information, call 315-646-1700.

Visit Tibbets Point Lighthouse at the outlet of Lake Ontario and at the head of St. Lawrence River, 3 miles west of Cape Vincent. Constructed in 1827, it's still used as a sailor's beacon, and its keeper's cottage is now used as a youth hostel. Tour the aquarium at Cape Vincent, open daily 1:00–5:00, May–October. For information, call 315-654-2147.

In Clayton, tour the Antique Boat Museum, housing the largest collection of antique freshwater vessels in the world. For information, call 315-686-4104. The museum hosts an antique raceboat show and fishing tournaments. Anglers can fish for pike, walleye, bass, and muskie.

Other town events include concerts on the waterfront, bluegrass and hot air balloon festivals, and a Fiddler's Fling. For information, call 315-686-3771 or 1-800-252-9806.

Downtown Clayton is designated as an historic district because of its 31 buildings built between 1854–1920. Get a map from the Chamber of Commerce.

INFORMATION
Cedar Point State Park
R.D. 2, Box 166, Route 12E
Clayton, New York 13624
315-654-2522 or 315-686-4472

CHENANGO VALLEY STATE PARK
6

LOCATION - The park is 13 miles northeast of Binghamton on New York 369.

FEATURES - Lily and Chenango lakes are kettle lakes formed by receding Ice Age glaciers.

ACTIVITIES - The park is open year-round. Camp in the 216-site campground, 51 with electrical hookups and trailer dump station, or stay in one of 24 cabins. Snacks are available at the snack bar.

Attend a summer concert and go hiking and bicycling. Enjoy swimming, fishing for trout, pike, bass, and walleye, and go boating in Chenango Lake with rowboat rentals available. Play golf on the eighteen-hole course. For a tee-off time, call 607-648-9804.

During the winter, go camping, cross-country skiing on 13 kilometers of trails, sledding, snowshoeing, ice skating, tubing, and tobogganing.

In Binghamton, attend the summer music festival. For a schedule, call 607-777-ARTS. The Binghamton Symphony Orchestra also performs at the Forum. For information, call 607-772-0400.

Flower lovers can tour Cutler Botanic Gardens at 840 Front Street in Binghamton. Guided tours may be scheduled in advance by calling 607-772-8953.

In March, attend the Irish Festival or Spring Antique Show. In May, attend Two Rivers Ethnic Festival. For information, contact the Visitor Bureau at 1-800-836-6740.

Take a ride on the wood-carved Ross Park carousel from Memorial Day through Labor Day. Admission is a piece of litter.

Incoming pilots can land at Binghamton Regional Airport, located 7 miles north of Binghamton. Rental cars are available.

INFORMATION
Chenango Valley State Park
R.D. 2
Chenango Forks, New York 13746
607-648-5251

COLES CREEK STATE PARK
7

LOCATION - The park is on the St. Lawrence River, 5 miles east of Waddington on New York 37, on the south shore of Lake St. Lawrence.

FEATURES - Lake St. Lawrence is 25 miles long and 4 miles wide, formed upriver from the Robert Moses Power Dam.

ACTIVITIES - Coles Creek is open mid-May through Labor Day. Camp in the 235-site campground, including 154 with electrical hookups, with a trailer dump station and groceries.

Go fishing for bass, pike, walleye, and panfish, swimming from the beach, and boating from the ramp in the St. Lawrence River with rental boats available at the marina.

Nearby attractions include Eisenhower Lock, Robert Moses Power Dam, an Upper Canada Historic Village, and the Frederic Remington Art Museum at 303 Washington Street in Ogdensburg. For information, call 315-393-2425. In Ogdensburg, attend the International Seaway Festival in mid-July.

INFORMATION
Coles Creek State Park
Route 37, Box 442
Waddington, New York 13694
315-388-5636

CONNETQUOT RIVER STATE PARK PRESERVE
8

LOCATION - The preserve is near Oakdale and Bohemia on New York 27 on Long Island.

ACTIVITIES - The preserve is open Tuesday–Sunday from 7:00–4:30. Entry and equestrian permits must be obtained in advance by writing Long Island State Park and Recreation Commission Headquarters, P.O. Box 247, Babylon, New York 11702.

The large 3,473-acre preserve supports many species of animals and plants. It offers horseback riding along bridle paths, river fishing, guided nature walks, and interpretive tours offered Tuesday–Sunday.

INFORMATION
Connetquot River State Park Preserve
Oakdale, New York 11769
516-581-1005

CRANBERRY LAKE STATE PARK
9
ROGERS ROCK STATE PARK
10
NICK'S LAKE STATE PARK
11
LAKE GEORGE BEACH STATE PARK
12

LOCATION - Cranberry Lake is in Adirondack Park off New York 3, 1.5 miles south of Cranberry Lake Village.

Rogers Rock State Park is at the northwest end of 32-mile-long Lake George on Forest Bay in the southeastern Adirondacks.

Lake George Beach State Park is on the southern end of Lake George.

Nick's Lake State Park is south of Old Forge off New York 28.

FEATURES - The state parks are in 6-million-acre Adirondacks Park. The northeastern part of the park has 46 "high peaks," with 42 rising over 4,000 feet. Mount Marcy is the highest at 5,344 feet.

ACTIVITIES - One Adirondack Park Visitor Interpretive Center is located in Newcomb. To reach it, take New York 28N 14 miles east of Long Lake. Watch the multimedia presentation and take guided trail walks. For information, call 518-582-2000.

A second visitor center is in Paul Smiths on New York 30, 12 miles north of Saranac Lake. Hike several miles of surfaced trails. Naturalists lead walks in July and August. Attend their multi-image presentation, see park exhibits, and obtain park-wide information by calling 518-327-3000.

Adirondack Park offers boating, horseback riding, and 2,000 miles of hiking trails, including a north-south wilderness trail that covers 146 miles from Lake Placid to Northville. Visitors can fish for bass, trout, and panfish, go swimming, water-skiing, and scuba diving. During the winter, go cross-country skiing on summer hiking trails or on nearby Peavine Swamp Ski Trail. Also enjoy ice boating, snowmobiling, and snowshoeing.

Cranberry Lake State Park is open mid-May through Labor Day. Camp in the 173-site campground with a camp store. Go fishing, swimming, and boating with power boats permitted. Boat rentals are available. The Oswegatchie River, headwaters of Cranberry Lake, has 16 miles of canoeing water beginning from the inlet.

Many canoers' favorite route begins at Old Forge and follows a string of waterways nearly 140 miles to Tupper Lake and the Saranac Lakes. Another favorite is the St. Regis Canoe Area with 57 interconnecting lakes and ponds near Saranac.

Hikers can climb Bear Mountain via a 2.4-mile loop trail or explore a 17.4-mile loop trail system nearby. Five Ponds Wilderness Area has over 50 miles of hiking trails.

At Nick's Lake State Park, go boating, hike forest trails, and go fishing for trout, pike, bass, and whitefish. The park is near McCauley Mountain Ski Slope where you can downhill ski during the winter.

At Old Forge, enjoy a narrated cruise along the Fulton Chain of Lakes' historic coastline where you pass President Benjamin Harrison's summer home. For information, call 315-369-6473.

Go kayaking on the Moose River. Put in 11 miles south of Old Forge on Moose River Road and take out before the Fowlersville Bridge. This is rated one of the most technical whitewater runs in the Northeast with Class 4 and 5 action. Scouting is recommended.

In Indian Lake, hikers can climb Snow Mountain, hike to remote ponds, or follow the Northville-Placid Trail. Climb Chimney Mountain with its ice caves. During the winter, go alpine skiing on nearby Gore Mountain, Oak Mountain, Big Tupper, or Whiteface Mountain near Lake Placid, which was the site of the 1980 winter Olympics.

Snowmobilers come to Indian Lake to enjoy groomed trails, part of Hamilton County's 750-mile trail system. For Indian Lake information, call 518-648-5112.

Go kayaking along the Hudson River. Put in at the Abanakee Dam in Indian Lake and take out at North River along New York 28. The rapids are Class 3 and 4.

Tour Adirondack Museum one mile north of Blue Mountain Lake on New York 28N/30 from the end of May through mid-October. The museum of history and art has both indoor and outdoor exhibitions. A 35-minute movie is shown hourly. For information, call 518-352-7311.

While in Blue Mountain Lake, hike to the summit of 3759-foot Blue Mountain. The trailhead is .5-mile north of the museum and gains 2,000 feet in 3 miles. It is very rocky with many tree roots and can be muddy. Hiking boots and insect repellent are advised. Pick up a free map of the area's other 60 miles of trails. Take a canoe trip, rent a boat, or enter a sailfish race. For information, call 518-352-7715.

In late June, attend their annual No-Octane Regatta for Wooden Boats. For information, contact the Adirondack Museum at 518-352-7311.

Visit Adirondack Lakes Center for the Arts at Blue Mountain Lake. It offers concerts, films, and theater. For schedules, call 518-352-7715.

Bicyclists can ride the Adirondack "bikeway" between Blue Mountain Lake and Indian Lake.

Rogers Rock State Park's campground has 314 sites. Rogers Rock hiking trail begins 3.5 miles north of Hague on New York 9N. The trailhead isn't clearly marked, so ask for assistance prior to setting out. It climbs 500 feet and involves a 2.5-mile round trip.

Lake George Beach State Park offers swimming from the beach and is the start of the Warren County Bikeway. This generally flat ride goes through the woods, ending up at Glens Falls in 8.5 miles. For a map, call 1-800-365-1050, ext. 2750.

For a unique experience, rent an island campsite in the lake. Some islands have large campgrounds, while others have only a single site. Contact Ticketron for information.

While in Lake George, enjoy a narrated steamboat ride aboard *Mine-Ha-Ha*, an authentic sternwheeler steamboat, or aboard the *Mohican*, *Ticonderoga*, or the 1,500-passenger *Lac du Saint Sacrement*. For information, call 518-668-5777. Take a shoreline cruise to learn about the owners of mansions fronting the lake.

Rent a speedboat, take a horse-drawn carriage ride, or a parasail ride from their floating dock. Go scuba diving, boating, fishing for trout, landlocked salmon, bass, pike, and pickerel. Enjoy swimming, bike the mountain bike trails, play golf and tennis, and go whitewater rafting.

Drive up 5.5-mile, 2,021-foot Prospect Mountain Scenic Highway for a 100-mile view of five states. The highway is open Memorial Day through early October. If you prefer to hike up the mountain, the trail begins near the wharf where you can ask for directions.

For general area information, call 1-800-365-1050, ext. 1818. For information on the operas and festival orchestra concerts, call 518-793-3858.

Tour Fort William Henry and museum on the south end of Lake George, a restored fort dating from the French and Indian War. Observe musket/cannon firings and living history demonstrations. The fort is open from May–October. For information, call 518-668-5749.

Tour nearby Fort Ticonderoga on New York 74 from mid-May through mid-October. It's 18 miles east of I-87, Exit 28. Fort Ticonderoga was built by the French in 1755 at the outset of the French and Indian War to block the British on Lake Champlain. It houses an outstanding collection of military memorabilia from the eighteenth-century—paintings, furniture, and articles of daily life of soldiers garrisoned here.

Take a history cruise aboard M/V *Carillon* on Lake Champlain. A French and Indian War reenactment and encampment occurs the last weekend in June.

Take a guided tour, listen to fife and drums July–August. For general information, call 518-585-2821.

Drive over Burgoyne Trail and visit both Mount Hope and Mount Defiance which were constructed as perimeter fortifications for the fort.

Visit Olympic Village in Lake Placid where you can attend weekly Lake Placid sinfonietta concerts on Wednesday from early July through early August and on Sundays at the Lake Placid Center for the Arts. Play golf and enjoy water activities on Lake Placid. Attend various entertainment events at the Olympic Center and watch our future Olympians practicing in the ice arenas. For details, contact the Lake Placid Visitor Bureau at 518-891-1990. For a complete calendar of summer and fall events in Lake Placid, call 1-800-462-6236.

To take a guided tour of the various Olympic sites, stop by the Olympic Center or call either 518-523-1655 or 1-800-462-6236.

Take a chair lift-elevator ride up the 90-meter ski jump tower used for Olympic and World Cup events. From here, you can see Mount Marcy, the state's highest mountain.

Watch summer and fall practice competition performed on plastic mats in the Kodak Sports Park off New York 73. The complex is also site of the U.S. freestyle aerial training center. Athletes take off from 20 to 50 feet above a large pool as they perfect their inverted aerials, since such maneuvers must be mastered in water before being attempted on land.

Take a trolley car ride up Mount Van Hoevenberg to get a close-up look at the mile-long Olympic track and its companion Olympic luge runs.

Enjoy a mountain bike ride along the old Central Railroad tracks from Lake Placid to Saranac Lake. The 14-mile trail begins at the Train Station Museum on Averyville Road in Lake Placid and ends at the old train pullout before Saranac Lake.

Pick up a trail description at the visitor center of the various hikes available in Lake Placid as well as in the surrounding Adirondacks. We hiked the trail to Owen, Copperas, and Winch ponds and, although beautiful, found the area full of insects. Be sure to bring along plenty of repellent! Boots would be helpful since there are many muddy places, especially following a rain storm.

For a fantastic view of the countryside around the Adirondacks, drive up Whiteface Mountain Veterans' Memorial Highway. Park in the lot and take the elevator in the center of the mountain to the summit for a 360-degree view of the mountains and lakes beneath your feet. A restaurant is on top, but time your departure since all cars need to be off the summit by 6:30.

Take an aerial chair lift ride up Whiteface Mountain from 9:00–4:00 to the top of 3,600-foot Little Whiteface to see the Olympic racing trails from mid-June through mid-October.

Take a self-guided tour of High Falls Gorge located on New York 86 between Lake Placid and Wilmington. Walk along steel bridges and paths for overlooks into the waters of the Ausable River as it rushes through the gorge.

Go for a self-guided tour of John Brown's farm, home of the abolitionist. The farm is off New York 73, south of Lake Placid. For information, call 518-523-3900.

Incoming pilots can land at the Lake Placid Airport, one mile south of the village, or at the Adirondack Airport at Saranac Lake, 16 miles from Lake Placid.

INFORMATION

Cranberry Lake State Park
Lone Pine Road
Cranberry Lake, New York 12927
315-848-2315

Rogers Rock State Park
Route 9
Hague, New York 12836
315-585-6746

Lake George State Park
518-668-3352
Adirondack Park Agency
518-891-4050

CROWN POINT STATE HISTORIC SITE
13

LOCATION - Crown Point is by the Lake Champlain Bridge, 4 miles east of New York 9N and 22.

FEATURES - The ruins of two forts are located above Lake Champlain. Fort St. Frederic was begun in 1734 by the French, but was captured by the British 25 years later during the French and Indian War. The British then constructed one of the largest fortifications in colonial America, His Majesty's Fort of Crown Point. This fort was captured by the Americans in 1775.

ACTIVITIES - Take a self-guided tour of the grounds and fort ruins year-round. Tour the visitor center's exhibits and watch their audio-visual show. The fort is open June–October on Wednesday–Sunday, including Independence Day and Labor Day. The rest of the year, it's open by appointment only.

INFORMATION

Crown Point State Historic Site
R.D. 1, Box 219
Crown Point, New York 12928
518-597-3666

CUMBERLAND BAY STATE PARK
See under LAKE CHAMPLAIN STATE PARKS

DARIEN LAKES STATE PARK
14

LOCATION - The lakes are ¼ mile north of New York 20 on Harlow Road, west of Darien Center, and 3 miles west of Darien Lake Amusement Park. Go 12 miles south of Exit 48A off I-90.

ACTIVITIES - The campground has 150 sites and a trailer dump, open from the second weekend in June through Labor Day. The park has approximately 19 miles of multiple-use trails for hiking, horseback riding, and during the winter, cross-country skiing and snowmobiling.

Go bass fishing in Harlow Lake and swimming from the guarded beach from mid-June through Labor Day. No boats are permitted.

In Batavia, enjoy an evening of harness racing at Batavia Downs and watch the Batavia Clippers' farm club play at Dwyer Stadium. Genesee County Airport has a ten-day summer skydiving event. For information, call 716-343-6200.

Darien Lake Theme Park has roller coasters, the world's largest Ferris wheel, and sponsors famous entertainers and summer concerts. For performance information, call 716-343-9313.

The Farmer's Market is held in Batavia on Tuesday and Friday during summer and early fall.

INFORMATION
Darien Lakes State Park
10289 Harlow Road
Darien Center, New York 14040
716-547-9242

DELTA LAKE STATE PARK
15

LOCATION - The park is 6 miles northeast of Rome on New York 46.

ACTIVITIES - Camp in the 101-site campground, hike and bike the trails, go boating with rentals available, bass fishing, and swimming.

In Rome, tour 1840s Erie Canal Village, site of Fort Bull on New York 49 West. Take a ride on the 1840 horse-drawn packet boat. The village is open May–September from 10:00–5:00. For information, call 315-337-3999.

Tour Fort Stanwix National Monument at 112 East Park. The reconstructed Revolutionary War fort has costumed guides, a film, and museum open from April 1–December 31. For information, call 315-336-2090.

Attend a Broadway musical or drama at Beck's Grove Dinner Theater, 4286 Oswego Road, Blassvale, from March–December. For information, call 315-336-7038.

INFORMATION
Delta Lake State Park
Route 46
Rome, New York 13440
315-337-4670

FAIR HAVEN BEACH STATE PARK
16

LOCATION - The beach is one mile north of Fair Haven off New York 104A north of the Finger Lakes.

ACTIVITIES - Fair Haven State Park is the second largest of the Finger Lakes state parks. Camp in the 195-site campground, 44 with electrical hookups, with groceries and a trailer dump station. It's open mid-April through mid-October. You can also stay in one of 33 cabins.

Go trout, steelhead, salmon, perch, bass, and pike fishing, boating from the ramp with rentals available, and swimming in Lake Ontario. Hike the nature trails.

During the winter, go ice skating, snowmobiling, and cross-country skiing on 9 kilometers of trails. Their annual Winter Carnival is held in February.

INFORMATION
Fair Haven Beach State Park
Route 104A
Fair Haven, New York 13064
315-947-5205

FILLMORE GLEN STATE PARK
17

LOCATION - The park is one mile south of Moravia on New York 38.

FEATURES - Fillmore Glen was named for President Millard Fillmore and is noted for its unique rock formations, breath-taking gorges, and waterfalls.

ACTIVITIES - Camp in the 57-site campground from mid-May through mid-October. It has a trailer dump station. Stay in one of three cabins, go swimming in the gorge-fed pools, and hike trails both in the gorge and through the woods. The park boasts five waterfalls, including the Pinnacle.

Enjoy fishing in Owasco Lake and Inlet. Play golf on the eighteen-hole course adjacent to the park.

During the winter, go hiking and cross-country skiing on unplowed park roads. However, gorge trails are closed then.

In late July, attend the annual Fillmore Days festival in the park. The Fillmore Auto Show is held Labor Day Sunday in the park.

In Moravia, tour the birthplace of Millard Fillmore on Summer Hill, north of New York 90 and 5 miles east on Skinner Hill Road. It's open daily from May–October. For information, call 315-497-1055.

INFORMATION
Fillmore Glen State Park
R.D. 3
Moravia, New York 13118
315-497-0130

GILBERT LAKE STATE PARK
18

LOCATION - Gilbert Lake State Park is 12 miles northwest of Oneonta off New York 205 in the Catskill Mountains.

ACTIVITIES - The park is open from early May through mid-October. Camp in the campground with 221 sites, 17 with electrical hookups, a trailer dump station, and limited groceries. Rent one of the 33 cabins. Go bicycling and hiking on 12 miles of trails. Enjoy boating from the ramp with rentals available. Go fishing and swimming from Memorial Day weekend through Labor Day.

Golfers can play the nine-hole golf course overlooking the state park. For tee-off times, call 607-432-2713. For a different kind of challenge, check out their Frisbee-disc golf course.

During the winter, go cross-country skiing, sledding, snowmobiling, and winter camping.

Tour the National Soccer Hall of Fame at 5-11 Ford Avenue in Oneonta. For information, call 607-432-3351.

Nearby Cooperstown has several places to visit, including the Farmers' Museum, James Fenimore Cooper House, and the Baseball Hall of Fame. For details, see Glimmerglass State Park.

Incoming pilots can land at Oneonta Municipal Airport, 3 miles north of Oneonta. Rental cars are available.

INFORMATION
Gilbert Lake State Park
R.D. 1, Box 145
Laurens, New York 13796
607-432-2114

GLIMMERGLASS STATE PARK
19

LOCATION - The park is 4 miles south of New York 20, east of East Spring-field. Take New York 31 south to the park entrance. The park has 8,000 feet of shoreline along Otsego Lake.

FEATURES - Glimmerglass got its name from a lake described by author James Fenimore Cooper in *The Deerslayer.*

ACTIVITIES - Camp in the 39-site campground with a trailer dump and groceries. A large raccoon population lives here, so secure all food.

Go swimming from the beach from mid-June through Labor Day and enjoy bass, trout, salmon, and perch fishing. Go boating in Otsego Lake in canoes and car-top boats. Go bicycling and enjoy hiking through the forest to get a spectacular view of Otsego Lake. Concessions are available.

Tour Hyde Hall, a 45-room nineteenth-century home, from June–September on weekends from 1:00–5:00. For information, call 607-547-5098.

During the winter, go cross-country skiing, snowmobiling, ice fishing, sledding, primitive winter camping, and ice skating.

Tour Farmers' Museum on Lake Road, New York 80, in Cooperstown. It re-creates a nineteenth-century village. See the Cardiff Giant, America's most famous hoax. For information, call 607-547-2593.

Glimmerglass Opera's performances run from late June–August. For a schedule, call 607-547-5704 or 607-547-2255.

Cooperstown Theatre Festival, located 7 miles from the village, performs in July and August, Tuesday–Sunday. For information, call 607-547-2335.

National Baseball Hall of Fame and Museum is in Cooperstown. For information, call 607-547-9988. Tour Corvette Americana Hall of Fame on New York 28 to see Corvettes and slides of movies from the past 40 years. For information, call 607-547-4135.

Fenimore House on Lake Road has life masks of the nation's founding fathers. For information, call 607-547-2533.

For a one-hour cruise around Glimmerglass Lake, contact Lake Otsego Boat Tours at 607-547-5295 or Glimmerglass Boat Tours at 607-547-2790. For a rail excursion, particularly during the fall color season, contact Susquehanna Steam Engine 141 Tourist Operations at 607-547-2555, ext. 501.

In May, attend the annual three-day Susquehanna River General Clinton Canoe Regatta in General Clinton Park. The Annual Del-Se-Nango Fiddlers Festival is held in the Beaver Valley Campground in August. The annual Glimmerglass triathlon, featuring running, biking, and canoeing, is in September. Contact the Chamber of Commerce at 607-547-9983 for details.

Hanford Mills Museum is in East Meredith. It's at the intersection of Delaware County 10 and 12, 10 miles east of Oneonta. The museum features demonstrations of nineteenth-century mill work and antique gasoline engines. For information, call 607-278-5744.

INFORMATION
Glimmerglass State Park
R.D. 2 Box 580
Cooperstown, New York 13326
607-547-8662

GRAFTON LAKES STATE PARK
20

LOCATION - The lakes are 12 miles east of Troy on New York 2.

ACTIVITIES - Grafton Lakes State Park is open year-round. Go swimming from the beach in Long Pond or in the pool from Memorial Day through Labor Day. Enjoy trout fishing in Grafton Lakes, Long Pond, and Second Pond, all stocked annually with trout. Martin-Dunham Reservoir has good bass and walleye fishing. Go bicycling and boating without motors. Boat rentals are available.

Hike the trail encircling Long and Shaver ponds and explore Woodland or Shaver Pond's nature trails. Special events are offered throughout the year.

A January winter festival features pond ice fishing and ice skating with night skating available Friday and Saturday nights. Go orienteering, snowshoeing, and cross-country skiing on the 8-mile hiking trail. The park also has snow-mobile trails with shelters.

INFORMATION
Grafton Lakes State Park
Route 2E
Grafton, New York 12082-0163
518-279-1155

GRASS POINT STATE POINT
21

LOCATION - The park is 5 miles south of Alexandria Bay off New York 12 in the heart of Thousand Islands. From I-81, take Clayton Exit 50 south to New York 12 and go one mile toward Clayton to reach Grass Point.

FEATURES - Grass Point offers panoramic views of many islands and of the Rock Island Lighthouse, a National Register's historic site.

ACTIVITIES - The park is open from mid-May through mid-September. Camp in the 78-site campground, 18 with hookups, with a trailer dump station. Bird watchers enjoy birding in the large marsh area.

Go boating from the launch, swimming, and fishing in the St. Lawrence River for bass, pike, muskellunge, and panfish. Northern pike and walleye season begins in May. Black bass season extends from late June–November, and muskie are caught from July–December.

Watch freighters from all over the world traveling the St. Lawrence Seaway from the Atlantic Ocean to Duluth, Minnesota.

Take a scenic cruise aboard the *Empire*, including a stop to tour Boldt Castle. For information, call 315-482-9511 or 1-800-542-2628.

In Clayton, tour the Antique Boat Museum, housing the largest collection of antique freshwater vessels in the world. Attend their annual Antique Race Boat Regatta or a fishing tournament. Other annual events include concerts on the waterfront, hot air balloon and bluegrass festivals, and a Fiddler's Fling. For details, call 315-686-3771 or 1-800-252-9806.

INFORMATION
Grass Point State Park
R.D. 1, Box 166, Route 12S
Clayton, New York 13624
315-686-4472

GREEN LAKES STATE PARK
22

LOCATION - The park is 4 miles northeast of Fayetteville on New York 290.

FEATURES - Two beautiful aquamarine bodies of water were formed by receding glaciers during the Ice Age. Only a few lakes of this type exist in the world.

ACTIVITIES - Camp in the 137-site campground, 42 sites with electrical hookups and a trailer dump station, or stay in one of seven cabins. Go trout fishing and boating with rentals available. Go swimming from the beach, purchase a snack, go hiking, biking, and play golf. For a tee-off time, call 607-637-5515.

In the winter, go cross-country skiing, snowshoeing, and sledding.

INFORMATION
Green Lakes State Park
Routes 290 and 5
Fayetteville, New York 13066
315-637-6111

HAMLIN BEACH STATE PARK
23

LOCATION - The beach is 5 miles north of Hamlin on Lake Ontario State Parkway.

ACTIVITIES - Camp in the 264-site campground with all sites offering electrical hookups, a trailer dump, and limited groceries. Go hiking, bicycling, and trout fishing. Go swimming from late June through Labor Day and boating in cartop boats in Lake Ontario. In the winter, go cross-country skiing and snowmobiling.

INFORMATION
Hamlin Beach State Park
Hamlin, New York 14464
716-964-2462
914-351-2360 (Sebago Cabin Camp)

HARRIMAN STATE PARK
See under PALISADES INTERSTATE PARKS

HECKSCHER STATE PARK
24

LOCATION - The park is one mile south of East Islip off the Southern State Parkway on Long Island.

ACTIVITIES - Ride the bridle trails and go camping in the 63-site campground. Enjoy bicycling and hiking the trails and purchase a snack. Go boating from the ramp, saltwater fishing, and swimming in the pool or from the beach. During the winter, go cross-country skiing.

Hike 34-mile Suffolk Greenbelt Trail, stretching along the shores of the Nissequogue and Connetquot rivers from Sunken Meadow State Park to Heckscher State Park.

In August, attend Islip Jazz Festival in the park in August and the Antique Auto Show in September.

INFORMATION
Heckscher State Park
P.O. Box 247
Babylon, New York 11702
516-581-2100

HIGLEY FLOW STATE PARK
25

LOCATION - Higley Flow is nestled at the foothills at the northern edge of the Adirondack Mountains. Follow New York 56 to South Colton. Go west on Cold Brook Drive for 2.5 miles.

ACTIVITIES - The park is open from Memorial Day through Labor Day. Camp in the 135-site campground with 43 electrical hookups. Swim in the Racquette River and go boating from the boat launch. Since the river is 3 miles long, all types of boats are permitted, with canoeing especially popular. The park has 3 miles of hiking trails. Fish in the Racquette River and reservoir for walleye, pike, and panfish.

During the winter, enjoy 15 miles of snowmobile and cross-country skiing. You can also go snowshoeing and ice fishing.

INFORMATION
Higley Flow State Park
R.D. 1
Colton, New York 13625
315-262-2880

HITHER HILLS STATE PARK
26
MONTAUK POINT STATE PARK
27

LOCATION - Hither Hills is 8 miles west of Montauk on New York 27.

Montauk Point State Park is east of Hither Hills, 4 miles east of Montauk, on the south shore of eastern Long Island.

FEATURES - Montauk, named by the Indians, means "hilly country." The area holds 30 world fishing records registered in the 1980 *International Game Fish Association Record Book*.

ACTIVITIES - Hither Hills has 7 campsites, a trailer dump, and a food store. Go hiking and visit the walking dunes. Cycle the bicycling trails, go swimming, and play tennis or golf. Charter a boat from June–October and go saltwater fishing from June–October for tuna, marlin, shark, and swordfish. Surf cast for bluefish, blackfish, cod, flounder, and bass from April–November with some of the best catches made late in the fall.

Montauk Point also has hiking, an Indian cemetery, and fishing in both the Atlantic Ocean or Lake Montauk.

Take the ferry from Montauk to Block Island, Rhode Island, where you can enjoy a picnic, go fishing, and swimming at Block Island State Recreation Area.

Visit the Montauk Point Lighthouse and museum located at the end of Montauk Highway. The lighthouse was commissioned by President George Washington in the 1790s and is the fourth oldest active lighthouse.

Incoming pilots can land at Montauk Airport, 3 miles northeast of Montauk in Montauk Point State Park. Rental cars are available.

INFORMATION

Hither Hills State Park
Old Montauk Highway
Montauk, New York 11946
516-668-2461

Montauk Point State Park
Route 27, Old Montauk Highway
Montauk, New York 11946
516-668-3781

JACQUES CARTIER STATE PARK
28

LOCATION - The park is 2 miles west of Morristown off New York 12.

ACTIVITIES - Jacques Cartier State Park is open from May 30 through Columbus Day weekend. Camp in the 92-site campground with 22 sites providing electrical hookups, a dump station, and groceries. Go swimming in the bay and enjoy unlimited boating opportunities from the boat launch. Go fishing in the nationally known St. Lawrence River for pike, muskellunge, bass, and walleye, while watching ships from all over the world navigating the seaway. In the winter, go ice fishing.

INFORMATION

Jacques Cartier State Park
P.O. Box 135
Morristown, New York 13664
315-375-6371

JOHN BOYD THACHER STATE PARK
29

LOCATION - The park is 4 miles north of New Salem on New York 157 and 15 miles southwest of Albany.

FEATURES - John Boyd Thacher State Park provides a panoramic view of the Hudson-Mohawk valleys, the Adirondacks, and of the Green Mountains.

The Mohawk Indians used the pass over the Helderbergs to go from the Albany trading post to their homes in the Schoharie valley. Part of their path, now called Indian Ladder Trail, is accessible to park visitors. The original ladder was a notched tree trunk laid against the cliff and used to scramble up.

ACTIVITIES - The park is open year-round. Hike the geological trail that is located along the Helderberg Escarpment where you're in one of the richest fossil-bearing formations in the world. Go swimming in the Olympic-size pool and enjoy a snack.

During the winter, the trail network south of New York 157 is used for cross-country skiing, snowshoeing, tobogganing, snowmobiling, and downhill skiing without a lift. Heated comfort stations are at Hop Field and Mine Lot picnic areas.

Incoming pilots can land at Albany County Airport 6 miles northwest of Albany. Rental cars are available.

INFORMATION
John Boyd Thacher State Park
R.D. 1
Voorhees, New York 12186
518-872-1237

JONES BEACH STATE PARK
30

LOCATION - Jones Beach is on the ocean shore of Long Island off Meadowbrook or Wantagh Parkway.

FEATURES - Jones Beach has a 6-mile beach along the Atlantic Ocean.

ACTIVITIES - Go supervised surf bathing and swimming in Zach's Bay or in one of two pools. Walk the 2-mile boardwalk along the shoreline. Go roller-skating in the outdoor rink and play golf. Go boating, fishing, and ride the bicycle trails. Food is available.

Concerts are presented summer nights in the band shell and in Jones Beach Marine Theater. For information, call 516-785-1600.

INFORMATION
Jones Beach State Park
P.O. Box 247
Babylon, New York 11702
516-785-1600

KEEWAYDIN STATE PARK
31

LOCATION - The park is one mile west of Alexandria Bay on New York 12.

FEATURES - Keewaydin State Park was once a private estate built in 1894 by James Wesley Jackson of Summit, New York.

ACTIVITIES - Camp in the 41-site campground from mid-May through Labor Day, swim in the pool and go fishing in nationally known St. Lawrence River for pike, muskellunge, bass, and walleye. Enjoy a picnic and go boating from the ramp by the marina from mid-May through mid-October. In the winter, go ice skating, ice fishing, cross-country skiing, and snowmobiling.

INFORMATION
Keewaydin State Park
Route 12N, Box 247
Alexandria Bay, New York 13607
315-482-2593

KEUKA LAKE STATE PARK
32

LOCATION - The park is 6 miles southwest of Penn Yan off New York 54A in the Finger Lakes.

ACTIVITIES - Go camping in the 150-site campground. Enjoy hiking, boating from the launch site, trout fishing, and swimming in Keuka Lake. During the winter, go cross-country skiing and snowmobiling.

Incoming pilots can land at Penn Yan Airport, located one mile south of town. Rental cars are available.

INFORMATION
Keuka Lake State Park
Route 54A
Bluffpoint, New York 14478
315-536-3666

KNOX'S HEADQUARTERS STATE HISTORIC SITE and WASHINGTON'S HEADQUARTERS STATE HISTORIC SITE
33
NEW WINDSOR CANTONMENT STATE HISTORIC SITE
34

LOCATION - Washington's Headquarters are located at 84 Liberty Street in Newburgh. To reach it from the New York Thruway, take Exit 17. From I-84, take Exit 10 to New York 17K to downtown Newburgh. Then follow signs.

Knox's Headquarters are on Forge Hill Road and New York 94 east of Vails Gate. From Newburgh, follow New York 94 for 4.5 miles southwest to Vails Gate.

New Windsor Cantonment State Historic Site is located one mile north of Vails Gate on Temple Hill Road.

FEATURES - Washington's Headquarters, Hasbrouck House, circa 1750, served as his Revolutionary War headquarters when he and his staff stayed here in 1782–83.

Knox's Headquarters was built in 1754 and was occupied during the American Revolution by Continental officers, including Generals Henry Knox and Horatio Gates.

New Windsor is the site of the Continental army's last camp.

ACTIVITIES - Washington's Headquarters State Historic Site's museum includes artifacts of the Continental army. Take a guided house tour from mid-April through October, Wednesday–Saturday from 10:00–5:00, Sunday 1:00–5:00, and by appointment. Visit the 1887 Tower of Victory monument.

At Knox's Headquarters, follow paths along the gorge by Silver Stream to see ruins from Ellison's eighteenth-century grist mill. The grounds, including the Jane Colden Native Plant Sanctuary, are open year-round, but the house is only open by appointment Wednesday–Sunday from April 1 through the end of October.

At New Windsor, walk through the blacksmith shop and watch living history reenactments and military demonstrations. The site is open Wednesday–Sunday from 10:00–5:00 beginning in late April through late November.

Tour historic downtown Newburgh with buildings dating from the eighteenth and nineteenth centuries. Guided tours leave on Sunday afternoons from the town's visitor center at 87 Liberty Street and by appointment. For information, call 914-565-6880. You can also pick up a map for a self-guided tour at the Chamber of Commerce at 72 Broadway. For information, call 914-562-5100.

Incoming pilots can land at Stewart International Airport, located 3 miles northwest of Newburgh. Rental cars are available.

INFORMATION

Knox's Headquarters State
  Historic Site
P.O. Box 207
Forge Hill Road and New York 94
Vails Gate, New York 12584
914-561-5498

Washington's Headquarters State
  Historic Site
84 Liberty Street
Newburgh, New York 12550
914-562-1195

New Windsor Cantonment State Historic Site
Temple Hill Road
Newburgh, New York 12550
914-561-1765

KRING POINT STATE PARK
35

LOCATION - The park is 10 miles northeast of Alexandria Bay via New York 12.

FEATURES - Kring Point is located on a narrow peninsula with its south shore facing Goose Bay and its north shore facing the St. Lawrence River.

ACTIVITIES - The park is open from the first Saturday in May through Columbus Day. The park has 8 cabins, a 108-site campground with 33 providing electrical hookups, plus 13 walk-in sites.

Enjoy boating, swimming, and fishing in the St. Lawrence River for pike, bass, and panfish. An annual Small Fry Fishing Derby is held the last Saturday in June.

A nearby attraction is Ironside Island with the river's largest great blue heron rookery.

Take a cruise aboard the *Empire* with a stop at Boldt Castle, a 120-room replica of a Rhineland castle, open from mid-May through mid-October. For information, call 315-482-9511 or 1-800-542-2628.

INFORMATION
Kring Point State Park
P.O. Box 247
Alexandria Bay, New York 13607
315-482-2444

LAKE CHAMPLAIN STATE PARKS

CUMBERLAND BAY STATE PARK
36
MACOMB RESERVATION STATE PARK
37
POINT AU ROCHE STATE PARK
38

LOCATION - Cumberland Bay is one mile north of Plattsburgh off U.S. 9. Take Exit 39 off I-87 onto New York 314.

Macomb Reservation is 3 miles west of Schuyler Falls off New York 22B.

Point Au Roche is 4 miles north of Plattsburgh and east of New York 9.

ACTIVITIES - At Cumberland Bay, camp in the 210-site campground from early May through early October. Fish and swim in the lake from with a 2,700-foot beach and purchase a snack.

Ausable Chasm is 12 miles south of Plattsburgh on U.S. 9. Take Exit 34 or 35 from Adirondack Northway I-87. The chasm is open daily for tours mid-May through early October. Visitors go through the chasm first on foot along a gorge trail and then by boat to an awaiting bus. For information, call 518-834-7454.

Macomb Reservation is open from mid-May through Labor day and has 180 campsites. Hike the trails, go fishing, swimming, and boating on the lake in rowboats and canoes. During the winter, go cross-country skiing, snow-shoeing, snowmobiling, and ice skating.

Point Au Roche is open year-round and is open for day-use only. Enjoy a picnic and hike 8 miles of trails. Go boating, fishing, and swimming. Ride the bicycle trail, tour the visitor center, and purchase a snack. Go cross-country skiing and snowshoeing during the winter.

Take a scenic 12-minute ferry ride across Lake Champlain to Grand Isle, Vermont. For a schedule, call 802-864-9804. Enjoy a narrated boat tour from Miller Street in Plattsburgh from June–September. For information, call 518-516-8970 or 1-800-388-8970.

Tour Clinton County Historical Museum at 48 Court in Plattsburgh to see 300 years of Champlain Valley history. Watch races at the Airborne Park Speedway on Saturday evenings. For information, call 802-244-6964.

Tour Plattsburgh Air Force Base Museum. Take Exit 36 off I-87. The museum is the oldest combat-ready military installation in the U.S. and offers tours on Monday–Friday from 2:00–4:00. For information, call 518-565-6165.

INFORMATION

Cumberland Bay State Park
MR 1, Box 1
Plattsburgh, New York 12901
518-563-5240

Macomb Reservation State Park
Schuyler Falls, New York 12985
518-643-9952

Point Au Roche State Park
R.D. 2, Box 278
Plattsburgh, New York 12901
518-563-0369

LAKE ERIE STATE PARK
39

LOCATION - The park is on the eastern shoreline of Lake Erie 2 miles north of Brockton on New York 380. It's also 7 miles west of Dunkirk on New York 5.

ACTIVITIES - Lake Erie has a 95-site campground, 6 sites with water, 44 with electrical hookups, and a dumping station. You can also stay in one of 10 cabins. Enjoy fishing in Lake Erie for trout, record-size walleye, bass, and salmon. Go swimming, hiking, and bicycling.

Go boating from the park or public boat-launch facilities at Westfield and Dunkirk.

An Artist-in-Residence from Allegany State Park brings music programs and storytelling to the park once a week.

During the winter, go snowmobiling and cross-country skiing with rentals available.

Dunkirk Historical Lighthouse, circa 1875, and Veterans' Park Museum is off New York 5 on Lighthouse Point Drive North. Lighthouse tours are offered from June–August from 10:00–4:00, and from September–November from 10:00–3:00 except on Sunday and Wednesday. For information, call 716-366-5050. Anglers fish in Dunkirk Harbor.

Chautauqua Institution, a National Historic Landmark, is located halfway between Buffalo and Erie and offers summertime entertainment. For details, call 1-800-836-ARTS. Play on the 27-hole golf course. Go jogging and bicycling. Enjoy boating, swimming, and fishing in Chautauqua Lake for bass, muskellunge, and walleye. Several fishing derbies are held each year.

Take a steamboat excursion from Mayville aboard the *Chautauqua Belle* from May–September. For reservations, call 716-753-2403.

Incoming pilots can land at Chautauqua County Dunkirk Airport 3 miles east of Dunkirk. Rental cars are available.

INFORMATION
Lake Erie State Park
R.D. 1
Brocton, New York 14716
716-792-9214

LAKE GEORGE BEACH STATE PARK
See under CRANBERRY LAKE STATE PARK

LAKE SUPERIOR STATE PARK
See under PALISADES INTERSTATE PARKS

LAKE TAGHKANIC STATE PARK
40

LOCATION - The lake is 12 miles southeast of Hudson. It's accessible from the Taconic State Parkway, one mile south of the New York 82 Interchange.

ACTIVITIES - Go hiking and camp in the campground from mid-May through the end of October or stay in one of the 43 cabins or cottages. Enjoy swimming, boating with rentals available, and fishing for bass and norlings. Snacks are available. The second Sunday after Labor Day attend the annual Columbia County Day fishing derby. During the winter, go ice fishing, skating, cross-country skiing, and snowmobiling.

In Kinderhook, tour Martin Van Buren National Historical Site on New York 9H. The house was built in 1797 and is open from May–October. For information, call 518-758-9689.

Hudson-Athens Lighthouse, circa 1874, is on the Hudson River off South Bay and is best seen from Promenade Hill Park on Front Street in Hudson.

Clermont State Historic Site on New York 9G is a 500-acre estate that was home to seven generations of the Livingston family. Enjoy beautiful views of the Hudson River and Catskills, 4 miles of hiking trails, and picnic facilities. It's open for guided tours from April–October on Wednesday–Sunday. For information, call 518-537-4240.

Shaker Museum on Shaker Museum Road off New York 13, Old Chatham, features exhibitions of Shaker industries spanning over 200 years. Their annual antique festival is the first Saturday in August. For information, call 518-794-9100.

Olana State Historic Site is off New York 9G, one mile south of the Rip Van Winkle Bridge in Greenport, south of Hudson. The nineteenth-century home of landscape painter Frederic Edwin Church has guided tours from April–October, but is closed Mondays and Tuesdays. Hike extensive grounds' trails with spectacular views of the Hudson Valley. Call 518-828-0135 for a schedule of special events.

Incoming pilots can land at Columbia County Airport, located 4 miles northeast of Hudson. Rental cars are available.

INFORMATION
Lake Taghkanic State Park
R.D. 1, Box 74
Ancram, New York 12502-9731
518-851-3631

LAKESIDE BEACH STATE PARK
41

LOCATION - The beach is between Lake Ontario State Parkway and Lake Ontario, 1½ miles east of Kuckville on New York 18.

ACTIVITIES - Camp in the 274-site campground, all equipped with electrical hookups, with a trailer dump station and purchase limited groceries in the camp store from late April through late October. Fish and boat in Lake Ontario where rentals are available and go hiking and bicycle riding. In August, participate in the trout and salmon derby in Lake Ontario.

During the winter, go cross-country skiing, hiking, and snowmobiling.

In Medina, take a ride on the Erie Canal aboard *Miss Apple Grove*, a mule-drawn packet boat. For information, call 716-798-2323.

Incoming pilots can land at Pine Hill Airport, located 5 miles southwest of Albion. Rental cars are available.

INFORMATION
Lakeside Beach State Park
Route 18
Waterport, New York 14571
716-682-5246 (May–October)
716-682-4888 (November–April)

LETCHWORTH STATE PARK
42

LOCATION - The park is 2 miles north of Portageville. Follow New York 19A to Denton's Corners, then go 2 miles east. It's also accessible from I-390, Exit 7, to Mount Morris. Follow New York 408 south. Mount Morris offers the park entrance closest to the Highbanks Recreation Area and is the location of the Mount Morris dam.

To get directly to the campground area from Warsaw, go east 6.5 miles on 20A to Perry Center. Turn right onto New York 246, heading south. In Perry, turn left on Covington, right on Gardeau for one mile, and left on Schenk Road.

FEATURES - The park is often referred to as the Grand Canyon of the East and is known for its three beautiful waterfalls in the Genesee River Gorge. Middle Falls, dropping 107 feet, is lit at night from dusk until 11:00 PM. The 7-mile gorge's walls rise 600 feet, and the gorge is visible from a number of lookouts.

ACTIVITIES - The park is open from mid-May through late October. Stay in the motel, one of 82 cabins, Pinewood Lodge, or historic Glen Iris Inn, open from April through early November.

Camp in the 270-site campground, all with electrical hookups, a trailer dump station, and limited groceries. Food is also available in three snack bars and two restaurants.

Enjoy canoeing, tubing, whitewater rafting from Lee's Landing Area, and trout fishing in the Genesee River. Go swimming in two guarded pools in the Highbanks Area, bicycle riding, or horseback riding with rentals available. Attend philharmonic concerts, lectures, and guided walks.

Hikers have access to 42 miles of terrain along 22 scenic trails. Seven-mile gorge trail passes the three main waterfalls. These falls are easily seen by short hikes from the park road. The Upper Falls are behind the Glen Iris Inn, and if you continue up the trail from the inn, you get a closer look at them.

One of the trails, Gardeau Trail, drops down a steep, heavily eroded trail to reach the river in approximately one mile. Inspiration Point has the park's most spectacular view and an interpretive trail. For an even longer hike, take the 21.5-mile Finger Lakes Trail with several access points making it possible to take shorter hikes along its route.

Besides the three well-known falls, the park has approximately 50 other falls in the park, with 23 described in a park brochure entitled "Letchworth Waterfall Guide."

Half the trails are available for winter hiking. In addition, you can go cross-country skiing and snowmobiling.

For an unusual view of the gorge, take a balloon ride at sunrise or sunset. For information, call 716-468-5538.

In Portageville, tour Letchworth Pioneer and Indian Museum from May–November.

In Mount Morris, tour the General William August Mills House at 14 Main. Listed on the National Register of Historic Places, it's open from June 1 through Labor Day, Friday–Sunday from noon–4:00. For information, call 716-658-3292.

Castile Historical House, 17 East Park Road, has Victorian furniture, military collections, and genealogical materials. It's open Tuesdays. For information, call 716-493-5370.

Airplane buffs can tour the National Warplane Museum located ½ mile west of Geneseo on New York 20A. See World War II planes, including a B-17 Flying Fortress. In August, attend the three-day 1941 Wings of Eagles air show. For information, call 716-243-0690.

Incoming pilots can land at Perry Warsaw Airport 3 miles northwest of Perry. Rental cars are available.

INFORMATION
Letchworth State Park
1 Letchworth State Park
Castile, New York 14427-1124
716-493-2611
716-493-2622 (Glen Iris Inn)
716-237-3303 (campground)

LONG POINT STATE PARK
43

LOCATION - The park is 12 miles south of Three Mile Bay, on Point Peninsula on Chaumont Bay in Lake Ontario. Chaumont is on New York 12E south of Cape Vincent.

ACTIVITIES - Camp in the 88-site campground by Long Bay, 18 with electrical hookups and a trailer dump station. Enjoy swimming, bicycling, walking, salmon fishing, and picnicking. In the winter, go ice fishing, cross-country skiing, and snowmobiling.

Go boating on Lake Ontario or Chaumont Bay, which also has excellent fishing for bass, salmon, pike, walleye, and trout. Annual events include bass derbies, ice fishing competitions, and a triathlon. On July 4th, come for the Annual Pit Roast Beef Dinner. For details, call 315-649-2265.

Nearby attractions include Sackets Harbor Battlefield Historic Site, overlooking the only natural harbor at the east end of Lake Ontario, on the west side of Sackets Harbor village. Two battles were fought over this military stronghold during the War of 1812.

Tour the visitor center in the 1817 Union Hotel from late May through late September. For information, call 315-646-3634. Other attractions include Wellesley Island Shipyard Museum, Cape Vincent Aquarium open daily from 9:00–5:00 from May–October, and Fort Henry in Kingston, Ontario.

Take a boat cruise aboard the *Empire*, with a stop to tour Boldt Castle. For information, call 315-482-9511 or 1-800-542-2628.

Cape Vincent is known as the "home of the gamey black bass" where anglers have captured world title river muskies from mid-June until fall.

Tibbett's Point Lighthouse is at the outlet of Lake Ontario and head of the St. Lawrence River, 3 miles west of Cape Vincent. Built in 1827, it's still a beacon for sailors. The former keeper's cottage is now a youth hostel.

INFORMATION
Long Point State Park
P.O. Box 220
Three Mile Bay, New York 13693
315-649-5258

LONG POINT ON LAKE CHAUTAUQUA STATE PARK
44

LOCATION - Long Point is along a peninsula on the eastern shore of Lake Chautauqua, off New York 430 near Bemus Point.

FEATURES - Long Point was formed by retreating glaciers and extends into the lake where the water is deepest. Lake Chautauqua, 18 miles long and 1,308 feet above sea level, is one of the most navigable bodies of water in the U.S.

ACTIVITIES - Open for day-use only, visitors enjoy hiking its wooded trails, swimming from the guarded beach, and boating from the marina. Chautauqua Lake is noted for its muskellunge, muskie, and walleye fishing. A walleye contest runs from mid-May through mid-June. Charter services are available.

Chautauqua Institute is on the west side of the lake and is considered one of the United States' leading summer cultural centers. Chautauqua is listed as a National Historic Landmark and is accessible via I-90 at the Westfield exit and then by following New York 394 south.

The Chautauqua Institute was founded here in 1876 and is one of five still active in the U.S. In its heyday, over 300 independent Chautauquas were open.

Admission is charged to tour the spacious grounds with its many historic Victorian homes and beautiful gardens. Tickets are sold for day tours, and if purchased in the evening, permit you to attend a concert in the amphitheater. For information, call 716-357-6250. For information concerning the institution's various programs, call 1-800-836-ARTS.

Golfers can play on Chautauqua Golf Club's 27-hole public course. Come to play tennis, go jogging and biking, and swimming from 4 beaches. Go fishing, water-skiing, and boating on the lake.

Cruise aboard a steam-powered sternwheeler, *Chautauqua Belle*, near Mayville off New York 394. For information, call 716-753-7823.

Come to Mayville in February for the Ice Castle Extravaganza in Lakeside Park or in September for Septober Fest. For details, contact the Chamber of Commerce at 716-753-7823.

Incoming pilots can land at Chautauqua County/Jamestown Airport 4 miles north of Jamestown. Rental cars are available.

INFORMATION
Long Point on Lake Chautauqua State Park
Route 430, R.D. 3, Box 160
Bemus Point, New York 14712
716-386-2772 or 716-386-2688

MACOMB RESERVATION STATE PARK
See under LAKE CHAMPLAIN STATE PARKS

MAX V. SHAUL STATE PARK and
SCHOHARIE CROSSING STATE HISTORIC PARK
45

LOCATION - Max V. Shaul State Park is in the Schoharie Valley on New York 30 at the base of Toe Path Mountain, 5 miles south of Middleburgh.

Schoharie Crossing State Historic Site is on New York 5S at Fort Hunter at the confluence of the Mohawk River and Schoharie Creek. From Thruway Exit 27, Amsterdam, follow signs to New York 5S West. Turn right on Main Street and left on Railroad Street.

ACTIVITIES - At Max V. Shaul State Park, camp in one of 32 wooded campsites. Picnic and attend a movie shown every Saturday night from Memorial Day through Labor Day. Special events are offered summer and fall.

Schoharie Crossing State Park is open Wednesday–Saturday from mid-May through the last Sunday in October. The park has visible remnants from all three stages of the Erie Canal development. Visitors can go boating, fishing, take guided tours, or enjoy a free mule-drawn boat ride on Saturdays from Memorial Day through mid-October.

Take a hike or bike the 3-mile trail along the banks of the present-day Barge Canal or along the original Erie Canal. Guided walking tours are available at 11:00 and 2:00 from Wednesday–Friday.

Tour Old Stone Fort Museum complex along the bank of Fox Creek near its confluence with Schoharie on New York 30A, 3 miles south of I-88, Exit 23. It's open May 1–October 31, but closed Mondays. For information, call 518-295-7192.

Tour the 1743 Palantine House, now a living museum listed on the National Register of Historic Places. It's open weekends in June, September, and October from 1:00–5:00 and Thursday–Monday in July and August. For information, call 518-295-7585.

The Train Car Museum on Depot Lane in Schoharie is open weekends from June–October from 1:00–5:00 and is listed on the National Register of Historic Places.

Tour Howe Caverns east of Cobleskill off I-88. Take Exit 22 to New York east. Go one mile, making a left onto Caverns Road. Explore the caverns both on foot and take an underground cruise on Lake of Venus. For information, call 518-296-8990. During the winter, the caverns' ski center sets 15 kilometers of tracks and has rentals, a warming hut, food, and lodging.

Tour Secret Caverns north of Howe Caverns featuring a 100-foot underground waterfall. For information, call 518-296-8558.

Bramanville Grist Mill Museum is located one mile before the Caverns and has water-powered mill stones for grinding corn and three floors of milling equipment.

INFORMATION

Max V. Shaul State Park
P.O. Box 23, Route 30
Middleburgh, New York 12071
518-827-4711

Schoharie Crossing State
Historic Site
Fort Hunter, New York 12157
518-829-7516

MILLS MANSION STATE HISTORIC SITE and MILLS–NORRIE STATE PARK
46

LOCATION - Mills Mansion is on Old Post Road in Staatsburg, 5 miles north of Hyde Park off New York 9. It's also 4 miles south of Rhinebeck off New York 9.

Mills–Norrie State Park is on the Hudson River next to the mansion.

FEATURES - Mills Mansion, an 1895 Beaux Arts mansion, is a 79-room country estate situated on a hill overlooking the Hudson. Take a guided tour given every half hour with the last tour departing at 4:30. For tour hours, call 914-889-8851.

Mills–Norrie State Park has bass fishing, hiking on the riverside trails, camping in 55 campsites, and boating from the ramp. Cycle the bicycle paths, play golf, and get a meal in the restaurant or refreshments from the concession stand. Go cross-country skiing in the winter.

INFORMATION

Mills Mansion State Historic Site   Mills–Norrie State Park
Old Post Road   914-889-4646
Staatsburgh, New York 12580
914-889-8851

MINE KILL STATE PARK
47

LOCATION - The park is in Schoharie Valley on New York 30, 20 miles south of I-88. It's also 15 miles south of Middleburgh.

FEATURES - Mine Kill was opened in 1973 when adjacent New York Power Authority's Blenheim-Gilboa Pumped Storage Project was begun. The park overlooks the storage project's lower reservoir.

ACTIVITIES - Picnic overlooking the reservoir and camp in the campground. Go boating, water-skiing, and fishing for trout, bass, walleye, carp, and panfish in Mine Kill Reservoir. Go boating from the launch.

Go swimming in the Olympic-sized pool. Swimming is not permitted in the reservoir. An overlook on the south end of the lake provides views of Mine Kill Falls.

Special events and performances are presented in the park through the summer. Hike an extensive trail network.

During the winter, go snowmobiling, tobogganing, cross-country skiing, and sledding.

A one-mile-long hiking trail leads to New York Power Authority's Lansing Manor complex, nineteenth-century estate of Supreme Court Justice John Lansing. Lansing Manor is open to tour from Memorial Day through Columbus Day except Tuesdays. For information, call 518-827-6121.

The Old Blenheim covered bridge in North Blenheim, circa 1855, is the United States' longest single-span covered bridge and one of six remaining double-tunnel bridges in the U.S.

Tour the Blenheim-Gilboa Power Project Visitor Center on New York 30 near North Blenheim. Located in a converted nineteenth-century barn, the center has hands-on displays and a laser video show. It's open Monday–Sunday 10:00–5:00. For information, call 1-800-724-0309.

INFORMATION
Mine Kill State Park
P.O. Box 923
North Blenheim, New York 12131
518-827-6111

MONTAUK POINT STATE PARK
See under HITHER HILLS STATE PARK

MOREAU LAKE STATE PARK
48

LOCATION - Moreau Lake State Park is 18 miles north of Saratoga off New York 9 in the foothills of the Adirondacks.

FEATURES - Moreau Lake covers 150 acres and is 50 feet at its deepest point. The park's "kettlehole" was formed by a glacier approximately 20,000 years ago.

ACTIVITIES - Camp in the 144-site campground, hike the trails, and enjoy a picnic. Fish for perch, catfish, trout, and bass. Launch your cartop boat or rent a rowboat. No motors are allowed on the lake.

Throughout the summer, attend various special events featuring musicians, drama, and storytellers. During the winter, go cross-country skiing and ice fishing for perch and pickerel.

Petrified Gardens is on New York 28 and is listed as a National Registered Landmark. It contains a reef of ancient petrified plants plus glacial crevices and potholes. It's open from 11:00–4:00 on Friday–Monday or by appointment by calling 518-584-7102.

In Saratoga Springs, tour the Historical Society's Museum and Walworth Memorial Museum and Casino in historic Congress Park. The museum highlights nineteenth-century resort life. For information, call 518-584-6920.

Stay in the Gideon Putnam Hotel in Saratoga Springs, open year-round, which is a National Historic Landmark. For reservations, call 518-584-3000. Attend performances in the Saratoga Performing Arts Center.

Tour President Grant's home, Grant Cottage, a State Historic Site. It's open from Memorial Day through Labor Day Wednesday–Sunday from 10:00–4:00. For information, call 518-587-8277.

Incoming pilots can land at Saratoga County Airport 3 miles southwest of Saratoga Springs. Rental cars are available.

INFORMATION
Moreau Lake State Park
605 Old Saratoga Road
Gansevoort, New York 12831
518-793-0511

NEW WINDSOR CANTONMENT STATE HISTORIC SITE
See under KNOX'S HEADQUARTERS STATE HISTORIC SITE

NIAGARA RESERVATION STATE PARK and OLD FORT NIAGARA STATE PARK
49

LOCATION - Niagara Reservation State Park is at the foot of Falls Street in Niagara Falls.

Old Fort Niagara is north of Niagara Falls along the Robert Moses Parkway in Youngstown.

FEATURES - Niagara Falls began approximately 12,000 years ago when glacial ice covering much of North America melted. Gradually, water has eroded the falls back almost 7.5 miles to its present location. American Falls are 175 feet high with a 1,110-foot-long brink. Canadian Horse Falls are 167 feet high with a brink of 2,500 feet.

Water flowing over Niagara Falls comes from four of the Great Lakes. From here, the Niagara River flows north to Lake Ontario and then on to the Atlantic Ocean by way of the St. Lawrence River. Niagara Falls has been producing power since the 1800s and is one of the largest producers of electric power in the world.

ACTIVITIES - Niagara Reservation State Park, established in 1885, is America's oldest state park, open from late May through Labor Day. Terrapin Point on Goat Island provides one of the best views of Horseshoe Falls.

Go up the 100-foot observation tower at Prospect Point on Goat Island to get a spectacular view of the falls. Elevators descend from here into the gorge at the base of American Falls. Prospect Park has a visitor center showing "Niagara Wonders" hourly, Great Lakes gardens, tennis, fishing, kinetic water sculpture, snacks, and a theater. During the winter, go cross-country skiing.

Dine in Top of the Falls restaurant for a great view from all tables. To arrange for tours or special gatherings, call 716-285-3311.

Old Fort Niagara is open year-round. Its historic buildings were occupied by the military of several nations from 1726 until after World War II. It features cannon and musket firings, battle reenactments, eighteenth-century living demonstrations, and archeological programs. For information, call 716-745-7611.

Don a raincoat to visit Cave of the Winds at the base of Bridal Veil Falls on Goat Island. Tour Schoellkopf Geological Museum and take a Viewmobile ride through the park.

Go hiking into Niagara Gorge. Walk across Rainbow Bridge into Canada to a vantage point of the falls.

Take a Maid of the Mist boat tour, beginning from the base of the Observation Tower. Half-hour-long tours leave every 15 minutes from mid-May through late October. For information, call 716-284-8897. Boat tours also leave from the Canadian side of the falls.

The Aquarium of Niagara Falls at 701 Whirlpool overlooks Niagara Gorge and presents hourly dolphin and sea lion shows. For information, call 716-285-3575.

Whirlpool State Park features the raging Lower Niagara River as it forms a massive whirlpool in the Niagara Gorge. Come for a picnic, stop at several observation points, hike the nature trails, and go fishing.

Devil's Hole State Park features picnicking, observation points, an historical site, nature trails, and fishing.

Many fishing competitions are held in Lake Ontario and the Niagara River. For dates, call 1-800-338-7890. Fish Niagara River for trout, salmon, bass, pike, muskellunge, and panfish. For a current fishing report, call 716-433-5606.

Attend Niagara Falls' annual Festival of Lights held the end of November through early January to see hundreds of colored lights, old-fashioned animated displays, light shows, and entertainment nightly from 5:00–11:00.

Learn the story of Niagara Falls' electrical power generation at Power Vista on New York 104, Lewiston Road. The site is open year-round.

Wintergarden, located near the Convention Center on Rainbow Boulevard, is a glass-enclosed tropical park with ponds, waterfalls, and 7,000 trees. It's open year-round. For information, call 716-285-8007.

Bicycle enthusiasts can see the exhibit Pedaling History at the Burgwardt Bicycle Museum at 3943 North Buffalo Road on New York 240/277. It's the only all-bicycle museum in the U.S. For information, call 716-662-3853.

Many Niagara visitors go to Canada where the views of the Horseshoe Falls are more dramatic. The Canadian side has more commercial development with shops and restaurants. Attend an IMAX adventure and witness *Niagara: Miracles, Myths, and Magic.*

Campers who prefer leaving their cars behind while they tour can stay at the Niagara Glen-View Campground in Canada and catch a shuttle into the park from June through Labor Day. From the campground, hikers, joggers, and bicyclists can access the Niagara River Recreation Trail paralleling the Niagara River. It begins at Anger Avenue in Fort Erie and goes to Fort George at Niagara-on-the-Lake, 35 miles away.

Also from the Canadian side, walk through the Table Rock scenic tunnels behind Horseshoe Falls or ride aboard the Spanish aero car, a cable car carrying passengers 250 feet above Whirlpool Rapids. Take a Whirlpool Jet whitewater boat ride 1½ miles below the falls. If you prefer your thrills vicariously, experience Ride Niagara, a computer controlled, simulated ride over the falls.

Treat yourself to dinner at the Skylon Tower in the revolving dining room. For a spectacular view of the falls lit at night, plan to dine close to dusk. For reservations, call 416-356-2651.

For a unique view of the falls, take a helicopter ride over the falls. Helicopters are based by the Niagara Glen-View Campground in Canada.

Incoming pilots can land at Niagara Falls International Airport 4 miles east of Niagara Falls. Rental cars are available.

INFORMATION

Niagara Reservation State Park
716-278-1770

Niagara County Tourism
139 Niagara Street
Lockport, New York 14094
1-800-338-7890

Old Fort Niagara State Park
  Association, Inc.
P.O. Box 169
Youngstown, New York 14174
716-745-7611

Niagara Falls Visitor Information
716-278-1796

NICK'S LAKE STATE PARK
See under CRANBERRY LAKE STATE PARK

OLD ERIE CANAL STATE PARK
50

LOCATION - The park is on Andrus Road near Kirkville.

FEATURES - Old Erie Canal State Park covers a continuous 35-mile stretch of the Canal Recreationway in central New York from Rome to DeWitt.

ACTIVITIES - Enjoy biking, fishing, picnicking, canoeing from the canoe launch, and hiking along the towpath. During the winter, enjoy snowmobiling, snowshoeing, and ice skating along the canal.

Picnic sites are available along the canal at Central Bay Park and Poolside. Go to Green Lakes State Park to camp overnight.

The Erie Canal Trail is adjacent to the present-day Barge Canal and extends for 60 miles. Enjoy biking or hiking the trails or take a boat cruise. Free maps are available either from the state parks in Albany or from the New York State Department of Transportation, 1530 Jefferson Road, Rochester, New York 14623.

In Oneida, tour Cottage Lawn Museum, located at 435 Main Street. Constructed in 1849, it contains artifacts from the Erie Canal. It's open June 1–August 31. For information, call 315-363-4136.

INFORMATION
Old Erie Canal State Park
Andrus Road
Kirkville, New York 13082
315-687-7821

OQUAGA CREEK STATE PARK
51

LOCATION - The park is 9 miles south of Sidney off New York 206.

ACTIVITIES - Camp in the 95-site campground with a trailer dump station. Food is available at the snack bar. In Artic Lake, go swimming from the beach, trout fishing, boating, and canoeing from the ramp with rentals available. Hike and bike the trails. During the winter, go cross-country skiing, snowshoeing, tobogganing, and ice skating.

Incoming pilots can land at Sidney Municipal Airport one mile west of Sidney. Rental cars are available.

INFORMATION
Oquaga Creek State Park
R.D. Box 2, Box 255, Route 206
Bainbridge, New York 13733
607-467-4160

PALISADES INTERSTATE PARKS

BEAR MOUNTAIN STATE PARK
52
HARRIMAN STATE PARK
53

LAKE SUPERIOR STATE PARK
54
ROCKLAND LAKE STATE PARK
55
TALLMAN MOUNTAIN STATE PARK
56

Palisades Interstate Parks run from the George Washington Bridge north to Bristol Beach and west to Lake Superior, covering nearly 83,000 acres of woods, lakes, wetlands, mountains, and historic sites. For general information and special event schedules, stop at the information center located south of the Anthony Wayne Recreation Area, located in the center median of Palisades Interstate Parkway, open from Memorial Day weekend through October.

BEAR MOUNTAIN STATE PARK

LOCATION - The park is 5 miles south of West Point off U.S. 9W. It's 45 miles north of New York City on the Palisades Parkway.

ACTIVITIES - Stay at Bear Mountain Inn and eat in the dining room open year-round. Call 914-786-2731 for reservations.

Tour the park's four museums: Geology, Nature Study, Small Animals, and History. Hike nature trails with many outdoor exhibits and animal enclosures. Enjoy views of the Hudson River and highlands from various rocky outlooks. Visit the Outer Redoubt of Fort Clinton.

Go swimming in the pool and fishing and boating on the Hudson River where rentals are available or in nearby Hessian Lake. Hike around Hessian Lake or along the Appalachian Trail that passes through here. Play tennis and golf. Go ice skating in the rink from fall to spring. For a unique activity, go square dancing.

Drive up Perkins Memorial Drive to the 1,305-foot mountaintop to an observation tower.

In the winter, go cross-country skiing and sledding. The park also has a ski jump.

Visit West Point off New York 9W, 10 miles south of Newburgh. Tour restored fortifications and walk through the visitor center exhibits. Check here for parade dates, guided tours, and athletic schedules or call 914-938-2638.

Take a self-guided tour of the cadet chapel to see one of the largest organs in the world. Tour Fort Clinton, Trophy Point, and West Point Museum in Olmsted Hall on the South Post. Revolutionary War Fort Putnam is open daily 9:00–4:00, but closed during the winter.

Escorted tours of West Point are offered by West Point Tours in Highland Falls. For information, call 914-446-4724.

INFORMATION
Bear Mountain State Park
Bear Mountain, New York 10911
914-786-2701

HARRIMAN STATE PARK

LOCATION - The state's second largest state park is 5 miles north of Hamlin on Lake Ontario and 30 miles north of New York City off the Palisades Parkway.

Beaver Pond is 5 miles west of Stony Point on Gate Hill Road. Lake Sebago Beach and Anthony Wayne are off the Palisades Parkway, Exit 16 on 7 Lakes Drive and Lake Welch Drive.

Silver Mine is on 7 Lakes Drive, one mile west of Palisades Parkway. Lake Tiorati Beach is 10 miles north of Sloatsburg on 7 Lakes Drive. Lake Welch Beach is accessed from Exit 13 from Palisades Parkway and is 2 miles east on South Mountain Road.

ACTIVITIES - Lake Welch's ½-mile-long beach is one of the largest inland beaches in the U.S. where you can go fishing for bass, perch, and sunfish, boating with rentals available, and swimming. A refreshment stand is open summers. Camping is available in 200 campsites at the adjacent Beaver Pond Campground.

Go hiking, biking, fishing, and boating in Lake Ontario. Stay in one of 42 cabins at Lake Sebago Beach. During the winter, go ice fishing and snow-mobiling.

Day-use areas include Silver Mine, Lake Tiorati Beach, Anthony Wayne, and Lake Welch Beach. Lake Tiorati has picnicking, fishing, boating, swimming, and group camping.

Anthony Wayne Recreation Area, named for Revolutionary War General "Mad Anthony" Wayne who gained fame by leading a surprise attack on the Stony Point fortification held by the British, has a 2.7-mile hiking trail, picnicking, and access to several other hiking trails. Seven kilometers of trails are open for cross-country skiing in the winter.

INFORMATION
Harriman State Park
Bear Mountain, New York 10911
914-786-2701

Anthony Wayne Recreation Area
914-942-2560

Lake Tiorati
914-351-2568

Lake Welch Beach/Beaver Pond
914-947-2444

LAKE SUPERIOR STATE PARK

LOCATION - Lake Superior State Park is on Dr. Duggan Road, accessible from New York 17B and 55, west of Monticello.

ACTIVITIES - Lake Superior, not one of the Great Lakes, is open for day-use only. Go swimming, launch non-motorized boats from the boat launch, and go fishing. Enjoy a picnic, take a hike, and purchase food from the concession stand open June through Labor Day.

Incoming pilots can land at Sullivan County International Airport 6 miles northwest of Monticello. Rental cars are available.

INFORMATION
Lake Superior State Park
Bear Mountain, New York 10911
914-794-3000, ext. 5002

ROCKLAND LAKE STATE PARK

LOCATION - From New York City via the George Washington Bridge, take Palisades Interstate Parkway north to Exit 4. Then follow New York 9W for 12 miles to reach the park.

FEATURES - Rockland Lake is on a ridge of Hook Mountain above the west shore of the Hudson River.

ACTIVITIES - Swim in one of the two Olympic-sized pools from late May through Labor Day and purchase a snack at the refreshment stand. Fish in Rockland Lake for norlunge, bass, and perch. Go boating in your cartop boat or rent a rowboat from April through the end of November.

Play golf on the championship golf course from early April through late November. Play tennis on one of six courts. Work out on the 3.4-mile fitness trail or hike or bike around Rockland Lake. Hike along the Hudson River or up Hook Mountain.

During the winter, cross-country ski or go sledding on the golf course.

INFORMATION
Rockland Lake State Park
P.O. Box 217
Congers, New York 10920
914-268-3020

TALLMAN MOUNTAIN STATE PARK

LOCATION - From the Saw Mill River Parkway, New York 9, cross the Tappan Zee Bridge and head south on New York 9W.

ACTIVITIES - Open for day-use only, bring your bicycle to cycle the bike trail. Swim in the pool, run on the track, play tennis and badminton, and get a snack from the snack bar. Go cross-country skiing during the winter.

INFORMATION
Tallman Mountain State Park
Sparkill, New York 10976
No phone available

POINT AU ROCHE STATE PARK
See under LAKE CHAMPLAIN STATE PARKS

ROBERT MOSES STATE PARK
57

LOCATION - The park is on the west end of Fire Island on the Atlantic Ocean. Fire Island stretches 32 miles from Robert Moses State Park on the west to Smith Point Park on the east and is accessible via the Robert Moses Causeway from Captree State Park. It's 2 miles north of New York 37 on Barnhart Island in the St. Lawrence River and is 3 miles north of Massena.

FEATURES - Fire Island's barrier island separates the Atlantic Ocean from the Great South Bay. The park overlooks several lock operations and provides access to the Moses-Saunders Power Dam.

ACTIVITIES - Visitors can play pitch and putt-putt golf, go boating with rentals available, swimming in the ocean, and pan fishing in Lake St. Lawrence. Hike out to the Fire Island Lighthouse at the east end of the park. The keeper's quarters house a museum, and tours up the 192-step tower are offered one day a week June–August with reservations required. Contact the tourist bureau at 516-563-8448.

Camp in the 169-site campground, 28 offering electrical hookups, with a trailer dump station and food. You can also stay in one of 15 cabins.

Tour the visitor center at the Moses-Saunders Power Dam and watch their orientation film.

Incoming pilots can land at Massena International-Richards Field Airport 2 miles east of Massena. Rental cars are available.

INFORMATION
Robert Moses State Park
P.O. Box 48
Massena, New York 13662
516-669-0449

ROCKLAND LAKE STATE PARK
See under PALISADES INTERSTATE PARKS

ROGERS ROCK STATE PARK
See under CRANBERRY LAKE STATE PARK

ST. LAWRENCE STATE PARK
58

LOCATION - The park is 4 miles west of Ogdensburg on New York 37.

ACTIVITIES - The park is open April 20 through Columbus Day weekend. Purchase concessions and play golf on its nine-hole course. Tee times may be reserved two days earlier by calling 315-393-2286. In the winter, go cross-country skiing.

A week-long Ogdensburg International Seaway Festival is held in mid-July, featuring free museum tours and musical concerts.

Incoming pilots can land at Ogdensburg International Airport 2 miles southeast of Ogdensburg. Rental cars are available.

INFORMATION
St. Lawrence State Park
P.O. Box 247
Alexandria Bay, New York 13607
315-393-1977

SAMPSON STATE PARK
59

LOCATION - Sampson is 5 miles north of Ovid on New York 96A and 11 miles south of Geneva. It's on the east side of Seneca Lake.

ACTIVITIES - The park is one of the state's largest. Camp in the 245-site campground—all sites offering electrical hookups, a trailer dump station, and groceries. Go biking, hiking, and play tennis. Enjoy boating from the marina in Seneca Lake, swimming, and trout fishing.

The National Lake Trout Derby is held annually Memorial Day weekend at Seneca Lake.

Nearby Geneva was rated thirty-fifth in the *100 Best Small Towns in America*, published in 1993 by Prentice Hall. The Historical Museum offers both a walking and driving tour of its historic city homes.

INFORMATION
Sampson State Park
Ovid, New York 14541
315-585-6392

SARATOGA SPA STATE PARK
60

LOCATION - The park is south of Saratoga Springs.

FEATURES - Because of its classical architecture, the spa is listed as a National Historic Landmark. Mineral waters originate in a layer of limestone 100–1,000 feet below the surface and emerge through the Saratoga fault.

ACTIVITIES - Saratoga Spa has walking paths along the stream and through a hemlock forest. Runners have a 5- and 10-kilometer certified course where running events are held spring and fall. Several mineral springs are located near the picnic area.

Roosevelt Spa has mineral waters where you can get a massage and take a mineral bath. For reservations, call 518-584-2011. Lincoln Baths also offer mineral baths and massages in July and August. For reservations, call 518-583-2880.

Stay in Gideon Putnam Hotel. For reservations, call 518-584-3000. Dine in the Park Place Restaurant. Play eighteen holes of golf on one of the two championship golf courses. Call 518-584-2008 for a tee-off time. Go swimming in one of the two pools, play tennis, and have a picnic.

Attend a performance in the Saratoga Performing Arts Center from June–August. The Spa Little Theatre and National Museum of Dance provides performances and exhibits year-round. Call 518-584-9330 for information.

Saratoga National Historic Park's entrances are 30 miles north of Albany on U.S. 4 and New York 32. Stop by the visitor center to get a map of the Saratoga Battlefield and learn details of the Campaign of 1777. Drive a 9½-mile route and walk self-guided paths. Tour the Philip Schuyler House, country home of General Philip Schuyler.

Saratoga Lake is one of northeastern New Yorkers' favorite bass fishing holes. During the winter, 4.2-mile Wilkinson Trail is open for cross-country skiing. For additional park information, call 518-664-9821.

A winter festival in February features free horse-drawn sleigh rides, dog cart rides, and snow sculptures. Cross-country ski along the golf course or on 20 kilometers of groomed trails. Ice skate on the Victoria Mall near the pool complex. A warming hut is available.

In Saratoga Springs, tour the National Museum of Dance, the only museum of its kind in the nation. See costumes celebrating the lives and works of great contributors to American professional dance. It's open May–October from Tuesday–Sunday. For information, call 518-584-2225.

Tour President Grant's cottage, 8 miles north of Saratoga Springs off New York 9. It's open from Memorial through Labor Day on Wednesday–Sunday from 10:00–4:00. For information, call 518-587-8277.

Attend Saratoga polo matches on Seaward Street on Tuesdays, Friday–Sunday in August. For information, call 518-584-8108. Horse racing occurs year-round at Saratoga Harness Raceway at Crescent Avenue and Jefferson in Saratoga Springs, February–November. For information and track tours May through Labor Day, call 518-584-2110.

Incoming pilots can land at Saratoga County Airport 3 miles southwest of town. Rental cars are available.

INFORMATION
Saratoga Spa State Park
Saratoga Springs, New York 12866
518-584-2000

SCHOHARIE CROSSING STATE HISTORIC PARK
See under MAX V. SHAUL STATE PARK

SCHUYLER MANSION STATE HISTORIC SITE
61

LOCATION - The mansion is in Albany on 32 Catherine Street, 2 blocks west of South Pearl Street.

FEATURES - A National Historic Landmark, the eighteenth-century Georgian mansion of General Philip Schuyler, a noted Revolutionary War general, boasts a collection of New York and New England furniture from the Colonial and Federal periods.

ACTIVITIES - The mansion is open mid-April through December, Wednesday–Saturday from 10:00–5:00 and Sunday from 1:00–5:00.

Incoming pilots can land at Albany County Airport 6 miles northwest of Albany. Rental cars are available.

INFORMATION
Schuyler Mansion State Historic Site
32 Catherine Street
Albany, New York 12202
518-434-0834

SELKIRK SHORES STATE PARK
62

LOCATION - The park is 5 miles west of Pulaski on New York 3.

ACTIVITIES - Camp in the 145-site campground, 88 offering electrical hookups, with a trailer dump station and groceries. Stay in one of 16 cabins. Go salmon fishing in Lake Ontario, boating, swimming, hiking, and biking the trails. During the winter, go cross-country skiing.

INFORMATION
Selkirk Shores State Park
Route 3
Pulaski, New York 13142
315-298-5737

SOUTHWICK BEACH STATE PARK
63

LOCATION - The park is 32 miles southwest of Watertown off New York 3 on the eastern shore of Lake Ontario.

ACTIVITIES - Southwick Beach is open mid-May through mid-October. Camp in the 112-site campground with 44 electrical hookups and a trailer dumping station. Go swimming and boating in carry-in boats only. Hike the nature trails. Concessions are available. In the winter, go cross-country skiing and snowshoeing.

Southwick is adjacent to Lakeview Wildlife Management Area's hiking trails and coastal sand dunes.

In Watertown, wander through historic downtown. On Thursday evenings during the summer, go to the "Square" for a weekly concert. For whitewater excitement, experience the Black River with 14 major rapids packed into an 8-mile stretch of river. Experienced guides are available. Contact the Hudson River Rafting Company at 315-782-7881 or Mountain River Expeditions at 315-788-8111.

Annual Watertown events include the Bravo Italiano Fest every September. B'Gosh and B'Gorah is celebrated in March during its annual Irish festival. The Snowtown U.S.A. Winter Festival is held 10 days each winter. For information, call 315-788-4400.

Canoe the Indian River Canoe Route. Begin at the rest stop on New York 11, south of Antwerp. For details, contact the town clerk at NYSDEC, 317 Washington, Watertown, New York 13601.

Incoming pilots can land at Watertown International Airport 5 miles west of Watertown. Rental cars are available.

INFORMATION
Southwick Beach State Park
Box 60A, Route 1
Woodville, New York 13698
315-846-5338

STONY POINT BATTLEFIELD STATE HISTORIC SITE
64

LOCATION - The State Historic Site is on Park Road off New York 9W, 2.5 miles north of Stony Point.

FEATURES - The storming of Stony Point by American forces under the command of General "Mad Anthony" Wayne was one of the most brilliant exploits of the American Revolution. The British post, which overlooks a strategic colony ferry crossing, was captured in a daring midnight raid by American light infantry in July 1779.

ACTIVITIES - The site is open from April 15–October and the rest of the year by appointment only. The grounds are open Wednesday–Sunday from 10:30–5:00, and the museum is open 11:00–4:00. Exhibits and walking tours explain the daring raid. Picnic at sites overlooking the Hudson River.

INFORMATION
Stony Point Battlefield State Historic Site
Park Road off Route 9W
Stony Point, New York 11720
914-786-2521

TALLMAN MOUNTAIN STATE PARK
See under PALISADES INTERSTATE PARKS

TAUGHANNOCK FALLS STATE PARK
65
CAYUGA LAKE STATE PARK
66

LOCATION - Taughannock Falls are 8 miles north of Ithaca on New York 89.

Cayuga Lake State Park is 3 miles east of Seneca Falls on the Lower Lake Road off New York 89 on the northern end of Seneca Lake.

FEATURES - Taughannock Falls, one of the highest continuous waterfalls in the east, drop 215 feet within a rock amphitheater flanked by 400-foot walls. Taughannock is an Algonquin or Iroquois word meaning "the great falls in the woods."

Cayuga Lake is one of eleven Finger Lakes carved by the continental glaciers as they ground their way south from Canada. Cayuga is the largest of these lakes, measuring 38.1 miles long and 474 feet deep at its deepest spot. At Cayuga State Park, however, the lake is only 5 feet deep.

ACTIVITIES - At Taughannock Falls, camp in the 76-site campground, 16 with electrical hookups and a trailer dump station, or stay in one of 16 cabins. Go bass fishing in Taughannock Creek and Cayuga Lake. Enjoy swimming from the beach, water-skiing, and boating from the ramp or marina. Food is available.

Hike a ¾-mile-long trail beside Taughannock Creek through the gorge to reach the base of the falls. No swimming is permitted in the gorge. Two other trails follow the rim above the gorge and another multi-use trail goes through the woods from the north rim trail.

Attend concerts at their summer music festival and participate in a camper recreation program.

During the winter, ride the free rope tow up the bunny slope, cross-country ski or ice skate, and warm up in the warming hut.

In Ithaca, located at the southern tip of Cayuga Lake, you'll find more deep gorges carrying Six Mile, Fall, and Cascadilla creeks. The Cayuga Wine Trail starts here and heads north on New York 89 on its way past several wineries located on the lake's western shore.

At Cayuga Lake State Park, camp in the 286-site campground with 36 electrical hookups, a trailer dump station, and groceries. You can also stay in one of 48 cabins.

Go bass, carp, and bullhead fishing, swimming from the beach, bicycling, boating from the ramp or marina. During the winter, go cross-country skiing.

The northern end of the lake joins Montezuma Marsh, a National Wildlife Refuge that supports nesting sites for ducks and other waterfowl, located along the migratory route for thousands of geese.

A long section of the Erie Canal Recreationway Trail begins here and continues for 108 miles to Lockport. Much of this trail is designated as a bike trail and passes nine canal lift-locks.

In Seneca Falls, tour Women's Rights National Historical Park at 116 Fall Street, site of the home of Elizabeth Cady Stanton. It has a visitor center and guided tours.

The National Women's Hall of Fame at 76 Fall Street honors women of the past and present for their many contributions. Special events held in Seneca Falls include Women's Rights Convention Days, an annual Pageant of Bands, Women's Equality Days, strawberry and wine festivals, and concerts.

Visitors can take a boat cruise on Seneca Lake from the Urban Cultural Park in Seneca Falls. For information, call 1-800-343-BOAT.

Incoming pilots can land at Tompkins County Airport 4 miles northeast of Ithaca. You can also land at Finger Lakes Regional Airport one mile south of Seneca Falls on New York 414. Rental cars are available at both airports.

INFORMATION

Taughannock Falls State Park	Cayuga Lake State Park
R.D. 3	2678 Lower Lake Road
Trumansburg, New York 14886	Seneca Falls, New York 13148
607-387-6739	315-568-5163

WASHINGTON'S HEADQUARTERS STATE HISTORIC SITE
See under KNOX'S HEADQUARTERS STATE HISTORIC SITE

WATKINS GLEN STATE PARK
67

LOCATION - Watkins Glen is in the village of Watkins Glen at the south end of Seneca Lake. It's 25 miles west of Ithaca on New York 79.

FEATURES - The park's 1½-mile-long gorge has 832 steps climbing 700 feet as it passes 19 waterfalls.

ACTIVITIES - The park is open from mid-May through mid-October. Camp in the 303-site campground with a trailer dump. Snacks or breakfast and lunch are available. Go fishing in the lake and swimming in their Olympic-sized pool.

Hike up gorge trail to the top of the gorge. Shuttles are available for visitors not wishing to climb. Guided tours are offered at 9:30 and 1:30 from June 20 through Labor Day. Gorge trails are closed from November 10 through mid-May.

Additional hiking trails include the North Country National Scenic Trail, Indian Trail heading north above the gorge, and South Rim Trail that joins Finger Lakes Trail next to the picnic area by the campground. We followed South Rim's wooded trail for several miles as it wound along the gorge's south rim, passing Punch Bowl Lake. For additional information and a map on any of these trails, contact the visitor center in Watkins Glen.

Attend Timespell, a unique laser interpretive show giving the area's history from 45 million centuries ago to the present. It's given daily in the gorge each evening from May–October at dusk. Visitors climb 83 steps to view the show on towering rock walls. For reservations, call 607-535-4960.

To watch auto racing from June–September, Thursday–Sunday, go to Watkins Glen International Race Track located 4 miles southwest of Watkins Glen via New York 414. For a schedule, call 607-535-2481.

Go for a cruise on Seneca Lake. A 10-mile trip departs from the foot of Franklin Street on the hour from 10:00–8:00, from May 15–October 15. For reservations, call 607-535-4541 or 607-535-4680.

Take a winery tour at Chateau Lafayette Reneau 6 miles north of Watkins Glen on New York 414. The tour takes 15 minutes and is followed by wine tasting. For information, call 607-546-2062.

At Seneca Lake, fish from the pier, charter a fishing boat to fish for deep water lake trout, go scuba diving, sailing, or rent a motorboat.

Go to Montour Falls to see Chequaga Falls which are almost as high as Niagara Falls. Hector Falls are on the east side of Seneca Lake near Hector.

Tour the Corning Museum of Glass in nearby Corning. It's rated as one of top three attractions in New York. Allow at least three hours to tour this very comprehensive glass museum, the hall of science and industry, and the Steuben factory where Steuben glassware is made. It's open seven days a week, 9:00–5:00, except July–August when it's open until 8:00 PM. For information, call 607-974-8271.

INFORMATION
Watkins Glen State Park
P.O. Box 304
Watkins Glen, New York 14891
607-535-4511

WELLESLEY ISLAND STATE PARK
68

LOCATION - The park is 4 miles west of Alexandria Bay via Thousand Islands Bridge linking the U.S. to Canada. From New York 81, take Exit 51.

ACTIVITIES - Camp in the 430-site campground, which has 74 sites with electrical hookups, 57 with full hookups, and a camp store. Hike to one of 12 carry-in sites or stay in one of 10 cabins.

Tour Minna Anthony Common Nature Center and hike along 10 miles of trails. For a tee-off time on the nine-hole golf course, call 315-482-9622.

Swim and go boating from the marina or launch a boat from four other sites. Enjoy fishing in nationally known St. Lawrence River for pike, muskellunge, and bass.

During the winter, go cross-country skiing and ice fishing.

Take a boat cruise aboard the *Empire* with a stop to tour Boldt Castle, a 120-room replica of a Rhineland castle. For information, call 315-482-9511 or 1-800-542-2628.

Wellesley Island State Park also operates Waterson Point State Park, a boat-only park surrounded by Wellesley Island. Visitors go to fish for pike, muskellunge, and black bass in nearby Lost Channel.

DeWolf Point State Park, located on Lake of the Isles off Cross Island Road, is also operated by Wellesley. It has 14 cabins, 12 campsites, and a boat launch into Lake of the Isles.

Tour Thousand Island Park to see hundreds of wooden Victorian homes. For information, call 315-482-7700.

INFORMATION
Wellesley Island State Park
Route 1, Box W437
Fineview, New York 13640
315-482-2722

WESTCOTT BEACH STATE PARK
69

LOCATION - The beach is 4 miles southwest of Sackets Harbor off New York 3 on Lake Ontario.

ACTIVITIES - The park is open from mid-May through October. Camp in the 168-site campground with 85 electric sites and dumping station. Go swimming from the 2,000-foot guarded beach. Hike approximately 6 miles of trails. Concessions are available. Go fishing and boating from the ramp in Lake Ontario. Special events occur throughout the summer.

During the winter, go cross-country skiing and snowshoeing.

Tour the visitor center housed in the 1817 Union Hotel. The center is open 10:00–5:00 Wednesday–Saturday and 1:00–5:00 Sunday from late May through late September. In July, attend the annual Can-Am War of 1812 Festival when muskets are fired and tall ships fill the harbor. For information, call 315-646-3634.

INFORMATION
Westcott Beach State Park
P.O. Box 339
Sackets Harbor, New York 13685
315-938-5083

WHETSTONE GULF STATE PARK
70

LOCATION - The park is 3 miles south of Martinsburg off New York 26.

FEATURES - The park is built in a 3-mile-long gorge, Whetstone Gulf, that cuts into the eastern edge of Tug Hill plateau.

ACTIVITIES - Whetstone is open Memorial Day through Labor Day and from December 15–March 15. Camp in the 56-site campground with a trailer dump station. Hike one of the three trails, including the 5-mile gorge rim trail. A shorter trail runs along the gorge creek.

Swim in the pool, fish for muskies and bass, and canoe in Whetstone Gulf Reservoir.

The park is in New York's heaviest snowbelt, averaging 300 inches of snow. You can snowmobile and cross-country ski along the park's 14 miles of trails that connect to others in the Tug Hill plateau. Warm up in the heated recreation building.

INFORMATION
Whetstone Gulf State Park
R.D. 2
Lowville, New York 13367
315-376-6630

WILDWOOD STATE PARK
71

LOCATION - The park is 3 miles east of Wading River off New York 25A on Long Island.

ACTIVITIES - Camp in the 322-site campground, 80 sites having electrical and sewer hookups, with a trailer dump station. Go fishing and swimming in Long Island Sound and bike the bicycle trails. Food service is available.

Come to cross-country ski in the winter.

INFORMATION
Wildwood State Park
P.O. Box 247
Babylon, New York 11702
516-929-4314

PENNSYLVANIA

Pennsylvania has 114 state parks, many located in wooded mountains. The main parks are located in the Poconos, Allegheny National Forest, and Laurel Highlands. Water sports are popular in the Laurel Highlands, at Lake Wallenpaupack in the Poconos, at Pine Creek Gorge, and at Pymatuning Reservoir. Whitewater enthusiasts can explore the Youghiogheny River at Ohiopyle State Park and the Lehigh River in Lehigh Gorge State Park.

With over 45,000 miles of flowing water, anglers have many fishing opportunities in the lakes and streams stocked with trout, muskellunge, bass, perch, and crappie. During the winter, go snowmobiling, downhill and cross-country skiing.

Pennsylvania's state parks offer over 7,000 family campsites, 281 cabins, 56 major recreational lakes, 61 swimming beaches, and over 1,000 miles of trails. For a free map of the state parks, call the park service at 1-800-63-PARKS or 717-787-8800.

BALD EAGLE STATE PARK
1

LOCATION - Bald Eagle is located on Foster Joseph Sayers Dam along Bald Eagle Creek. It's midway between Milesburg and Lock Haven off Pennsylvania 150 and is accessible via I-80. Eastbound travelers exit at Interchange 23 and travel north 10 miles on Pennsylvania 150. Westbound travelers exit at Interchange 26 and go north on U.S. 220 and then south 13 miles on Pennsylvania 150. It's also accessible at Howard off Pennsylvania 26.

FEATURES - The park, Bald Eagle Mountains, and valley were named for Indian Chief Bald Eagle of the Leni-Lenape tribes.

ACTIVITIES - Visitors can swim from the guarded beach with concessions available from Memorial Day through Labor Day. Enjoy a picnic in Schencks Grove picnic area and Skyline Drive's picnic area.

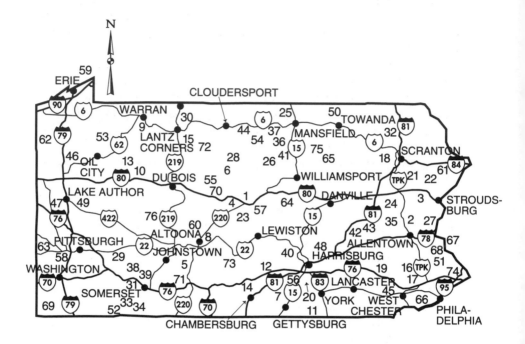

N

ERIE 59

CLOUDERSPORT

WARRAN
30   25
         9   44   37   50 TOWANDA
62 79 53   15 72   MANSFIELD   32   81
        62 LANTZ   54 36   6   SCRANTON
46 OIL   CORNERS   28   41 75   18
   CITY 13   6   26   65   61 84
        10 DU BOIS 55   WILLIAMSPORT   21 22
        80   70   1   80 DANVILLE   TPK
LAKE AUTHOR   4   64   3 STROUDS-
47 49   76 219 220 23 57   24   BURG
76   422   60   15   81 35 2 27
63 PITTSBURGH 22 ALTOONA 8 LEWISTON   42 43 78 67
58   29 JOHNSTOWN   22 40 48 ALLENTOWN 68
WASHINGTON   38 5   73   12 HARRISBURG 76 19 16 TPK 51
70   39   14   76   17 74
69 79 52 33 71 81 56 83 LANCASTER   45 95
        34 76 220 70 7 15 20 YORK WEST 66 PHILA-
CHAMBERSBURG   GETTYSBURG 11 CHESTER   DELPHIA

Hikers can explore a 3.5-mile-long lakeside trail located near the camping area. Come in the fall to hike among the hardwoods when they take on their fall foliage. Anglers can fish for warm water fish including crappie, bass, and northern pike.

Campers have access to 35 tent sites and 25 vehicle sites from the second Friday in April through the third Sunday in October. A dump station is available.

Boaters have six launch ramps. Two are open all night to provide night fishing access. The marina has rental dockage slips, boat rentals, and fishing supplies.

During the winter, go sledding, tobogganing, ice fishing, ice boating, ice skating, and snowmobiling along 17 miles of trails.

Nearby attractions include Curtin Mansion and Eagle Ironworks at Curtin, the Pennsylvania Military Museum at Boalsburg, Woodward Caves near Millheim, and fish hatcheries at Pleasant Gap and Lamar. Scenic views are located at Penn's View near Coburn, at Skytop on Pennsylvania 322, on Pine Grove Mills Mountain, and on Centre Hall Mountain on Pennsylvania 144.

A nearby attraction is Penn's Cave near Centre Hall. The cave is the country's only all-water cavern and features the "Statue of Liberty" and "Niagara Falls." Visitors can take a 60-minute tour, a ride on Lake Nitanee, and stroll through the wildlife sanctuary. For an added attraction, take a plane ride over nearby Amish farms. For information, call 814-364-1664.

INFORMATION
Bald Eagle State Park
R.D. 1, Box 56
Howard, Pennsylvania 16841
814-625-2775

BELTZVILLE STATE PARK
2

LOCATION - The park is 6 miles east of Lehighton on U.S. 209, accessible from the northeast extension of the Pennsylvania Turnpike immediately off Exit 34. Turn left and follow signs.

FEATURES - Beltzville is located along the Pohopoco Creek and on Beltzville Lake.

ACTIVITIES - The park is for open for day-use only and has picnicking at Pine Run West. Anglers can fish for bass, walleye, muskellunge, and perch in stocked Beltzville Lake. Much of the shoreline is accessible from Pennsylvania 397. Feeder streams are stocked with trout.

Boats of all types are permitted on the lake, and the park has a boat-launch ramp, courtesy docks, and parking at Pine Run East along the lake's north shore. Areas above Preacher's Camp and Pine Run Cove are restricted to "no-wake" speeds and thus are excellent for sailing and canoeing.

Hikers have access to 11 miles of trails, including a self-guided interpretive trail that has remains of a raceway for a grist mill and a slate quarry dating back to the 1700s.

Swim from the guarded sand beach from Memorial Day weekend through Labor Day. Concessions are sold near the beach. A covered bridge is between the picnic areas and beach. For a good look at the dam and lake, stop at the Overlook Rotunda off Pennsylvania T-397.

Incoming pilots can land at Beltzville Airport, located 3 miles east of Lehighton. No rental cars are available. However, cars are available at Jake Arner Memorial Airport, located 3 miles southwest of Lehighton.

INFORMATION
Beltzville State Park
R.D. 3, Box 242
Lehighton, Pennsylvania 18235
215-377-0045

BIG POCONO STATE PARK
3

LOCATION - The park is 13 miles west of Tannersville off I-80 on the slopes of Camelback Mountain. Entrance to the park is from Pennsylvania 715, Exit 45 at Tannersville. Because of the steep grade, vehicles towing trailers are advised not to attempt this route.

ACTIVITIES - Big Pocono State Park is open for day-use. Enjoy a picnic at one of the park's 50 picnic tables. Hikers have access to 10 miles of trails. Prior to hiking either of the two most difficult trails, Indian and North trails, hikers are advised to check on conditions with park office naturalists.

Equestrians share two of the hiking trails: South Trail and Old Railroad Grade Trail. Their trailhead is at the west end of the park near the park entrance. A restaurant located near Camelback's summit is reached either by park road or chair lift. During the winter, ski at Camelback Ski Area located north of the park.

Nearby attractions include the Pocono Mountains resorts, Gouldsboro State Park, Hickory Run State Park, and Delaware Water Gap National Recreation Area, located in Bushkill. When visiting the National Recreation Area, stop by the Kittatinny Point Information Station on I-80 in New Jersey or at Dingmans Falls Visitor Center off Pennsylvania 209. The area offers fishing, swimming, canoeing, and hiking. For information, call 717-588-6637.

INFORMATION
Big Pocono State Park
P.O. Box 173
Henryville, Pennsylvania 18332
717-629-0320 or 717-894-8336

BLACK MOSHANNON STATE PARK
4

LOCATION - The park is located 9 miles east of Philipsburg on Pennsylvania 504.

FEATURES - Moshannon is an Indian name meaning "moose stream."

ACTIVITIES - Only boating in non-powered boats and registered electric-powered boats is permitted. Rental boats are available.

Anglers can fish for warm water game fish in Black Moshannon Lake or for trout in Black Moshannon Creek, Six Mile Run, Black Bear Run, Smays Run, and Bald Eagle Creek.

Hikers have access to 15 miles of trails. One trail passes through Black Moshannon Bog Natural Area.

Campers have 80 campsites open from the second Friday in April through the end of antlerless deer season in late December when thirteen cabins are available for weekly rentals. Half-week rentals are only available during spring and fall but rentals are only available to Pennsylvania residents during the summer. Concessions are available.

Attend seasonal interpretive evening campfire programs and take guided nature hikes from Memorial Day through Labor Day.

During the winter, enjoy ice skating, cross-country skiing on 7 miles of trails, and snowmobiling both in the park and in the nearby state forest.

Incoming pilots can land at Mid-State Airport at Philipsburg, located 8 miles east of town. No rental cars are available.

INFORMATION
Black Moshannon State Park
R.D. 1, Box 183
Philipsburg, Pennsylvania 16886
814-342-1101 (office)
814-342-5777 (campground)

BLUE KNOB STATE PARK
5

LOCATION - Blue Knob is located 5 miles northwest of Pavia off Pennsylvania 869.

FEATURES - Blue Knob State Park is named for its 3,146-foot quartzite peak, Blue Knob, the state's second highest point.

ACTIVITIES - Swim in the guarded pool from Memorial Day through Labor Day. Enjoy a picnic at one of the two hundred tables. Anglers can fish for trout in Bob's Creek.

Camp in one of 75 campsites open from the second Friday in April through the third Sunday in October.

The park has a 17-mile trail system through the forest that passes by pioneer homesteads. Backpackers have access to Lost Turkey Trail, a 22-mile back-country trail.

During the winter, go ice skating on a lighted area by the Burnt House picnic area, sledding, and cross-country or downhill skiing. For ski information, contact the Blue Knob Ski Resort at 814-239-5111.

Nearby attractions include State Game Land 26, located adjacent to the park, where you can enjoy additional hiking.

Incoming pilots can land at Bedford Airport, located 3 miles north of Bedford. You can also land at Altoona-Blair County Airport, located 12 miles south of Altoona, or at Johnstown-Cambria County Airport, located 3 miles northeast of Johnstown. All three airports have rental cars available.

INFORMATION
Blue Knob State Park
R.D. 1, Box 230A
Imler, Pennsylvania 16655
814-276-3476

BUCKTAIL STATE PARK
6

LOCATION - The park provides a 75-mile scenic drive from Emporium along Pennsylvania 120 to Lock Haven.

FEATURES - Bucktail Trail was named for the famous Civil War Regiment of Woodsmen who were called the Bucktails or Bucktail Rangers because of their bucktail insignia.

The park is bounded by two state forests, Elk and Sproul, and is known as Big Woods Country. The West Branch of the Susquehanna River and Sinnema-honing Creek flow through Bucktail Canyon.

ACTIVITIES - Visitors coming here in the fall are treated to outstanding color displays in the hardwood forests. Come to Renovo in October to attend the Flaming Foliage Festival. Come in the spring to see mountain laurel in bloom. The state forests are known for their excellent fishing in stocked streams.

Several major hiking and backpacking trails are located in the park, including 75-mile-long Quehanna Trail, 30-mile Bucktail Path Trail, 52-mile Donut Hole Trail, and 50-mile Chuck Keiper Trail.

Incoming pilots can land at William T. Piper Memorial Airport, located one mile east of Lock Haven, where rental cars are available.

INFORMATION
Bucktail State Park
Regional Park Office
R.D. 1, Box 1-A
Emporium, Pennsylvania 15834
814-486-336

CALEDONIA STATE PARK
7

LOCATION - The park is located 4 miles east of Fayetteville, midway between Chambersburg and Gettysburg on U.S. 30.

FEATURES - Caledonia, one of Pennsylvania's oldest parks, is on the blue ridge known as South Mountain. This ridge separates the great valley to the west from the piedmont in the east.

In 1837, a charcoal iron furnace operated here, but it was destroyed in 1863 by Confederate cavalrymen. The pastures were utilized as field dressing stations for wounded brought here from Gettysburg. Today these pastures are used for children's play fields.

ACTIVITIES - Camp in one of the two campgrounds' 185 sites with a dump station. They open the second Friday in April through the end of the antlerless deer season in late December.

Go swimming in the large pool with a snack concession open from Memorial Day weekend through Labor Day weekend.

A seasonal naturalist presents campfire programs and guided hikes. Tour the historical center located in the Thaddeus Stevens blacksmith shop.

Hikers have access to over 10 miles of trails, including part of the Appalachian Trail traversing the central section of the park. Picnickers can picnic at one of over 450 picnic tables available year-round.

Anglers fish for trout and native brookies in the Conococheague Rock Mountain Creeks and surrounding state forest lands.

The oldest and most scenic course in south-central Pennsylvania is an eighteen-hole, par 68 public golf course located on the park grounds. For a tee-off time, call 717-352-7271.

Totem Pole Playhouse offers daily entertainment during summer months. For information, call 717-352-2164.

During the winter, go sledding, tobogganing, and cross-country skiing.

Nearby attractions include Michaux State Forest and Gettysburg National Military Park, 14 miles away. At Gettysburg, visitors can follow an 18-mile auto tour route to sites from the Civil War's bloodiest battle or walk around the 130-year-old battlefield. At nearby Gettysburg National Cemetery, President

Abraham Lincoln delivered his famous "Gettysburg Address" on November 19, 1863.

Come to Chambersburg the end of July to attend Chamberfest with its Civil War Seminar, Old Market Day, "Almost Anything Goes" games, Gospel Sing and Pageant. For information, call 717-264-7101.

In early August, Chambersburg holds the Cumberland Valley Antique Engine and Machinery Show at Twin Bridges Campground, featuring over 600 antique gas engines and tractors. For information, call 717-263-5588. In mid-August, attend the Franklin County Fair. For information, call 717-263-9335.

Country music fans come to Chambersburg's Capitol Theater to hear "The Appalachian Jubilee" presented on most Saturday nights throughout the year.

Incoming pilots can land at Chambersburg Municipal Airport, located 2 miles north of town. Rental cars are available.

INFORMATION
Caledonia State Park
40 Rocky Mountain Road
Fayetteville, Pennsylvania 17222
717-352-2161

CANOE CREEK STATE PARK
8

LOCATION - Canoe Creek is 12 miles east of Altoona and 10 miles northeast of Hollidaysburg off U.S. 22.

ACTIVITIES - The park is open for day-use only. Go swimming from the guarded area in Canoe Lake from Memorial Day through Labor Day. Picnickers have access to 450 picnic tables.

Anglers can fish for stocked walleye, muskellunge, bass, trout, and catfish. Boat in non-powered boats or registered electric-powered boats. Launch sites are available on both sides of the lake, with mooring spaces along the eastern shoreline.

The park is laced with trails for hikers, equestrians, and bicyclists. No rental horses are available.

Two concessions are located in the park, a beach food stand and a boat concession with rental boats.

During the winter, come to trout fish, ice skate, sled, or go cross-country skiing and ice boating.

Nearby attractions include the Beaver Dam State Game Lands 166, located one mile north of the park on Beaver Dam Road. The Allegheny Portage Railroad National Historic Site is near Cresson on Pennsylvania 22.

An hour's drive from the park brings you to the Johnstown Flood National Memorial located along U.S. 219 and Pennsylvania 869. It's 10 miles northeast of Johnstown near St. Michael. Here you'll see the remnants of the earthen South Fork Dam that burst in 1889, causing a devastating flood of Johnstown and nearby communities. For information, call 814-886-8176.

Revolutionary War Fort Roberdeau, established to mine lead for the Revolutionary army, is 9 miles east of Altoona via Kettle Road. A military reenactment occurs in July, and in early October, attend their autumn nature festival. Hike nature trails in the adjacent nature area and inspect rocks and minerals in the museum. For information, call 814-695-5541.

To see an engineering feat, go to the parking lot by Horseshoe Curve 5 miles west of Altoona to see a curve in the railroad track where the two ends of the arc are almost parallel.

Incoming pilots can land at Altoona-Blair County Airport 12 miles south of Altoona. Rental cars are available.

INFORMATION
Canoe Creek State Park
R.D. 2, Box 560
Hollidaysburg, Pennsylvania 16648
814-695-6807

CHAPMAN STATE PARK
9

LOCATION - Chapman is 5 miles west of Clarendon off U.S. 6, adjacent to Allegheny National Forest. The park includes a lake on the West Branch of Tionesta Creek.

ACTIVITIES - Camp in the campground open year-round with 83 campsites and a trailer dump station. Picnickers have access to over 200 picnic tables located throughout the park. Snacks and boat rentals are available on the beach or you can eat in the restaurant.

Anglers can fish for stocked trout, bass, sunfish, crappie, perch, and suckers.

Go swimming from the guarded sand beach from Memorial Day weekend through Labor Day. Go boating in non-powered and electric-powered boats. Two boat launches, seasonal mooring spaces, and boat rentals are available.

A naturalist offers guided walks and slide programs on summer weekends.

The park has a 12-mile hiking trail system with 3 miles of self-guided trails. Backpackers often begin from the park to hike into the nearby national forest.

Trail bikers have access to 18 miles of trails through Allegheny National Forest. Trail maps are available at the park office. Visitors also have access to State Game Land 29 where you can go birding and hiking.

During the winter, go snowmobiling through the national forest with a 123-mile trail network open to registered snowmobiles following the end of antlerless deer season in late December. Also go ice skating, sledding, tobogganing, ice fishing for stocked fish, and ice boating. Cross-country ski on 7 miles of trails within the park and on nearby forest land trails. A warming hut is open.

INFORMATION
Chapman State Park
R.D. 1, Box 1610
Clarendon, Pennsylvania 16313
814-723-5030

CLEAR CREEK STATE PARK
10

LOCATION - The park is 5 miles north of Sigel off Pennsylvania 949 and occupies a scenic portion of Clear Creek Valley. It's also 12 miles north of Brookville.

ACTIVITIES - Overnight in one of 22 rustic cabins from the second Friday in April through the end of antlerless deer season in late December. The cabins are rented on a weekly basis except for half-week rentals during the spring and fall.

Camp in the campground open year-round with 53 wooded campsites and a trailer dump station.

Hikers have access to 15 miles of trails, including Island Run's self-guided nature trail. Attend summer interpretive programs.

The Clarion River, classified as a Class C waterway, offers excellent canoeing, especially during the spring and fall. A popular 10-mile canoe trip leaves Clear Creek and goes to Cook Forest State Park. Rental canoes are available.

Anglers can fish for brook trout in Clear Creek and for pike, bass, and walleye in the Clarion River. Nearby streams also provide good trout fishing.

Adjacent Kittanning State Forest offers fishing and hiking. For scenic views of the surrounding area, go to Bear Town Rocks and Hays Lot Fire Tower.

From Memorial Day weekend through Labor Day, swim in the small man-made lake. Food concessions are available. Picnickers have access to over 300 picnic tables.

During the winter, go sledding, cross-country skiing, and tobogganing.

INFORMATION
Clear Creek State Park
R.D. 1, Box 82
Sigel, Pennsylvania 15860
814-752-2368

CODORUS STATE PARK
11

LOCATION - Codorus State Park has 26 miles of shoreline along Lake Marburg and is 5 miles southeast of Hanover. From town, drive east for 4 miles on Pennsylvania 216 to Dubs Church Road. Go south one more mile.

ACTIVITIES - Camp in the 198-site campground with a dump station which is open the second Friday in April through the third Sunday in October. Hike the 5-mile trail system. A park naturalist offers guided hikes and slide talks during the summer season. Equestrians have access to a 10-mile bridle trail network.

Fish for stocked trout, perch, bluegill, pike, bass, catfish, and muskies. One of the nation's largest swimming pools is open from Memorial Day weekend through Labor Day weekend.

Non-powered and registered power boats up to 10 horsepower are allowed on Lake Marburg. Two boat rental concessions and eight launch ramps are located around the lake.

Picnickers have access to two picnic pavilions and 755 tables. Several park concessions have food available.

Registered snowmobilers can explore the park after the end of antlerless deer season in late December. Cross-country skiers have access to a 16-mile network. Winter visitors can also enjoy sledding, tobogganing, ice fishing, ice skating, and ice boating.

Incoming pilots can land at Hanover Airport, located one mile west of town. No rental cars are available, but taxis are.

INFORMATION
Codorus State Park
R.D. 3, Box 118
Hanover, Pennsylvania 17331
717-637-2816

COLONEL DENNING STATE PARK
12

LOCATION - The park is 8 miles north of Newville off Pennsylvania 233 and 9 miles south of Landisburg.

FEATURES - The park honors the Revolutionary War hero, Colonel William Denning, who invented an iron cannon which he refused to sell to the English. Instead, he provided cannons for the colonists.

The park is in Doubling Gap, named for the S-turn formed when Blue Mountain doubles back on itself, visible from the Doubling Gap Vista on state forest land.

Doubling Gap Hotel, now operating as a church camp, was originally a plush resort hotel around the turn of the century.

ACTIVITIES - Swim from the guarded area from Memorial Day through Labor Day. Concessions are available near the beach during the summer. Fish for trout in Doubling Gap Lake.

Over 10 miles of hiking trails lace the park, including a 2.5-mile trail to Flat Rock where you get a scenic view of the Cumberland Valley. The 105-mile Tuscarora Trail passes through the western end of the park and leads to the Appalachian Trail. Tuscarora State Forest surrounds the park, providing additional hiking possibilities.

Picnic at one of the 200 picnic tables. The campground has 64 sites, open year-round. Tour the visitor center and get their schedule of events.

Hunters come here beginning with the fall dove season through March 31 except Sundays.

During the winter, go sledding, tobogganing, and cross-country skiing along existing roads and trails. You can also ice skate on Doubling Gap Lake.

INFORMATION
Colonel Denning State Park
R.D. 3
Newville, Pennsylvania 17241
717-776-5272

COLTON POINT STATE PARK
See under LEONARD HARRISON STATE PARK

COOK FOREST STATE PARK
13

LOCATION - The park is one mile north of Cooksburg off Pennsylvania 36. From the east, take Exit 13 off I-80 onto Pennsylvania 36 north to go directly to the park. If approaching from the west, take Exit 8 off I-80 onto Pennsylvania 66 north to Leeper. From Leeper, follow Pennsylvania 36 south for 7 miles.

ACTIVITIES - Camp in the campground with 226 campsites and a trailer dump station. You can also stay in one of 24 rustic cabins available from the second Friday in April through the end of the antlerless deer season in late December. Reservations are advised, particularly during the summer season.

Rent a canoe or bring your own to canoe the Clarion River, classed as a beginner's river under normal conditions. A canoe launch area and parking are available 3 miles upstream from Cooksburg along River Road.

Take a scenic drive to Seneca Point and climb the fire tower located 1.5 miles from the campground. Forest Drive and Tom's Run Road provide access to remote areas in the park.

The park has 27 miles of marked hiking trails, including 140-mile Baker Trail that passes through the park.

Seasonal naturalists lead daily walks. To see some of the largest primeval white pine and hemlock trees, hike Longfellow Trail from the Log Cabin Inn. The trees are from 200 to 350 years old and are nearly 200 feet tall.

Forest Cathedral Trail, accessed from Longfellow Trail, contains some of the largest primeval white pine and hemlock trees in Pennsylvania. These trees have been designated by the National Park Service as a National Natural Landmark.

Go swimming in the guarded pool and fishing in the Clarion River for trout, warm water game fish, and panfish. Equestrians have access to 4.5 miles of bridle trails and horse rentals are available from four riding stables adjacent to the park.

Tour the park museum housed in the former Log Cabin Inn where traditional crafts are sold. Picnickers have access to 340 picnic tables available year-round. Concessions are sold at the swimming pool and food at Log Cabin Inn. Anglers can fish for trout and panfish in the Clarion River. Many mountain trout streams and reservoirs are nearby.

During the winter, snowmobile along 20 miles of snowmobile trails or park roads, skate on the lighted pond near River Road, go sledding and cross-country skiing. Cross-country ski rentals are available.

INFORMATION
Cook Forest State Park
P.O. Box 120
Cooksburg, Pennsylvania 16217
814-744-8407

COWANS GAP STATE PARK
14

LOCATION - The park is 10 miles northeast of McConnellsburg off U.S. 30, between Chambersburg and McConnellsburg. If heading west on the Pennsylvania Turnpike, take Exit 13, Fort Littleton, onto U.S. 522 north to Burnt Cabins and follow signs to the park.

From the east, take Exit 14, Willow Hill, then Pennsylvania 75 south to Richmond Furnace and follow the signs. From U.S. 30, take Pennsylvania 75 north at Fort Loudon to Richmond Furnace and follow park signs.

FEATURES - Cowans Gap was named for Major Samuel Cowan, a British officer during the Revolutionary War.

ACTIVITIES - Swim from the beach from Memorial Day through Labor Day. Go boating on Cowans Gap Lake in non-powered and electric boats. Rentals of rowboats and paddleboats are available from the first day of trout season in April through mid-October.

Anglers can fish for trout, bass, perch, and panfish either in the lake or in the Little Aughwick Creek. Picnic at one of the 450 picnic tables.

Hike along 10 miles of hiking trails which link with additional trails on adjacent state forest land. Pick up a booklet at the park office for the one-mile Twin Springs Nature Trail. The 105-mile Tuscarora Trail goes through the park and connects to Big Blue Trail. This trail parallels the Appalachian Trail and intersects both it and the Darlington Trail near Deans Gap, north of Carlisle.

Cowans Gap has 260 campsites and an overnight boat-mooring area for registered campers. The campground is open from the second Friday of April to the day following antlerless deer season in December. You can also stay in one of 10 family cabins available spring–fall.

The park offers environmental interpretive programs Memorial Day through Labor Day, including nature walks, slide presentations, campfire activities, and historical tours.

During the winter, go sledding on Knobsville Road, ice skating, and cross-country skiing.

Nearby attractions include Buchanan's Birthplace State Park, birthplace of James Buchanan, our fifteenth President. It's in the foothills of the Tuscarora Mountains on the west side of the Cumberland Valley south of U.S. 30.

Country music fans can attend the Appalachian Jubilee, presented 50 Saturday nights of the year in old Capitol Theater in downtown Chambersburg. For ticket information, call 717-264-8349.

In July, attend Chamberfest in Chambersburg when Civil War seminars, Old Market Day, AirFest, and Skate Fest are featured. In August, the town presents the Franklin County Fair with a craft show, antique farm equipment, and a horse tractor pull. For details on Chambersburg events, contact the Chamber of Commerce at 717-261-1200.

Incoming pilots can land at Chambersburg Municipal Airport, located 2 miles north of town, where rental cars are available.

INFORMATION
Cowans Gap State Park
Star Route North
Fort Louden, Pennsylvania 17224
717-485-3948

ELK STATE PARK
15

LOCATION - Elk State Park is 9 miles east of Wilcox Legislative Route 24011, approximately 9 miles south of Clermont, and includes East Branch Lake.

ACTIVITIES - Camp in the 75-site campground open the second Friday in April through the end of antlerless deer season in late December. Picnickers have access to 12 picnic tables plus additional tables by the dam. Hike short White Tail Trail off Harrison Drive.

Fish for stocked muskellunge, walleye, and trout in the East Branch Clarion Reservoir or in one of the surrounding streams: Five Mile, Seven Mile, Straight Creek, Middle Fork, and Crook Creek.

Unlimited horsepower boating is allowed, and a boat launch plus seasonal mooring spaces are available. Launch areas are located at either end of the lake.

No swimming is allowed in the lake, but is available at Bendigo State Park, 13 miles away. During the winter, go ice fishing and ice boating.

INFORMATION
Elk State Park
c/o Bendigo State Park
P.O. Box A
Johnsonburg, Pennsylvania 25845
814-965-2646

EVANSBURG STATE PARK
16

LOCATION - The park is 25 miles from Philadelphia via the Schuylkill Expressway along Skippack Creek. It's also 5 miles northwest of Norristown.

ACTIVITIES - Go fishing for stocked trout, bass, catfish, carp, eel, and panfish in Skippack Creek. Hike 8 kilometers of scenic hiking trails, especially during the fall when the hardwoods change.

Stop by the Fried Visitor Center, housed in a building constructed in the early 1700s, to learn about the lifestyles of German Mennonites who lived here for 190 years. Pick up a self-guided trail booklet for Old Farmstead Trail.

Picnickers have access to over 200 picnic tables.

Equestrians have access to 10 miles of designated equestrian trails plus a trailhead parking area for horse trailers.

Play golf on eighteen-hole public Skippack Golf Course. For reservations, call 215-584-4653.

Eight Arch Bridge is located in the west side of the park on Germantown Pike, U.S. 422, and is listed as a National Historic Landmark.

A youth hostel operates within the park. For information, call 215-489-4326.

Nearby attractions include downhill skiing at Spring Mount. Plant lovers can visit Spring Meadow Farms and Otts Shwenksville's greenhouses to enjoy their seasonal displays.

Valley Forge National Historic Park is 20 miles west of Philadelphia and is the site of General Washington's Continental army encampment during the winter of 1777–78 during the Revolutionary War. Take a scenic drive through the park to see its many historical markers. Begin from the visitor center at the intersection of Pennsylvania 23 and North Gulph Road. You can rent bicycles from late spring through early fall weekends. For information, call 215-783-7700.

Incoming pilots can land at Wings Airport 4 miles northwest of town. You can also land at Northeast Philadelphia, located 10 miles northeast of town, or at Philadelphia International, located 7 miles southwest of town. All airports have rental cars.

INFORMATION
Evansburg State Park
P.O. Box 258
Collegeville, Pennsylvania 19426
215-489-3729

FORT WASHINGTON STATE PARK
17

LOCATION - Fort Washington State Park is between Fort Washington and Flourtown along the Bethlehem Pike, approximately 2 miles from Pennsylvania Turnpike Exit 26 and Pennsylvania 309.

FEATURES - The park was named for the fort built here in 1777 by Continental army soldiers fighting in the American Revolution. Fort Hill, located in the park, was the western end of the army. However, today no trace of the fort remains. Militia Hill, now a day-use area, was where the Pennsylvania militia held their positions.

Clifton House, north of Fort Hill on Bethlehem Pike, was built in 1801 and now houses a library and museum. Farmar's Mill, between Fort Hill and Militia Hill on Wissahickon Creek on the Skippack Pike, has a stone grist mill built in 1684.

ACTIVITIES - Picnic at either the Flourtown or Militia Hill day-use areas with over 300 picnic tables.

The park features 3.5 miles of trails passing through woods and fields, plus a .5-mile self-guided trail at the Militia Hill picnic area.

Fish in Wissahickon Creek for trout, carp, catfish, panfish, and suckers. Attend an interpretive program, take a guided walk, or attend a stream study session.

Hope Lodge is located south of Fort Hill on Bethlehem Pike. Constructed in 1750, the lodge was used as George Washington's headquarters and now contains antique art and furnishings. For information, call 215-646-1595.

Valley Forge National Historical Park is 15 miles south of the park and is where General Washington's forces camped for six months during the winter of 1777–78. Take a self-guided tour, a bus tour, or an auto tape tour from mid-May through October. Begin at the visitor center at the intersection of Pennsylvania 23 and North Gulph Road. You can rent bicycles from late spring through early fall. For park information, call 215-783-7700.

Tour Washington's headquarters from December–March and stop by Washington Memorial Chapel. Recitals on the carillon are offered Sundays at 2:00 PM and Wednesdays at 8:00 PM July–August. For information, call 215-783-0120.

INFORMATION
Fort Washington State Park
500 Bethlehem Pike
Fort Washington, Pennsylvania 19034
215-646-2942

FRANCES SLOCUM STATE PARK
18

LOCATION - The park is in northeastern Pennsylvania, 5 miles from Dallas off Pennsylvania 309 and 10 miles from Wilkes-Barre on Frances Slocum Lake.

FEATURES - Frances Slocum was a five-year-old Quaker child kidnapped by Indians, remaining with the tribe all her life. She was married twice to Indian chieftains and had four children.

ACTIVITIES - Go boating in non-powered or electric-powered boats from two boat launches. Rent rowboats and canoes and purchase refreshments from the boat concession.

Picnic year-round at one of the 400 picnic tables. Hike the 4.5-mile trail network. Go fishing in the lake for crappie, bluegill, perch, bass, and walleye. Swimmers can swim in the guarded pool from Memorial Day through Labor Day.

During the winter, go sledding, tobogganing, ice skating, and snowmobiling along the 7-mile trail system that joins other trails maintained by local snowmobilers.

Incoming pilots can land at Wilkes-Barre/Scranton International, located 6 miles southwest of town. Rental cars are available.

INFORMATION
Frances Slocum State Park
R.D. 3, Box 183
Wyoming, Pennsylvania 18644
717-696-3525

FRENCH CREEK STATE PARK
19

LOCATION - The park is in southeastern Pennsylvania, approximately 14 miles southeast of Reading via U.S. 422. From the Pennsylvania Turnpike, take

Exit 22 at the Morgantown Interchange and go 7 miles northeast on Pennsylvania 345.

FEATURES - French Creek has three lakes: Hopewell, Scotts Run, and Six Penny.

ACTIVITIES - Camp in the campground open year-round with 200 Class-A sites and 110 Class-B sites.

Picnickers have access to over 500 picnic tables. Climb Hopewell Fire Tower to get a good look at the surrounding countryside.

Go swimming in the guarded pool at Hopewell Lake from Memorial Day through Labor Day weekend. Concessions are available nearby.

Over 32 miles of hiking trails lace the park, including 6.5 miles of Horseshoe Trail which crosses the park. Because of the hardwood trees, flowering dogwood, pink azalea, and mountain laurel, this park is a colorful spot to visit during the spring and fall.

Scotts Run Lake is stocked with trout prior to Memorial Day and again during the winter trout season. Hopewell Lake offers fishing for pike, bass, walleye, and perch.

Boating is popular on Hopewell and Scotts Run lakes in non-powered boats and registered electric-powered boats. Boat rentals are available at Hopewell Lake.

A seasonal interpretive program, including evening campfire programs and guided nature hikes, is available.

During the winter, go cross-country skiing, ice skating, ice fishing, and ice boating on Hopewell Lake.

Nearby attractions include Hopewell Village National Historical Site, located east of the visitor center. July and August feature living history demonstrations. The village is open 9:00–5:00 year-round. For information, call 215-582-8773.

Three miles southeast of the park is State Game Land 43. Struble Lake, south of Morgantown and 10 miles from the park, has additional fishing.

Incoming pilots can land at Reading Regional-General Carl A. Spaatz Field, located 3 miles northwest of town, where rental cars are available.

INFORMATION
French Creek State Park
R. R. 1, Box 448
Elverson, Pennsylvania 19520
215-582-1514

GIFFORD PINCHOT STATE PARK
20

LOCATION - Gifford Pinchot is between York and Harrisburg. It's accessible from Harrisburg via Lewisberry Exit 15 off I-83 to Pennsylvania 177 south. It's also accessible from U.S. 15 at Dillsburg, where you intersect Pennsylvania 74. From York, follow Pennsylvania 74 or I-83. From I-83, take Exit 13 onto Pennsylvania 382 heading west to Pennsylvania 177 and go south.

ACTIVITIES - The campground is one of the state's largest with 340 campsites. It opens the second Friday in April through the third Sunday in October. It has two swimming beaches and a boat launching and mooring area. You can also stay in one of the park's cabins.

Swim from two large areas located in the Conewago and Quaker Race day-use areas. Concessions are located on both beaches.

Visitors can go hiking along the nature trail. Enjoy fishing for bass, muskellunge, pike, walleye, crappie, and sunfish. Go boating in non-powered or registered electric-powered boats. Boat rentals of canoes and rowboats are available.

Over 1,100 picnic tables are located throughout the park. Ride the bridle trails and tour the visitor center to pick up a guide for Straight Hill Area and learn about its unusual diabase boulders.

Come in the winter to go ice boating, sledding, tobogganing, cross-country skiing, ice skating on Pinchot Lake, or ice fishing for walleye, muskies, crappie, and sunfish.

Incoming pilots can land at Capitol City 3 miles southeast of Harrisburg or at Harrisburg International Airport, located one mile west of town. Both have rental cars.

INFORMATION
Gifford Pinchot State Park
2200 Rosstown Road
Lewisberry, Pennsylvania 17339
717-432-5011

GOULDSBORO STATE PARK
21

TOBYHANNA STATE PARK
22

LOCATION - Gouldsboro's park entrance is .5-mile south of Gouldsboro on Pennsylvania 507.

Tobyhanna's park entrance is 2.1 miles north of Tobyhanna on Pennsylvania 423. It's also accessible from I-84 to Pennsylvania 191. Then follow Pennsylvania 507 or Pennsylvania 423.

FEATURES - Tobyhanna is named for the creek that flows into the lake and is an Indian word meaning "dark waters" because of its tannic acid. Gouldsboro was named for an early wealthy settler, Jay Gould, who by 1892 owned one of every 10 kilometers of railroad in the county.

Both state parks are located in the famous Pocono Mountains resort area.

ACTIVITIES - In Gouldsboro State Park, go boating in non-powered boats or registered electric motorboats. Go fishing in Gouldsboro Lake for muskellunge, walleye, pickerel, bass, catfish, bluegill, and perch.

An almost level, one-mile hiking trail parallels the lake shoreline. Swim from the guarded swimming area from Memorial Day through Labor Day.

Over 350 picnic tables provide plenty of picnicking opportunities. Concessions of food and boat rentals are available.

In the winter, go ice fishing and ice skating.

Tobyhanna State Park offers additional boating in non-powered craft and registered boats with electric motors. Food concessions and rental boats are available.

Fishing is popular for bass, pickerel, perch, catfish, and bluegill. Additional trout fishing is available downstream in Tobyhanna Creek.

Tobyhanna has a 140-site campground open year-round. Since it's located 2,000 feet above sea level, nights can be cool.

Swim from the guarded swimming area from Memorial Day through Labor Day and enjoy a picnic at one of the 377 picnic tables.

Hikers and bicyclists can circle Tobyhanna Lake in 5 miles, and hikers can explore an additional 5 miles of easy hiking trails.

During the winter, enjoy ice skating, ice fishing, and snowmobiling on the 5-mile trail.

Nearby attractions to the parks include Lake Wallenpaupack, meaning "the stream of swift and slow water," which is one of Pennsylvania's largest man-made lakes. Tour the PP&L Visitor Center off Pennsylvania 6 near the dam. The lake is stocked with striped bass and trout. Test your skill at a fishing derby held in mid-spring. Participate in water sports such as canoeing, rafting, jet skiing, water skiing, and swimming. Boat rentals are available.

Take scenic boat tours and dinner cruises. Contact the Spirit of Paupack at 717-857-1251 or the Wallenpaupack Scenic Boat Tour at 717-226-6211.

State Game Land 127 and Delaware Water Gap National Recreation Area form a break in the Kittatinny Ridge of the Appalachian Mountains. The Delaware River runs the entire length of the national recreation area where you can go canoeing, hiking, swimming, and attend interpretive programs. Stop by the Kittatinny Point Station located on I-80 in New Jersey.

Dingmans Falls Visitor Center, open late April through October, is off Pennsylvania 209. For information, call 717-588-6637. Rent a canoe, go whitewater rafting, or go boating on the Delaware River. Rentals are available at Dingmans Ferry. For information, call 1-800-FLOAT-KC.

INFORMATION
Gouldsboro and Tobyhanna State Parks
P.O. Box 387
Tobyhanna, Pennsylvania 18466
717-894-8336 or 717-894-8337

GREENWOOD FURNACE STATE PARK
23

LOCATION - The park is in the mountains 5 miles northwest of Belleville on Pennsylvania 305.

FEATURES - Greenwood Furnace State Park was named for the Greenwood Iron Furnace that operated here from 1833–1904. In its 127 buildings, 300 employees produced pig iron. Several original structures remain intact, including stone blast furnaces. Look for remains of slag and charcoal along several trails, including Tramway Trail and Mid-State Trail.

ACTIVITIES - Tour the visitor center to learn how iron-smelting operations were conducted. Enjoy a picnic or go swimming from the sand beach from Memorial Day through Labor Day.

Campers have a 50-site campground in the woods open from the second Friday in April through the end of antlerless deer hunting season in late December. It has a trailer dump station. Concessions are sold in the park during the summer.

Fish in Greenwood Lake, regularly stocked with trout.

Hikers have access to several trails, including a spur of the Mid-State Trail leading to the Greenwood Fire Tower. Seasonal naturalists offer guided summer hikes.

During the winter, go snowmobiling over 50 miles of state forest trails open after antlerless deer season. You can also go ice skating and cross-country skiing.

Nearby attractions include Rothrock State Forest which surrounds most of the park. Come from May through July to see rhododendron and mountain laurel in bloom. Tour a virgin hemlock preserve at Alan Seegar Natural Area. For maps, call 814-643-2340.

On Wednesdays, visit Belleville when the Amish and Mennonite bring their produce and animals to the farmers' market.

Pennsylvania State University offers an annual arts festival in July and operates the Stone Valley Recreation Area where you can go sailing, boating, hiking, fishing, and visit the nature center.

Several caves are located within an hour's drive of the park.
INFORMATION
Greenwood Furnace State Park
R.D. 1, Box 118
Huntingdon, Pennsylvania 16652
814-667-3808

HICKORY RUN STATE PARK
24

LOCATION - Hickory Run is 6 miles southeast of White Haven on Pennsylvania 534. From I-80, take Exit 41.

From the northeast extension of the Pennsylvania Turnpike, take Exit 35 and go west on Pennsylvania 950 for 3 miles, then south on Pennsylvania 534 for 6 more miles.

ACTIVITIES - The large campground has 381 campsites (without hookups) and camping supplies. It is open from the second Friday in April through the end of antlerless deer season in late December.

Swim from the guarded sand beach in the Sand Springs Day-Use Area from Memorial Day weekend through Labor Day. A refreshment stand is located at the beach.

Picnickers have 475 picnic tables. A seasonal park naturalist offers weekend campfire programs and nature walks. Stop by the visitor center for schedules.

Visit Boulder Field, listed as a National Natural Landmark, with boulders extending as far as you can see, some as long as 26 feet.

Hikers have access to 30 miles of trails leading to Boulder Field and Hawk Falls, as well as through beautiful spring-blooming shrubs of mountain laurel and rhododendron. Come in mid-October to enjoy colorful fall foliage.

Anglers will find excellent fishing in the streams and lakes, including Lehigh River, Mud Run, Fourth Run, Sand Spring, Hickory Run, and Hickory Run Lake. Nearby Francis Walters Dam, 20 minutes from the park, offers additional boating and fishing opportunities.

During the winter, snowmobile or cross-country ski along 12 miles of designated trails, ice skate, sled, and toboggan.
INFORMATION
Hickory Run State Park
R.D. 1, Box 81
White Haven, Pennsylvania 18661
717-443-9991

HILLS CREEK STATE PARK
25

LOCATION - Hills Creek State Park is 7 miles northeast of Wellsboro off Pennsylvania 6.

ACTIVITIES - The park is open year-round. Tour the visitor center and check their schedule of activities. Go swimming from a guarded beach daily from Memorial Day through Labor Day. Concessions are available nearby.

The park has 3 picnic areas. The campground has 110 campsites and a dump station, open from the second Friday in April through late December. Rent one of 10 modern cabins available year-round. Advance reservations are required.

Hikers can hike the one-mile-long Lake Side Trail past two active beaver houses. Yellow Birch Trail is ½ mile long and passes through a hardwood forest.

Go boating on Hill Creek Lake in sailboats, rowboats, and canoes or with electric motors. No gasoline-powered motors are permitted.

Anglers can fish for muskellunge, walleye, bass, bluegill, sunfish, and perch. During the winter, go ice fishing, sledding, tobogganing, and ice skating.

Incoming pilots can land at Grand Canyon State Airport, located 4 miles southwest of Wellsboro. Rental cars are available.

INFORMATION
Hills Creek State Park
R.D. 1, Box 328
Wellsboro, Pennsylvania 16901
717-724-4246

HYNER RUN STATE PARK
26

LOCATION - The park, completely surrounded by Sproul State Forest, is 6 miles east of Renovo on Pennsylvania 120 and 3 miles north of Hyner on Hyner Run Road.

ACTIVITIES - Hyner Run is stocked annually with trout. Other mountain streams also provide excellent trout fishing.

Go camping in the campground with 30 sites open year-round. A trailer dump station is available. Picnickers have access to 172 picnic tables.

Enjoy hiking the park's self-guided Twin Valley Nature Trail or along trails on nearby Sproul State Forest land. The park serves as the eastern trailhead for the 50-mile Donut Hole Trail System, which is frequently enjoyed by backpackers.

Go swimming in the pool, open Memorial Day weekend through Labor Day. Concessions are available.

In the winter, go snowmobiling on the 64-mile Hyner Mountain Snowmobile Trail.

INFORMATION
Hyner Run State Park
P.O. Box 46
Hyner, Pennsylvania 17738
717-923-0257

JACOBSBURG STATE PARK
27

LOCATION - Jacobsburg is 6 miles north of Easton. Located at the foot of Blue Mountain, it's accessible from Pennsylvania 33 at the Belfast Exit near Nazareth.

FEATURES - The park was named for the early industrial village of Jacobsburg, which was located here in the late 1790s through the 1800s.

ACTIVITIES - Only group tent sites are available by reservation. Fish for trout in Bushkill Creek. Picnickers have access to two picnic areas. Tour the Environmental Education Center and attend their interpretive programs.

Hikers can explore the 2.5-mile Homestead Trail and the 3-mile Jacobsburg Trail. Stroll along Henry's Woods self-guided nature trail to learn the area's history. Historic sites include the eighteenth-century village of Jacobsburg, Henry Gun Factory, Boulton Gun Factory, Franklin Fort, and the Henry Homestead.

During the winter, go snowmobiling and cross-country skiing on 6.5 miles of trails.

Incoming pilots can land at Easton Airport, located 4 miles north of town. It has rental cars.

INFORMATION
Jacobsburg State Park
435 Belfast Road
Nazareth, Pennsylvania 18064
215-759-7616

KETTLE CREEK STATE PARK
28

LOCATION - The park is located in a mountain valley on Kettle Creek along Legislative Route 18003, 7 miles north of Westport and Pennsylvania 120.

ACTIVITIES - Go boating in non-powered or electric-powered boats on either Kettle Creek Reservoir or on Kettle Creek Lake. A launch ramp is located at the north end of the main reservoir.

Fish in Kettle Creek Reservoir for trout, bass, bullheads, suckers, and panfish. The park is surrounded by many excellent native trout fishing streams.

Campers have 2 campgrounds, each with 40 sites, and a dump station in the lower campground. The lower campground is open from early April through deer season in December. The upper campground opens with trout season in April through mid-December. Limited groceries are available.

Many trails lace the park and backpackers have access to the 53-mile Donut Hole Trail. This trail connects with several other backcountry trails, including the Susquehannock Trail System. Maps are available at the park office. A naturalist is on duty during the summer and offers guided walks.

Swimmers have access to a 250-foot beach at the northern end of the main reservoir from Memorial Day weekend through Labor Day. Picnickers have access to 200 tables.

During the winter, go sledding, tobogganing, ice fishing for stocked trout in Kettle Creek Reservoir, ice skating, snowmobiling, and cross-country skiing.

For a breathtaking view of the park, go to Kettle Creek Vista, located 3 miles west of the park. The second weekend in October, come to Renovo for their Pennsylvania Flaming Foliage Festival. For information, call 717-923-2411.

INFORMATION
Kettle Creek State Park
HCR 62, Box 96
Renovo, Pennsylvania 17764
717-923-0206

KEYSTONE STATE PARK
29

LOCATION - Keystone is on Keystone Lake, 3 miles southeast of New Alexandria on Pennsylvania 981.

ACTIVITIES - Camp in the campground open year-round with 100 sites available from mid-April through October and 40 sites remaining open from October through mid-April, weather permitting.

Go boating in non-powered or electric boats. Boat rentals and a launch ramp are available for rowboats, sailboats, and canoes. Go swimming from the guarded beach from Memorial Day through Labor Day. Concessions are nearby.

Tour the visitor center and enjoy a picnic on one of the 443 picnic tables. Hike the park trails or fish for trout in the lake. Equestrians have access to a 2-mile bridle trail.

During the winter, come to ice fish, skate, sled, and snowmobile on the 8-mile trail network.

A nearby attraction includes the Laurel Highlands in Ligonier.

INFORMATION
Keystone State Park
R.D. 2, Box 101
Derry, Pennsylvania 15627
412-668-2939

KINZUA BRIDGE STATE PARK
30

LOCATION - Kinzua is 3.5 miles northeast of Mount Jewett off U.S. 6.

FEATURES - A 2,053-foot bridge crosses 300 feet above the Kinzua River. When originally constructed in 1882, it was the highest railroad viaduct in the world and carried Erie Railroad trains transporting lumber, coal, and oil into the Alleghenies.

ACTIVITIES - Take a ride aboard the Knox Kane Railroad excursion train or walk across the bridge for a glimpse into the Kinzua Valley. Enjoy a picnic and go fishing or hiking. Concessions are available.

INFORMATION
Kinzua Bridge State Park
c/o Bendigo State Park
P.O. Box A
Johnsonburg, PA 15845
814-965-2646

KOOSER STATE PARK
31

LOCATION - Kooser is in the eastern foothills of the Laurel Mountains, 10 miles west of Somerset on Pennsylvania 31, midway between Donegal and Somerset turnpike interchanges.

ACTIVITIES - Visitors can rent one of nine rustic cabins available year-round. Summer rentals are for one week only, while during the other seasons, weekly and half-week rentals are available. Advance reservations are required.

Camp in one of 60 campsites open year-round. Picnickers have access to over 370 picnic tables.

Swim from the guarded swimming beach from Memorial Day through Labor Day, with a refreshment concession.

Many trails cross the park, including Kincora Trail and Laurel Highland's 70-mile backpacking trail. For information, contact Laurel Ridge State Park at 412-455-3744. Forbes State Forest is nearby where you can hunt, fish, and hike.

Fish for trout, bass, and bluegill in Kooser Lake.

During the winter, cross-country ski the 1.5-mile Kooser Trail or go snow-mobiling on the park's trail that joins 70-mile Forbes State Forest's trails. Snowmobile trails are closed from September 25 through the last day of antlerless deer season. Maps are available at the park office.

Incoming pilots can land at Somerset County Airport, 4 miles northeast of town. Rental cars are available.

INFORMATION
Kooser State Park
R.D. 4, Box 256
Somerset, Pennsylvania 15501
814-733-4218

LACKAWANNA STATE PARK
32

LOCATION - Lackawanna is 10 miles north of Scranton in northeastern Pennsylvania and is accessible off I-81. Take Exit 60 and go 3 miles west on Pennsylvania 524. If traveling on U.S. 6 and 11, follow Pennsylvania 438 north for 3 miles to Pennsylvania 407 and then continue east.

ACTIVITIES - Camp in the 96-site campground with a dump station from the second Friday in April through the third Sunday in October. Swim in the pool Memorial Day through Labor Day with a food concession located nearby.

Go fishing from 7.5 miles of shoreline of Lackawanna Lake for stocked trout, muskellunge, walleye, catfish, and bass. Canoers can enjoy canoeing Kennedy Creek. Picnic at one of over 200 picnic tables.

Boaters come to sail, canoe, and row. Only non-powered and electric boats are permitted. A concession near the swimming pool has rental boats.

A park naturalist presents weekend campfire programs and summer interpretive walks.

During the winter, ice skate, cross-country ski along the hiking trails, go ice fishing, tobogganing, and sledding.

Archbald Pothole State Park is located east of the park, 9 miles north of Scranton. From Exit 57 off I-81, follow U.S. 6 for approximately 6 miles to see the world's largest glacial pothole. It's 38 feet deep and was carved 15,000 years ago during the Wisconsin Ice Age as giant glaciers receded from the area.

To learn about the iron and coal industries that flourished here, tour one of four museums making up the Anthracite Museum complex. Pennsylvania Anthracite Heritage Museum is in McDade Park, 4.5 miles south of Scranton. After your tour, take a coal mine tour. For information, call 717-963-MINE.

Steamtown National Historic Site is in Scranton on South Washington Avenue off I-81, Exit 53. The site commemorates a decade of steam railroads from 1850–1950. Ride aboard an excursion train Friday–Sunday from late May through late October. For information, call 717-961-2033.

INFORMATION
Lackawanna State Park
R.D. 1, Box 251
Dalton, Pennsylvania 18414
717-945-3239 (main office)
717-563-9995 (campground)

LAUREL HILL STATE PARK
33

LOCATION - The park is 10 miles west of Somerset off Pennsylvania 31 near Trent. To reach the park from the Pennsylvania Turnpike, take Exit 10, Somerset Exit.

You can also reach the park from the Pennsylvania Turnpike's Exit 9 at Donegal. Turn left onto Pennsylvania 31 and head east to Pennsylvania 381/711. Turn right on Pennsylvania 381/711 and go south to Champion. Turn left and follow signs to Seven Springs and Laurel Hill State Park.

FEATURES - Federal troops camped in the park during the "Whiskey Rebellion" of 1794.

ACTIVITIES - Hikers have access to 12 miles of trails. As you hike, you'll see laurel, rhododendron, sugar maples, and tulip poplars. Watch for a small stand of virgin hemlock on Hemlock trail.

Camp in the campground with 270 campsites and snacks, open from the second Friday in April through mid-October. Go boating in non-powered boats and registered electric-powered boats. No boat rentals are available.

Anglers can try their luck at landing bass, trout, catfish, bluegill, perch, crappie, and sunfish in the lake. You can also fish for trout in Laurel Hill Creek and Jones Mill Run. A guarded swim area is open from Memorial Day through Labor Day weekend. Concessions are sold near the beach.

During the winter, go snowmobiling along 10 miles of park trails. These trails connect to a 60-mile trail system in Forbes State Forest. Pick up trail maps at the park office. Ice skaters go to Laurel Hill Lake, also open to ice fishing and ice boating.

Nearby attractions in Somerset include covered bridges at Barronvale and King's Bridge. Frank Lloyd Wright's home is at Ohiopyle in Fallingwater. Pennsylvania's highest point is at nearby Mount Davis.

Incoming pilots can land at Somerset County Airport, located 4 miles northeast of town. Rental cars are available.

INFORMATION
Laurel Hill State Park
R.D. 4, Box 130
Somerset, Pennsylvania 15501
814-445-7725

LAUREL RIDGE STATE PARK
34

LOCATION - The park stretches along the Laurel Mountains from the Youghiogheny River at Ohiopyle to the Conemaugh Gorge near Johnstown.

ACTIVITIES - Most visitors come to hike along the 70-mile Laurel Highlands Trail, which extends from Ohiopyle to Johnstown. The trail crosses several state parks, state forests, and state game lands. Many hikers come in June to see mountain laurel and rhododendron in bloom. Others come when the fall colors peak in mid-October.

Trail access points are located at every major highway crossing. For a trail map, contact the state park. Overnight shelters are located every 8 to 10 miles.

Hunters come for the fall archery season through March 31.

During the winter, snowmobilers have access to a 50-mile trail system open daily after the end of the antlerless deer season in late December. Approximately 35 miles of trail are open for cross-country skiing. A 10-mile loop is adjacent to Route 653's parking area.

Incoming pilots can land at Johnstown-Cambria County Airport, located 3 miles northeast of Johnstown. Rental cars are available.

INFORMATION
Laurel Ridge State Park
R.D. 3
Rockwood, Pennsylvania 15557
412-455-3744

LAUREL SUMMIT STATE PARK
See under LINN RUN STATE PARK

LEHIGH GORGE STATE PARK
35

LOCATION - The park extends from White Haven to Jim Thorpe in eastern Pennsylvania. Public access is only available along Coalport Road on the east side of Jim Thorpe at Rockport, Lehigh Tannery, and White Haven.

To access the park from Jim Thorpe, cross the Lehigh River on Pennsylvania 903 and continue straight at the stop sign onto Coalport Road. The park's main gate is approximately ½ mile on the left.

ACTIVITIES - The park extends 26 miles beside the Lehigh River. Mountain bikers enjoy biking along the gorge trail. Stop to take a short hike up to Glen Onoko Falls to enjoy bird watching. Additional mountain biking is available on top of the towering hills of the gorge through state game lands.

Anglers can go cold water fishing, and whitewater rafters come to float.

INFORMATION
Lehigh Gorge State Park
R.D. 1, Box 284
Drums, Pennsylvania 18222
717-443-7348

LEONARD HARRISON STATE PARK
36
COLTON POINT STATE PARK
37

LOCATION - Leonard Harrison State Park is on the eastern rim of Pennsylvania's "Grand Canyon." To reach its eastern rim, follow Pennsylvania 660 west from Wellsboro for 10 miles.

Colton Point State Park is on the western rim and is 5 miles south of U.S. 6 at Ansonia.

FEATURES - Both parks are especially spectacular in mid-October when the hardwoods take on their autumn foliage.

The "Grand Canyon" begins south of Ansonia along U.S. 6 and continues for 47 miles. At both state parks the canyon is 800 feet deep, and both areas provide some outstanding scenic overlooks. Nearby Pine Creek Gorge is registered as a National Natural Landmark.

ACTIVITIES - Leonard Harrison State Park has a 30-site campground open from the second Friday in April through the third Sunday in October. Hike Turkey Path's one-mile trail to the bottom of Pine Creek Gorge. If the stream is low, cross Pine Creek and continue on to Leonard Harrison State Park. To see a beautiful waterfall, hike Little Four-Mile Run.

Picnickers have access to 95 picnic tables. A park naturalist offers summer weekend campfire programs and interpretive walks. Concessions are available.

Colton Point State Park has a 25-site campground open from the second Friday in April through the third Sunday in October. Fish for trout, bass, and panfish in Pine Creek or in nearby Marsh Creek, Asaph, Straight, and Four-Mile Run. Picnic at one of 125 picnic tables and hike 4 miles of trails.

Snowmobiles can utilize a 20-mile trail network on state forest land following the end of the antlerless deer season.

Incoming pilots can land at Grand Canyon State Airport, located 4 miles southwest of Wellsboro. Rental cars are available.

INFORMATION
Leonard Harrison State Park
R.D. 6, Box 199
Wellsboro, Pennsylvania 16901
717-724-3061

LINN RUN STATE PARK
38
LAUREL SUMMIT STATE PARK
39

LOCATION - Linn Run State Park is 10 miles southeast of Ligonier. From Ligonier, follow U.S. 30 east for 2 miles. At the intersection of Pennsylvania 381, go south for 4 miles. Turn left on Linn Run Road at the small town of Rector.

Laurel Summit State Park is southeast of Linn Run.

ACTIVITIES - At Linn Run, rent one of 10 rustic cabins, with a limited number available year-round. Weekly and half-week rentals are available during the spring, fall, and winter. During the summer, only weekly rentals are available.

Picnickers have access to 137 tables in 2 picnic areas—Adams Falls and Grove Run. Additional picnic facilities are available at Laurel Summit State Park. Hikers have access to 5 miles of hiking trails. For additional fishing and hiking opportunities, go to adjacent Forbes State Forest. For an easy hike through a mixed hardwood forest past rhododendrons and through a "garden" of large boulders, follow Beam Run Trail.

Hikers can also access Laurel Highlands Hiking Trail which traverses nearby Laurel Ridge State Park. This 70-mile backpacking trail begins at Ohiopyle and, after crossing several other state parks and game lands, continues to Johnstown. For maps and shelter locations, contact the state park at 412-455-3744.

Downhill skiers can ski at Laurel Mountain Ski Area, located 8 miles east of Ligonier. For snow conditions, call 412-238-6688. Registered snowmobiles are permitted on the state forest's 65-mile trail system.

INFORMATION
Linn Run/Laurel Summit State Parks
P.O. Box 527
Ligonier, Pennsylvania 15658
412-238-6623

LITTLE BUFFALO STATE PARK
40

LOCATION - The park is off Pennsylvania 34 between New Bloomfield and Newport.

FEATURES - The park has several historical features, including a covered bridge, remnants of a narrow gauge railroad, grist mill, and a restored tavern.

ACTIVITIES - Go boating in Little Buffalo Lake where boat rentals of paddle-boats, canoes, and rowboats are available at the concession stand. Non-powered boats and registered electric-powered boats are permitted. Two boat ramps are provided, with one near the main entrance and the other near the mooring area.

Fish for stocked trout and other warm water game fish and panfish. Hike along 7 miles of trails, including a 1.5-mile-long self-guided trail. Go for a swim in the ½-acre swimming pool open from Memorial Day through Labor Day. Concessions are sold near the pool.

Picnickers have access to 500 tables. No camping is permitted in the park, but you can stay overnight at the Blue Ball Inn.

During the winter, ice skate on the east end of the lake at the main boat launch, go ice fishing, ice boating, and cross-country skiing on 2 miles of open hiking trails or along unplowed roads.

Nearby points of interest include the Box Huckleberry Natural Area, located one mile south of New Bloomfield off Pennsylvania 34.

INFORMATION
Little Buffalo State Park
R.D. 2, Box 256
Newport, Pennsylvania 17074
717-567-9255

LITTLE PINE STATE PARK
41

LOCATION - Little Pine is 3 miles north of Waterville off Pennsylvania 44, and 4 miles southwest of English Center on Pennsylvania 284.

ACTIVITIES - The park, open year-round, has 105 campsites and a trailer dump station. Go boating with rentals available. Anglers have 3.3 miles of shoreline and 4.2 miles of stream bank fishing for stocked and native trout, bass, bluegill, catfish, and carp.

Hikers have access not only to park trails but to adjoining state forest trails, offering a total of 22.8 miles of terrain. Half-mile-long Button Ball Trail is the park's shortest trail. For a longer hike, go to 10-mile Tiadaghton Trail.

Tour the visitor center and get a schedule for their guided nature hikes, night walks, and campfire programs presented Memorial Day weekend through Labor Day.

Go swimming from the guarded sandy beach where concessions are sold. Picnickers have access to 300 picnic tables.

Hyner View's overlook provides an excellent view of the Susquehanna River and Sproul State Forest, plus a starting point for hang gliders. To reach the overlook, go 6 miles east of Renovo on Pennsylvania 120 and 3 miles north of Hyner on Hyner Run Road.

During the winter, visitors can go cross-country skiing on a 10-mile trail, sledding, tobogganing, ice fishing for trout, ice skating, and snowmobiling over 100 miles of groomed trails.

Nearby is the beautiful Grand Canyon of Pennsylvania. For an overlook into the canyon, go to Colton Point State Park or Leonard Harrison State Park. The canyon is well known for its Flaming Foliage Festival and hang gliding competitions. Visitors also come for annual canoe and kayak races on Pine Creek. The 42.2-mile Black Forest Trail is open year-round for backpacking and cross-country skiing.

INFORMATION
Little Pine State Park
HC 63, Box 100
Waterville, Pennsylvania 17776-9705
717-753-8209

LOCUST LAKE STATE PARK
42
TUSCARORA STATE PARK
43

LOCATION - Locust Lake is approximately 7 miles north of Pottsville and 3 miles south of Mahanoy City via Exit 37 off I-81. From I-81, it's 2 miles southwest of the Pennsylvania 54 interchange.

Tuscarora State Park is 6 miles northwest of Tamaqua off Pennsylvania 209. It's also south of Barnesville on Pennsylvania 54. From I-81, take Hometown Exit 37E.

ACTIVITIES - At Locust Lake State Park, enjoy camping in the wooded campground with 282 campsites plus several walk-in sites. Attend evening campfire programs and take guided nature walks from Memorial Day through Labor Day.

Go boating on Locust Lake where only non-powered and registered electric-powered boats are permitted. Camping supplies, rental rowboats, and canoes are available at the concession stand.

Locust Lake, stocked with trout, also has pickerel, bass, and panfish.

Hike trails ranging in length from ¾ of a mile to the 4-mile Oak Loop Trail which circles the ridge. Swim in the lake on the western side. Bicyclists have a bicycle trail located in the northeastern part of the park.

During the winter, ice skate, ice fish for trout, and cross-country ski.

Nearby attractions include Pioneer Tunnel and several summer stock theaters in Ashland. Barnesville is the site of the Bavarian Festival, and Weiser State Forest offers additional hiking and snowmobile trails.

At Tuscarora State Park, fish in the lake for bass, muskellunge, walleye, catfish, perch, and trout. Boat in non-powered boats and registered electric-powered boats from the boat launching area. Rentals are available. Swim from the guarded beach with concessions located nearby.

During the winter, enjoy ice skating, ice fishing, and sledding.

Incoming pilots can land at Schuylkill County Airport, located 8 miles west of Pottsville. It has rental cars.

INFORMATION
Locust Lake State Park
c/o Tuscarora State Park
R.D. Box 1051
Barnesville, Pennsylvania 18214
717-467-2404
717-467-2772 (campground summer phone)

LYMAN RUN STATE PARK
44

LOCATION - The park is 15 miles east of Coudersport and 7 miles west of Galeton off U.S. 6.

FEATURES - A mixed northern hardwood forest of maple and cherry surrounds Lyman Run Lake.

ACTIVITIES - Go boating in non-powered and registered electric-powered boats. A launching ramp is available.

Go fishing in Lyman Run Lake for trout or flyfishing in an area adjacent to the park. Go swimming in the guarded lake from Memorial Day weekend through Labor Day weekend.

Camp in one of 50 campsites with snacks and a trailer dump station available.

Hikers have access to several trails throughout the park plus the 89-mile-long Susquehannock Trail that crosses the western edge of the park.

During the winter, enjoy snowmobiling. The park serves as a trailhead for a 43-mile trail that passes through Denton Hill State Park. Go ice fishing for trout and ice skating at the swimming area.

Go both downhill and cross-country skiing at Denton Hill, located off Pennsylvania 6 midway between Galeton and Coudersport. The area has refreshments, lodging, and cross-country ski trails on adjoining forest land.

Nearby attractions include the Pennsylvania Lumber Museum located on U.S. 6 between Coudersport and Galeton. Here you'll see an early logging camp with a sawmill, steam locomotive, blacksmith shop, and bunk house.

Incoming pilots can land at Cherry Springs Airport 9 miles southwest of Galeton, but no rental cars are available.

INFORMATION
Lyman Run State Park
P.O. Box 204
Galeton, Pennsylvania 16922
814-435-6444

MARSH CREEK STATE PARK
45

LOCATION - From the Pennsylvania Turnpike, follow Pennsylvania 100 to Eagle. Marsh Creek is approximately 2 miles west of Eagle. From Downingtown, follow U.S. 322 and Pennsylvania 282 north for 5 miles.

ACTIVITIES - Enjoy swimming from Memorial Day through Labor Day. Concessions are available nearby.

Go boating in non-powered boats and registered electric-powered boats from two launch areas. Rent rowboats, canoes, and sailboats. Participate in summer sailboat races. Enjoy fishing for tiger muskies, stocked bass, catfish, crappie, and walleye.

Picnickers have access to over 200 picnic tables. Take a hike along the 6-mile trail system. Walk to the 1881 Larkins Burr Arch covered bridge in the north side of the park. Equestrians have access to 6 miles of trails. Birders enjoy coming here, especially during the spring and fall waterfowl migrations.

Although the park has no overnight camping, two privately owned campgrounds are located within one mile of the park. A youth hostel is located within the park. French Creek State Park, 20 miles from the park, has year-round camping.

During the winter, go sledding, tobogganing, ice skating, ice boating, and ice fishing.

Incoming pilots can land at Bob Shannon Memorial Airport, located 2 miles southwest of Downingtown. Rental cars are available.

INFORMATION
Marsh Creek State Park
Park Road, R.D. 2
Downingtown, Pennsylvania 19335
215-458-8515

MAURICE K. GODDARD STATE PARK
46

LOCATION - The park is 4 miles west of Franklin off U.S. 62.

ACTIVITIES - Go boating on Lake Wilhelm in non-powered boats or registered motorboats with up to 10 horsepower. The marina has fuel, concessions, and boat rentals. The park has four launch areas, with three more on State Game Land 270.

Anglers can fish for bass, walleye, pike, and muskies. Picnickers have access to 275 tables scattered throughout the park. Go hiking on 7 miles of trails along the lakeshore and through wooded and open fields.

During the winter, go ice fishing, ice skating, and ice boating. A heated comfort station is kept open in Launch Area 3. Also enjoy cross-country skiing on 4 miles of trails and snowmobiling along park roads.

Visit the McKeever Environmental Education Center located in the south end of the park. For information on their programs, call 412-376-7585.

Incoming pilots can land at Chess-Lamberton Airport, located 2 miles southwest of Franklin. Rental cars are available.

INFORMATION
Maurice K. Goddard State Park
R.D. 3, Box 74
Sandy Lake, Pennsylvania 16145
412-253-4833

McCONNELLS MILL STATE PARK
47

LOCATION - McConnells Mill State Park is located in Slippery Rock Creek Gorge, 14 miles southeast of New Castle off U.S. 19, near the intersection of Pennsylvania 19 and U.S. 422.

FEATURES - The deep gorge of the Slippery Rock Creek is a result of the Wisconsin Ice Sheet that dammed up Muddy Creek and Slippery Rock Creek. When the ice melted, glacial Lake Arthur drained into the valley, carving a 400-foot gorge.

The mill, originally water powered, was one of the first rolling mills in the country, producing corn, oats, wheat, and buckwheat. It remained in operation until 1928.

ACTIVITIES - Go whitewater boating in rubber rafts, whitewater canoes, or kayaks. Begin from Rose Point, located at old U.S. 422's bridge outside of the park, and go to Eckert's Bridge 2.5 miles downstream. The route includes a portage around the dam at the mill. You can boat another 3.5 miles of white water from here to Harris Bridge. No rafts are available for rent in the park.

Go fishing for stocked trout and bass along Slippery Rock Creek but not from the dam.

No camping facilities or swimming is available in the park because the creek is too swift and dangerous. To go swimming, go to Moraine State Park, located 8 miles northwest of Butler off U.S. 422. Their picnic areas have 166 shaded tables. For a scenic view of the gorge, go to the Cleland Rock area.

Hikers have access to approximately 7 miles of rugged trails that traverse the gorge. A 2-mile self-guided section of the Kildoo Nature Trail provides easy access to the gorge. A trail at Hells Hollow leads to a waterfall and one of two remaining iron furnaces constructed in the mid-1800s.

Two climbing and rappelling areas are available. Beginners go to Rim Road across the creek from the mill, while more advanced climbers go to Breakneck Bridge.

Take a free guided tour of the restored grist mill from Memorial Day through Labor Day from 10:00–6:00. Off-season tours are available by appointment only.

The park's covered bridge was built in 1874 to protect the inner structure from rotting and rusting away.

Incoming pilots can land at New Castle Municipal, located 4 miles northwest of town. It has rental cars.

INFORMATION
McConnells Mill State Park
R.D. 1
Porterville, Pennsylvania 16051
412-368-8091

MEMORIAL LAKE STATE PARK
48

LOCATION - The lake is 3 miles northeast of Grantville off U.S. 22 and I-81.

ACTIVITIES - Enjoy a picnic, hiking, boating, and fishing on the 85-acre lake. Canoes, rowboats, sailboards, and sailboats may be rented. Go cross-country skiing during the winter.

Tour Indian Echo Caverns at 368 Middletown Road in Hummelstown, west of Hershey. It has 45-minute guided tours to see the Indian Ballroom with its 50-foot-high ceiling. Hershey Gardens, across the street from Hotel Hershey, features seasonal floral displays.

Hershey, known for its chocolate, is south of Grantville. Visit Hershey's Chocolate World on Park Boulevard to learn how chocolate is made. For information, call 717-534-4903.

Also in Hershey, visit the Hershey Museum of American Life to see a nineteenth-century collection of Pennsylvania Dutch antiques. For information, call 717-534-3439. Hersheypark, across the street off Pennsylvania 743 and U.S. 422, has roller coaster rides plus 47 other rides. Hersheypark Arena can accommodate 7,300 spectators at its various events. For schedules, call 717-534-3911.

INFORMATION
Memorial Lake State Park
R.D. 1, Box 7045
Grantville, Pennsylvania 17028
717-865-6470

MORAINE STATE PARK
49

LOCATION - The park is 8 miles northwest of Butler off U.S. 422. Take Exit 28 or 29.

FEATURES - Moraine State Park is named for the moraine deposited by the Wisconsin Ice Sheet. Lake Arthur dates back to a glacial lake located here over 10,000 years ago when most of northwestern Pennsylvania was covered by glaciers. When the glacier melted and retreated, lake waters were released with such force that McConnells Mill Gorge was created in a very short time.

Oil was discovered in Muddy Creek Valley in 1889 and coal was mined here, leaving behind many coal mines, coal strippings, gas, and oil wells. The area was left badly polluted and, after the 1950s, was gradually reclaimed. Deep mines were sealed off, strip mines were backfilled and graded, and 422 gas and oil wells were plugged. Today the swimming beach located in the Pleasant Valley Day-Use Area is situated on one of the former strip mines.

ACTIVITIES - Over 1,200 picnic tables are scattered throughout the park. Swimmers have access to two beaches, one in the Pleasant Valley Day-Use Area and the other in the Lakeview Day-Use Area on the North Shore. Lifeguards are on duty from Memorial Day weekend through Labor Day.

Anglers fish in Lake Arthur for a variety of fish, including muskellunge, pike, bass, walleye, catfish, crappie, and bluegill.

Eleven public boat-launching areas are located on Lake Arthur, with a boating limit of 10 horsepower. Boats with higher horsepower are permitted only if the motor is tilted out of the water. Sailing is popular on Lake Arthur, with races and regattas held during the summer. Two boat concessions and boat rentals are available at the Pleasant Valley boat launching area near the swimming beach and at the Crescent Bay boating area. Motorboats, pontoons and sailboats may be rented at the Crescent Bay boating area.

Hikers have 16 miles of trails to explore. Nine-mile Glacier Ridge Trail is the longest, going to nearby Jennings Environmental Center. One-mile Garden Trail and 2-mile Hilltop Nature Trail begin from the Pleasant Valley picnic area.

Go bicycling along a 7-mile paved bicycle trail beside Lake Arthur's north shore. Begin at the bicycle rental concession by the marina restaurant.

No family campgrounds are available in the park, but 10 modern cabins inside the park are available year-round.

Tour Jennings Environmental Education Center at the intersection of Pennsylvania 8, 528, and 173 in the northeastern section of the park to see a post-glacial prairie remnant.

During the winter, go ice skating, cross-country skiing, ice boating, ice fishing, snowmobiling, sledding, or take a winter nature hike.

Incoming pilots can land at Butler County Airport, located 5 miles southwest of town. It has rental cars.

INFORMATION
Moraine State Park
R.D. 1
Portersville, Pennsylvania 16051
412-368-8811

MOUNT PISGAH STATE PARK
50

LOCATION - The park is midway between Troy and Towanda, 2 miles north of U.S. 6 in the Endless Mountains at the base of 2,260-foot Mount Pisgah.

ACTIVITIES - Go fishing in Stephen Foster Lake for stocked perch, bass, pickerel, bluegill, and crappie. Go boating from the ramp on the lake's northern shore. Non-powered boats and registered electric-powered boats are permitted. Rentals are available.

Go swimming in the large pool, guarded from Memorial Day weekend through Labor Day weekend. Concessions are available. No swimming is permitted in the lake.

Go hiking on several trails that go around the lake, through the woods, on open farmland, and past marshy areas.

During the winter, cross-country ski, snowmobile, ice skate, or go ice fishing.

Nearby points of interest include the old Methodist church constructed in the early 1800s. It's located on Steamhollow Road, 2 miles from the park.

Incoming pilots can land at Towanda Airport, one mile south of town. Rental cars are available.

INFORMATION
Mount Pisgah State Park
R.D. 3, Box 362
Troy, Pennsylvania 16947
717-297-2734

NOCKAMIXON STATE PARK
51

LOCATION - The park is 5 miles east of Quakertown on Pennsylvania 313.

FEATURES - Nockamixon Lake is 6.8 miles long and has approximately 24 miles of shoreline.

ACTIVITIES - Go swimming in the pool from Memorial Day through Labor Day with refreshments available nearby. Enjoy a picnic at one of the 500 picnic tables. Go for a bicycle ride on the 2.8-mile trail or horseback ride the 7-mile bridle trail. Bicycle rentals are available.

Anglers can fish for pike, bass, muskie, and panfish. Boaters in non-powered boats and 10 horsepower boats are permitted on the lake. If your boat has more than 10 horsepower, you can go boating if you remove the propeller and leave it ashore. Boat rentals are available.

The park has no campground, but does have a youth hostel for overnight lodging open to the general public. During the winter, go ice fishing, ice skating, boating, and sledding.

State Game Land 157 has additional hiking trails. Also, go hiking or canoeing along a 60-mile section of the Delaware Canal—built during the early and mid-nineteenth century—which lies 10 miles east of Nockamixon State Park.

Incoming pilots can land at Quakertown Airport, located 2 miles west of town. Rental cars are available.

INFORMATION
Nockamixon State Park
R.D. 3, Box 125A
Quakertown, Pennsylvania 18951
215-847-2785 (park office)
215-536-5153 (boat rentals)
215-536-8282 (bike rentals)

OHIOPYLE STATE PARK
52

LOCATION - The park is 14 miles east of Uniontown on Pennsylvania 381.

FEATURES - Ohiopyle means "white frothy water." The gorge, 1,700 feet deep, was formed when the Youghiogheny River cut through Laurel Ridge. Fourteen miles of the Youghiogheny River Gorge pass through the center of the park, providing some of the best whitewater boating in the East.

The Delaware, Shawnee, and Iroquois Indians hunted here. In 1754, George Washington sought a water supply route to enable him to capture Fort Duquesne, now called Pittsburgh. However, when he reached the falls, he abandoned his plan.

During the early 1900s, the area became famous as a summer resort, and on Sundays, the Baltimore and Ohio Railroad ran excursion trains from Pittsburgh.

ACTIVITIES - Whitewater boaters can explore two segments of the river. The lower river run begins after Ohiopyle Falls and contains Class III and IV rapids. The upper section of the river contains Class I and II white water and open canoes often run this section. Four concessionaires offer guided river tours on the lower segment, and canoe rentals are available for use on the river's upper segment.

Stop by the visitor center to learn about park programs and guided nature walks. Picnickers have access to 100 picnic tables at either Cucumber Run or Tharp Knob with its scenic overlook of the lower gorge.

Bicyclists and hikers have access to a 17-mile hardpack trail paralleling the Youghiogheny River. Rentals are available. Some visitors like to combine bicycling or hiking with wilderness trout fishing. Hikers also have access to over 41 miles of additional hiking trails plus access to the southern end of 70-mile Laurel Highlands Trail.

Bear Run Nature Preserve is 3.5 miles northeast of Ohiopyle on Pennsylvania 381, adjacent to Fallingwater. It has over 20 miles of trails for hiking, backpacking, and cross-country skiing. Stop by the Youghiogheny River gorge overlook.

Camp in the campground that is open year-round with 223 campsites and a trailer dump station. Accommodations are also available at the Ohiopyle Youghiogheny Hostel.

Go fishing for stocked fingerling trout in the Youghiogheny River. Go to Meadow Run, Bear Run, or Jonathan Run to fish smaller streams.

During the winter, go snowmobiling, sledding, and tobogganing at Sugarloaf Knob. Cross-country skiers can ski Kentuck and Sproul trails which are closed to snowmobilers.

Fort Necessity National Battlefield lies 11 miles east of Uniontown on U.S. 40. Here Colonial troops commanded by Lieutenant Colonel George Washington were defeated in 1754.

Tour Fallingwater, 3 miles northeast of town on Pennsylvania 381. It's the only Frank Lloyd Wright house with its original setting and interior furnishings intact. For house touring reservations, call 412-329-8501.

INFORMATION
Ohiopyle State Park
P.O. Box 105
Ohiopyle, Pennsylvania 15470
412-329-8591

OIL CREEK STATE PARK
53

LOCATION - Oil Creek is 4 miles north of Oil City on Pennsylvania 8. The main park entrance is one mile north of Rouseville.

FEATURES - The park tells the story of the early petroleum industry and identifies oil boom towns, important oil well ruins, Indian oil pits, and events of the original oil boom of the 1860s.

ACTIVITIES - Tour the visitor center and attend one of their environmental programs.

Hikers and bicyclists have access to a 9.7-mile paved bicycle trail through Oil Creek gorge. In addition, 32 miles of other hiking trails take visitors through the park's historic and scenic sections. Bicycle rentals are available at the old Egbert Oil Office at Petroleum Center, and trailheads are located at both Petroleum Centre and Drake Well Museum. A concession has snacks from Memorial Day through Labor Day and on weekends during the fall and spring.

Canoers arrive in Oil Creek from March–June. The river is classified as a beginner's river under normal conditions. A canoe launch point is located near Drake Well and take-out points are at Petroleum Centre, Lower Day-Use Area, and at Rynd Farm. You can canoe 13.5 miles between Drake Well and Rynd Farm.

Anglers can fish for bass and trout in Oil Creek or go to Boughton Run, Toy Run, and Jones Run.

During the winter, cross-country skiers have 15 miles of track skiing on trails located between Petroleum Centre and Plumier, as well as along the bicycle trail. Snowmobilers also utilize the hiking and biking trails. The park has a warming hut.

Nearby attractions include Drake Well Museum, located at the north end of Oil Creek State Park near Titusville. It features a full-size replica of an engine shed and derrick built over an early oil well.

Tour the visitor center at Pithole, an oil boom town in 1865, located 6 miles from the park.

Fish in stocked Two Mile Run County Park. Boaters come in canoes, rowboats, electric-powered boats, and sailboats under 14 feet. Also go hiking, horseback riding, swimming, and camping.

Visit Franklin's Pioneer Cemetery with one of the earliest marked grave sites in northwestern Pennsylvania, iron furnaces from the early 1800s, and an orchard planted by Johnny Appleseed. Pick up a map at the Chamber of Commerce, 1282 Liberty Street, Suite 2, and take a walking tour of historic Franklin. Stop by the Hoge-Osmer house at South Park and Elk streets, built in 1865. Farmers' market day is held Wednesday and Saturday on Twelfth Street.

Take a 2.5-hour narrated train ride aboard the Oil Creek and Titusville Railroad. Either begin at Perry Street Station, a restored 1892 freight house in Titusville, or from Drake Well Park. The southern terminal is at Rynd Farm, 4 miles north of Oil City. Reservations may be made by calling 814-676-1733.

Play golf in Foxburg and walk through the clubhouse's American Golf Hall of Fame and museum. The course is the oldest one in continuous use in the U.S. and has operated since 1887. For information, call 412-659-3196.

The Allegheny River has canoeing, small craft boating, and fishing. Access to the river is in Emlenton, Franklin, Oil City, and Kennerdell.

Major events in Franklin include the Applefest, which is held the first full weekend of October. The four-day festivities include a 10K run and a quilt and antique show. For details, call 814-432-5823.

An Oil Festival is held in Titusville in mid-August for 10 days and includes a parade, fireworks, dancing, and music. For details, call 814-827-2941.

Oil Heritage Week is held the last full week in July in Oil City, with a parade, athletic events, and concerts. For information, call 814-676-8521.

Incoming pilots can land at Titusville Airport, located 3 miles west of town. Rental cars are available.

INFORMATION
Oil Creek State Park
R.D. 1, Box 207
Oil City, Pennsylvania 16301
814-676-5915

OLE BULL STATE PARK
54

LOCATION - Ole Bull is 3 miles southwest of Oleona off Pennsylvania 144.

FEATURES - The park area is called the Black Forest because of its dense tree cover and was named after Ole Bornemann Bull, a famous Norwegian violinist who toured the U.S. in the 1850s. He began a castle on the hill behind the park office, but was unable to complete it.

ACTIVITIES - The park has 2 campgrounds with 81 campsites along Kettle Creek. Area 2 has 20 sites with electric hookups. Year-round camping is available.

Check the naturalist schedule for guided walks and evening campfire programs. Swim from the guarded beach in Camping Area 1 from Memorial Day through Labor Day.

Picnickers have 3 large pavilions and 100 tables. Anglers will find good trout fishing in Kettle Creek and in Old Bull Run.

Hikers can follow Daugherty Loop Trail through the Black Forest. Ole Bull Trail goes to the historic foundation remains of Ole Bull's castle and provides a panoramic view of the park. Susquehannock Trail passes through the park.

During the winter, go cross-country skiing, snowshoeing, and snowmobiling along many miles of Susquehannock State Forest trails.

Local festivities include the Maple Festival at Coudersport in early May, the State Laurel Festival in Wellsboro in mid-June, Cherry Springs Woodsmen Carnival in Cherry Springs State Park the first weekend in August, and the State Flaming Foliage Festival in Renovo the second weekend in October.

To learn about the once-active lumbering industry, visit Pennsylvania Lumber Museum along U.S. 6, 10 miles west of Galeton. Pennsylvania Grand Canyon is off U.S. 6 at Ansonia, 20 miles east of Galeton. Downhill skiers can ski at the Denton Hill Ski Area on U.S. 6, 10 miles west of Galeton.

Incoming pilots can land at Cherry Springs Airport, located 9 miles southwest of Galeton. However, no rental cars are available.

INFORMATION
Ole Bull State Park
HCR 62, Box 9
Cross Fork, Pennsylvania 17729
814-435-2169

PARKER DAM STATE PARK
55

LOCATION - Parker Dam is 4 miles east of Penfield off Pennsylvania 153 in the heart of the Moshannon State Forest.

ACTIVITIES - Camp in the 107-site campground from the second Friday in April through late December at the eastern edge of the lake or stay in one of 16 rustic cabins. Summer rentals may be made for one week to Pennsylvania residents only, and spring and fall rentals are for the week or half week. Advance reservations are required.

Tour the nature center near the beach and attend interpretive programs presented during the summer and weekends the remainder of the year. Backpackers and hikers have over 75 miles of trails to explore, including the Quehanna Trail which joins the Susquehannock Trail System above Sinnemahoning.

Boaters can launch non-powered or electric-powered boats in Parker Dam Lake. Boat rentals are available.

Swim from the guarded beach Memorial Day through Labor Day, with refreshments and picnic facilities nearby.

Fish for stocked trout in the spring and winter and for bluegill, crappie, and catfish during the summer. During the winter, come to sled, toboggan, ice skate, ice fish, and cross-country ski. Snowmobile on an extensive snowmobile trail system on state forest lands. Cross-country skis and snacks are available near the ice-skating area.

Incoming pilots can land at Clearfield-Lawrence Airport, located 2 miles northeast of Clearfield. Taxi service is available.

INFORMATION
Parker Dam State Park
R.D. 1
Penfield, Pennsylvania 15849
814-765-5082

PINE GROVE FURNACE STATE PARK
56

LOCATION - The park is at Pine Grove Furnace on Pennsylvania 233.

FEATURES - Pine Grove Furnace State Park is named for the remains of the old iron furnace, circa 1764. Fuller Lake was originally a major iron ore hole, now registered on the National Register of Historical Places.

ACTIVITIES - The park is open year-round. Go camping in one of 74 sites. Swim in one of the two lakes from sand beaches from Memorial Day weekend through Labor Day. Enjoy a picnic at one of 365 picnic tables scattered throughout the park.

Go boating from the launch on Laurel Lake in non-powered boats or registered electric-powered boats.

Anglers can fish in both Laurel and Fuller lakes for pickerel, perch, and rainbow trout. Mountain Creek is stocked with trout.

Stop by the visitor center's exhibit and check the schedule for summer guided walks and campfire programs. The park has a store, bicycle and boat rentals, and two refreshment stands. Bicyclists can cycle on a 3-mile bicycle trail beginning at the furnace, following an old railroad bed past Fuller Lake.

Hikers can hike one of the short park trails or hook up with the Appalachian Trail along Quarry Road by the furnace. Creek Trail offers good hiking in early June when mountain laurel are in bloom and again in July when the rhododendron flower.

During the winter, come to cross-country ski both on park and nearby Michaux State Forest trails, snowmobile on the extensive trail system on state forest lands, and ice skate or ice fish in Laurel Lake.

Tour the visitor center at the Huntsdale Fish Hatchery off Pennsylvania 233 north of the park.

INFORMATION
Pine Grove Furnace State Park
R.D. 2
Gardners, Pennsylvania 17324
717-486-7174

POE VALLEY STATE PARK
57

LOCATION - To reach Poe Valley from Milroy, drive northwest 6 miles on U.S. 322 to Sand Mountain Road and then go northeast 11 miles.

It's also accessible from Potters Mills by driving east on U.S. 322 for 1.5 miles to near the top of Seven Mountains Scenic Area and then 10 miles on marked state forest roads. From Millheim, drive west on Pennsylvania 45 for 1.5 miles and then follow signs south another 12 miles.

FEATURES - The park is in a mountain valley surrounded by Bald Eagle State Forest.

ACTIVITIES - Go boating on Poe Lake from two launching areas in either non-powered or electric-powered boats. Rental boats are available.

Anglers can fish in Penns Creek or in the lake for trout, crappie, catfish, pickerel, sunfish, and perch. Several other fishing streams are nearby.

Visit the nature center located behind the beach and check their program of guided walks and evening amphitheater programs.

Swim from the guarded beach at Poe Lake from Memorial Day through Labor Day. Picnic at one of 150 picnic tables located near the lake. Camp in the 78-site campground, open year-round. Poe Paddy State Forest has 43 additional campsites. A boat and food concession stand is open from Memorial Day through Labor Day.

Hikers can hike several short park trails or along a stretch of 166-mile Mid-State Trail passing through the park. Additional trails are located in Poe Paddy State Forest. Hike through the 85-meter-long Paddy Mountain Railroad Tunnel, reached by following Mid-State Trail upstream along Penns Creek. It's near the Poe Paddy State Forest picnic area.

During the winter, come to cross-country ski, sled, toboggan, ice fish, ice skate, and snowmobile. Snowmobiles have access to designated park trails as well as to state forest trails.

Nearby attractions include several scenic vistas including Penns View, Eagles Eyre, and Ingleby View. Several natural limestone caverns are located within 25 miles of the park.

INFORMATION
Poe Valley State Park
R.D. 1, Box 276-A
Milroy, Pennsylvania 17063-9735
814-349-8778 or 717-667-3622

POINT STATE PARK
58

LOCATION - This historic state park is located at the tip of Pittsburgh's Golden Triangle at the confluence of the Allegheny and Monongahela rivers. To reach it from the east or west, follow I-376 and I-279. Take Pennsylvania 8 from the north and Pennsylvania 51 from the south.

FEATURES - The two rivers join to form the Ohio River. Here the armies of France and Britain clashed in the mid-1700s, and four forts were constructed as the conflict intensified.

ACTIVITIES - A computer-driven fountain is at the tip of the peninsula and sprays its pure water 150 feet into the air from 10:00 AM until 10:00 PM from Easter through mid-November.

Attend concerts presented by the Pittsburgh Wind Symphony or ride the Monongahela or Duquesne inclines to the top of Mount Washington for an overlook of the city. The Duquesne Incline's lower station is at 1197 West Carson Street, across the river from the state park. For information, call 412-381-1665. Monongahela Incline's lower station is on West Carson Street across from Station Square dock. For information, call 412-231-5707.

Go boating on the three rivers on one of the excursion boats operated by the Gateway Clipper Fleet from the dock at Station Square. For cruise schedules, call 412-355-7979.

Three of the original bastions from the fortification of old Fort Pitt have been restored. Monongahela Bastion houses the Fort Pitt Museum, and the adjacent blockhouse is the oldest structure found in western Pennsylvania. Watch the orientation film and wander through the museum to learn some history of western Pennsylvania.

The Royal American Regiment, a reenactment group of the British army of the eighteenth century, performs at 2:30 on Sundays from mid-June through Labor Day. For information, call 412-281-9284.

Attend baseball, football, and hockey games, theater performances, and musical concerts at nearby Civic Arena. It's on Washington Place at Center and

Bedford in the Golden Triangle and features the world's first and largest retractable dome roof. For event information, call 412-642-2062.

Visitors can tour Phipps Conservatory in Schenley Park with guided tours offered Monday–Saturday at 1:00 and 2:00. For information, call 412-622-6914. Visit the animals at the Pittsburgh Zoo and Aquazoo located in Highland Park or view extinct animals at Dinosaur Hall at the Carnegie Institute and Museum at 4400 Forbes Avenue on the University of Pittsburgh's campus.

Take a walking tour of the city. For maps, contact the Visitor Information Center in downtown Gateway Center or call 412-391-6840.

Incoming pilots can land at Allegheny County Airport, 4 miles southeast of Pittsburgh; at Greater Pittsburgh International, 12 miles northwest of town; or at Pittsburgh Metro, 10 miles southwest of town. All three airports have rental cars.

INFORMATION
Point State Park
101 Commonwealth Place
Pittsburgh, Pennsylvania 15222
412-471-0235

PRESQUE ISLE STATE PARK
59

LOCATION - The park is 5 miles north of Erie on Peninsula Drive, Pennsylvania 832. Ferry service provides access from the Erie Public Dock from 10:00–7:00 Memorial Day through Labor Day.

ACTIVITIES - Presque Isle State Park is a wildlife refuge and conservation area registered as a National Natural Landmark. Open for day-use only, it offers miles of beaches. Many visitors consider the isle one of the best spots in the world for viewing sunsets. Enjoy a picnic at one of the 825 picnic tables.

Look for the Perry Monument, commemorating when Commodore Oliver Perry took command of a small American fleet here to defeat the British in the Battle of Lake Erie in 1813.

Go boating from six ramps in both non-powered and registered powered crafts. Rental boats are available at the East Boat Livery.

Go water skiing and swimming from beaches guarded from Memorial Day weekend through Labor Day. The park has the state's only surf swimming.

Go fishing in Lake Erie for perch, coho, walleye, trout, and bass. Fish for panfish, perch, bass, muskellunge, walleye, pike, and coho in Presque Isle Bay.

Stop by the nature center near Beach 3. Hikers can hike a 7-mile trail network. Concessions are sold at the East Boat Livery, Beach 6, Pettinato Beach, Budny Beach, and at Beach 11.

Nearby attractions include Flagship Niagara Historic Site, located near Misery Bay. The Niagara was Commodore Perry's flagship used in his victorious battle over the British.

Incoming pilots can land at Erie International, located 5 miles southwest of town. It has rental cars available.

INFORMATION
Presque Isle State Park
P.O. Box 8510
Erie, Pennsylvania 16505
814-871-4251

PRINCE GALLITZIN STATE PARK
60

LOCATION - The park is 16 miles northwest of Altoona off Pennsylvania 53. If coming from the north through Frugality, follow LR-11055. From Flinton, follow LR-11052 for a more direct route to the campground.

It's also accessible from U.S. 219 at Carroltown. From U.S. 219 turn onto LR-11048 and continue to Patton. From Patton, follow LR-11050 to the park.

ACTIVITIES - Go boating on Glendale Lake from the launching sites in non-powered or registered powered boats up to 10 horsepower. Concessions and boat rentals are available.

Anglers can fish for bass, pike, muskellunge, and stocked trout in the lake's two major feeder streams. Go swimming from the guarded beach from Memorial Day through Labor Day. Picnickers have access to 1,314 picnic tables.

Stay in one of the 10 rental cabins available year-round. Advance reservations are required. Camp in the 437-site campground open from the second Friday in April through antlerless deer season in mid-December.

Hikers have access to 9 miles of trails. Equestrians have a bridle trail to explore.

Visit the Environmental Education Center to check their schedule of summer activities. During the winter, cross-country ski on 7 miles of marked trails. Registered snowmobiles have access to 20 miles of trails. Go sledding, toboganing, ice boating, ice skating, and ice fishing. An annual ice-fishing derby is held.

Incoming pilots can land at Altoona-Blair County Airport, located 12 miles south of Altoona. Rental cars are available.

INFORMATION
Prince Gallitzin State Park
R.D. 1, Box 79
Patton, Pennsylvania 16668

814-674-3691 (main office)
814-687-4355 (campground office)

PROMISED LAND STATE PARK
61

LOCATION - Promised Land is 10 miles north of Canadensis on Pennsylvania 390 in the heart of the Poconos.

ACTIVITIES - Camp in one of over 500 campsites in 4 campgrounds: the Pines, Lower Lake, Pickerel Point, and Deerfield. All campgrounds are close to swimming, boating, fishing, and hiking. Pickerel Point campground is open year-round.

Stay in one of 12 rustic cabins. During the summer, cabin rentals are restricted to Pennsylvania residents for one-week periods.

Swim from three guarded beaches from Memorial Day through Labor Day. A refreshment concession is in the picnic area near the main beach. Picnic at over 300 picnic tables scattered through the woods.

Anglers can fish in two lakes, Promised Land Lake and Lower Lake, for bass, pickerel, walleye, muskellunge, perch, and catfish.

Hikers have access to 23 miles of hiking trails. Bruce Lake Trail leads to a natural glacial lake. Equestrians can ride along snowmobile trails and hiking trails. During the summer, park naturalists offer daily nature hikes and weekend campfire programs. Tour the small nature museum.

Boaters can boat either in non-powered or registered electric-powered boats on both lakes. The park has five boat-launching areas, with boat rentals at Promised Land Lake.

During the winter, snowmobile on the park trail network, go cross-country skiing, ice fishing, and ice skating. Delaware State Forest, which surrounds the state park, has 80 miles of roads and trails designated for snowmobiling. Maps are available. Call 717-424-3001 for information.

Nearby attractions include George W. Childs Park and Lake Wallenpaupack, which offers boating and fishing for trout and warm water fish. Visit Delaware Water Gap National Recreation Area, located along Silver Lake Road 2 miles west of Dingman's Ferry. Tour the visitor center on I-80 in New Jersey and go fishing, swimming, canoeing, hiking, and rock climbing. For information, call 717-588-6637.

Incoming pilots can land at the Flying Dollar Airport, 2 miles north of Canadensis. No rental cars are available.

INFORMATION
Promised Land State Park
R.D. 1, Box 96
Greentown, Pennsylvania 18426
717-676-3428

PYMATUNING STATE PARK
62

LOCATION - The park's southern end is 4 miles north of Jamestown off U.S. 322. Its western end is near Linesville on U.S. 6.

FEATURES - The name Pymatuning is believed to be Iroquois and means "the crooked-mouthed man's dwelling place."

ACTIVITIES - Go boating on Pymatuning Reservoir. Boats with motors over 10 horsepower are permitted if the propeller is removed and left on shore. The park has boat rentals.

Go fishing in the lake for stocked walleye, muskellunge, carp, crappie, and bass. Visit the protected wildlife refuge to watch migratory waterfowl. Visit the dam, fish hatchery, two causeways crossing the lake, and the waterfowl museum. The Linesville "spillway" is where fish are fed and are so abundant that the ducks reportedly walk on the fishes' backs to compete for the food.

The campground is one of the largest in the state with 832 campsites located in four areas. Its group camping area can accommodate up to 400 campers. Modern tent and trailer campgrounds are in the Jamestown and Tuttle campgrounds where 85 sites have electrical hookups.

Visitors can picnic all around the lake, hike short trails near the dam, tour the visitor center, and eat in the park restaurant. Swimmers have access to four areas guarded from Memorial Day through Labor Day. Concessions are sold at three of the beaches: Tuttle, Jamestown No. 1, and Linesville.

Tour Pymatuning Wildlife Museum on Ford Island, south of Linesville, to see over 400 mounted birds and mammals.

During the winter, go ice boating, ice fishing, ice skating, sledding, cross-country skiing, and snowmobiling. The park hosts the Annual National Dog Sled Races and Annual Snow Fun Days. Winter concessionaires provide refreshments and rent ice skates, cross-country ski equipment, and snowmobiles.

Pymatuning State Park in Ohio is located on the western shore of Pymatuning Reservoir where additional fishing, hiking, camping, swimming, and boating are available. Pymatuning Deer Park is .5-mile east of Pennsylvania 322 on Pennsylvania 58 where you can see ostriches, mountain lions, and llamas. Also, stop by the petting zoo and take a train or pony ride. For information, call 412-932-3200.

INFORMATION
Pymatuning State Park
P.O. Box 425
Jamestown, Pennsylvania 16134
412-932-3141

RACCOON CREEK STATE PARK
63

LOCATION - Raccoon Creek is 2 miles north of Frankfort Springs on Pennsylvania 18 and 25 miles west of Pittsburgh via U.S. 22 and 30.

FEATURES - Raccoon Creek is one of the state's largest and most beautiful parks, and Historic Frankfort Mineral Springs was a nationally known health spa during the 1800s. Today you can still see the springs from a scenic self-guiding trail.

ACTIVITIES - Go boating in non-powered and electric-powered boats. A boat launch area, boat rentals, and refreshments are available.

Park naturalists offer guided walks from April–October plus summer weekend evening campfire programs.

Hikers have access to several miles of trails, including the Wildflower Reserve on the park's eastern boundary. Equestrians have access to 3 miles of trails. Camp in the campground with 161 campsites open year-round.

Swim from the guarded beach Memorial Day through Labor Day weekend. Refreshments are located nearby. Approximately 600 picnic tables are located in 5 picnic areas.

Anglers can fish for bluegill, bass, perch, catfish, and crappie. Trout are found both in the lake and in feeder streams. Visit State Game Lands 189 and 117 for additional recreational opportunities. During the winter, go ice fishing, ice skating, and sledding. Look for spectacular ice formations at the Frankfort Mineral Springs.

Incoming pilots have access to three airports near Pittsburgh: Allegheny County, 4 miles south of town, Greater Pittsburgh International, 12 miles northwest of town, and Pittsburgh Metro, 10 miles southwest of town. All three airports have rental cars available.

INFORMATION
Raccoon Creek State Park
R.D. 1, Box 329
Hookstown, Pennsylvania 15050
412-899-2200

RALPH STOVER STATE PARK
See under ROOSEVELT STATE PARK

RAYMOND B. WINTER STATE PARK
64

LOCATION - The park is located in central Pennsylvania on Pennsylvania 192, 16 miles west of Lewisburg.

ACTIVITIES - Come when the mountain laurel and rhododendron are in bloom and in the fall to enjoy the fall foliage.

Fish for stocked trout in Halfway Lake and along Rapid Run. Additional fishing is available in the lower portion of Penns Creek and in Walker Lake.

Camp in one of 60 campsites available from the second Friday in April through the end of antlerless deer season in late December. Seasonal concessions are available.

Hike along 6.3 miles of trails or begin your backpacking trip along Mid-State or Brush Hollow trails.

Picnickers have access to approximately 350 picnic tables. Swimming is available from a guarded beach from Memorial Day through Labor Day.

During the winter, cross-country ski along 5 miles of park trails which connect with additional trails and roads in the surrounding state forest. Snowmobilers have access to 30 miles of trails in the northern division of the Bald Eagle State Forest.

INFORMATION
R. B. Winter State Park
R. D. 2, Box 377
Mifflinburg, Pennsylvania 17844
717-966-1455

RICKETTS GLEN STATE PARK
65

LOCATION - The park is 4 miles north of Red Rock on Pennsylvania 487. Because the section of Pennsylvania 487 from Red Rock to Lake Jean is a very steep road, trailers are advised to enter the park via Pennsylvania 487 south from Dushore.

FEATURES - Ricketts Glen is named for Colonel Robert Bruce Ricketts who led Battery F for the Union army in Rickett's Charge during the Battle of Gettysburg.

The Glens Natural Area, a registered National Natural Landmark, is one of the park's main attractions. Two branches of Kitchen Creek run through deep gorges of Ganoga Glen and Glen Leigh and, after uniting at Waters Meet, continue through Ricketts Glen. Many trees in the park are over 500 years old and tower over 100 feet.

Over 30 waterfalls are found in the park, formed as Kitchen Creek winds through three steep park gorges. Ganoga Falls tumble 94 feet and are the highest of over 22 named waterfalls in the park.

ACTIVITIES - Boaters with non-powered boats and registered electric-powered boats are permitted on Lake Jean. Boat rentals of rowboats and canoes are available.

Anglers can fish in Lake Jean and several park creeks have trout. Mountain Springs Lake, adjacent to the eastern part of the park, has trout and panfish.

Camp in one of 101 campsites or rent one of 10 modern cabins available year-round. Advance reservations are required.

Swim from the guarded beach from Memorial Day through Labor Day. Concessions and picnic facilities are available nearby.

Equestrians have access to 5 miles of bridle trails and hikers can explore 20 miles of trails. Seven miles of trails parallel streams flowing to Glens Natural Area. Evergreen Trail provides an excellent view of a series of waterfalls. Five miles of trails follow Kitchen Creek as it winds through the park.

Naturalists offer summer campfire programs and guided nature walks. Picnickers will find extensive facilities in Lake Jean area and in the park's lower area off Pennsylvania 118. During the winter, snowmobile on the 21-mile-long snowmobile trail, ice fish in Lake Jean, ice skate, go sledding, and winter camp.

Incoming pilots can land at Bloomsburg Municipal Airport located east of town. Taxi service is available.

INFORMATION
Ricketts Glen State Park
R.D. 1, Box 251
Benton, Pennsylvania 17814
717-477-5675

RIDLEY CREEK STATE PARK
66

LOCATION - Ridley Creek State Park is 16 miles southwest of Philadelphia. The main park entrance is on Pennsylvania 3, 2.5 miles west of Newtown Square. Another access is from Gradyville Road east of Pennsylvania 352.

FEATURES - A small eighteenth-century village called Bishop's Mill and Upper Providence Corn Mill occupied the area now known as Sycamore Mills. The park is designated as the Ridley Creek Historic District by the National Register of Historic Places.

ACTIVITIES - The park is open for day-use only and has over 950 picnic tables located in 14 picnic areas. Anglers can fish in trout-stocked Ridley Creek. Sycamore Mills Dam at the mouth of Dismal Run is open for flyfishing only. Park naturalists offer year-round programs.

Hikers have access to 12 miles of trails. Those in the park's southern end join the Tyler Arboretum property which has horticultural collections and historical buildings open to the public. For information, call 215-566-5431.

Bicyclists can cycle along a 5-mile bicycle trail, while equestrians have a separate 4.7-mile trail. The park has a stable with rental horses. For information, call 215-566-0942.

During the winter, cross-country skiers use the hiking, bicycle, and bridle trails. Others come to sled and toboggan on the slope next to Picnic Area 13.

Tour the Colonial Pennsylvania Plantation to visualize life on a Delaware County Quaker farm in 1776. For information, call 215-566-1725.

Incoming pilots can land at Brandywine Airport, located 3 miles northeast of West Chester. Rental cars are available.

INFORMATION
Ridley Creek State Park
Sycamore Mills Road
Media, Pennsylvania 19603
215-566-4800

ROOSEVELT STATE PARK
67
RALPH STOVER STATE PARK
68

LOCATION - Roosevelt State Park is located along the Delaware Canal at Upper Black Eddy in eastern Pennsylvania.

Ralph Stover State Park is located along Tohickon Creek south of Roosevelt State Park, 2 miles north of Point Pleasant on State Park Road and Stump Road.

FEATURES - Delaware Canal, a National Historic Landmark, is the only continuously intact remnant of the towpath canals constructed in the early to mid-nineteenth century. When active, approximately 33 million tons of coal was transported along its length.

Ralph Stover State Park has a water-powered grain mill used in the late eighteenth century. Its High Rocks section features a horseshoe bend in Tohickon Creek that was named by the Lene-Lenape Indians and means "deer-bone creek."

ACTIVITIES - Come to Roosevelt State Park to enjoy picnicking, fishing, canoeing with rentals available, and hiking along the 60-mile-long canal. Go cross-country skiing in the winter. Ride on a mule-drawn boat from New Hope, south of the park. The boats cover approximately 4.5 miles and run from Memorial Day through Labor Day.

Ralph Stover State Park offers fishing for bass, sunfish, carp, eel, and stocked trout. Hike the trail to High Rocks overlook where experienced rock climbers climb the 200-foot sheer cliffs. Stay in one of 6 rental cabins available from the second Friday in April through the end of antlerless deer season in late December. Half-week rentals are available for the spring and fall.

When water is high, Tohickon Creek has white water for rubber rafts, closed deck canoes, and kayaks.

INFORMATION

Roosevelt State Park
Box 615A, R.R. 1
Upper Black Eddy,
   Pennsylvania 19872
215-982-5560

Ralph Stover State Park
R.D. 1, Box 209
Pipersville, Pennsylvania 18947
215-297-5090

RYERSON STATION STATE PARK
69

LOCATION - Ryerson Station is one mile south of Wind Ridge off Pennsylvania 21, on Pennsylvania Legislative 30039.

FEATURES - The park is open year-round. Camp in the 50-site campground from the second Friday in April through the end of antlerless deer season in late December.

Anglers can fish for stocked trout and warm water game fish in R. J. Duke Lake. Go boating in both non-powered and registered electric boats from the launch ramp near the park office. Gasoline motors are prohibited. Boat rentals are available next to the swimming pool.

Swim from the guarded pool from Memorial Day through Labor Day. Food concessions are sold in the pool area. Enjoy a picnic at one of over 300 picnic tables scattered throughout the park.

Park naturalists offer nature hikes and campfire programs on Saturdays and summer holidays. Hikers can hike a 10-mile hiking trail network.

Winter sports include ice skating, ice fishing, sledding, cross-country skiing along the hiking trails, and snowmobiling along 6 miles of trails.

Incoming pilots can land at Washington County Airport 3 miles southwest of town. Rental cars are available.

INFORMATION

Ryerson Station State Park
R.D. 1, Box 77
Wind Ridge, Pennsylvania 15380
412-428-4254

S. B. ELLIOTT STATE PARK
70

LOCATION - The park is 9 miles northwest of Clearfield on Pennsylvania 153, north of Exit 18 off I-80.

ACTIVITIES - Hikers have access to 20 miles of hiking trails. Originally a local road, 2½-mile-long Old Horse Trail offers a two-hour walk through mountain laurel and an original white pine and hemlock forest. To see lots of plant life, hike Lick Run Trail paralleling Lick Run Stream. Additional hiking is available on Quehanna Trail.

Tour the visitor center, camp in the 25-site primitive campground with a trailer dump station or rent one of 6 rustic cabins.

Enjoy uncrowded fishing conditions for native and stocked trout in several small mountain streams.

INFORMATION
S. B. Elliott State Park
c/o Parker Dam State Park
R.R. 1, Box 165
Penfield, Pennsylvania 15849
814-765-0630

SHAWNEE STATE PARK
71

LOCATION - Shawnee State Park is 9 miles west of Bedford off U.S. 30.

ACTIVITIES - Go boating in non-powered boats and registered electric boats from two boat-launch areas. Boat rentals are available. Attend evening campfire programs and nature walks conducted by park naturalists. Swim from the guarded beach from Memorial Day through Labor Day. Concessions are available nearby.

Camp in the 300-site campground, 19 with electrical hookups and a dump station. It's open from the second Friday in April through the end of the antlerless deer season in late December. A camp store is open from Memorial Day through Labor Day.

Fish in Shawnee Lake stocked with bass, pike, walleye, muskellunge, perch, and bullhead. Hikers have access to a 12-mile trail system, and picnickers can choose from 700 picnic tables.

During the winter, go ice skating, ice fishing, ice boating, sledding, tobogganing, and snowmobiling on an 11-mile trail network. Downhill and cross-country skiers can ski at Blue Knob Ski Area in Blue Knob State Park 25 miles from the state park.

Visit Coral Caverns at Manns Choice off Pennsylvania 31, 7 miles west of Bedford. In Bedford, stop by the historic Anderson House at 137 East Pitt Street. Pick up a guide to see over 50 historic houses. Espy House, circa 1766, is at 123 East Pitt and served as Washington's headquarters during the Whiskey Rebellion in 1794.

Fort Bedford is a reproduction of the 1700s British garrison, and Old Bedford Village features over 40 authentic buildings constructed between 1750–1850. The old village is on Pennsylvania 220 South, ½ mile south of Pennsylvania Turnpike's Exit 11. Pendergrass Tavern serves lunch daily, and summer stock theater presentations are offered summer weekends. The village is open 9:00–5:00 from the first Saturday in May until the last Sunday in October. For information, call 1-800-622-8005.

U.S. 30 is located along the old Forbes Trail which was once used as the main highway between Fort Bedford and Fort Ligonier in the 1700s. Along the way, you'll pass many small settlements and original inns plus 14 covered bridges.

Incoming pilots can land at Bedford Airport, located 3 miles north of town. Rental cars are available.

INFORMATION
Shawnee State Park
P.O. Box 67
Schellsburg, Pennsylvania 15559
814-733-4218

SINNEMAHONING STATE PARK
72

LOCATION - The park is 10 miles north of Sinnemahoning. Follow Pennsylvania 872 north 8 miles from its intersection with Pennsylvania 120 in Sinnemahoning.

FEATURES - Sinnemahoning is an Indian word meaning "rocky lick." The lick, located near the mouth of Grove Run, supplied game animals with salt.

ACTIVITIES - Go boating in non-powered boats and registered electric-powered boats. Go fishing in First Fork Sinnemahoning Lake for trout, bass, bluegill, walleye, and muskellunge. You can also fish the nearby creeks and runs.

Camp in the 40-site campground and hike the trails. Swim from the guarded beach from Memorial Day through Labor Day. Each July, the annual Sinnemahoning Rattlesnake Hunt attracts many participants.

Snowmobilers have access to park trails which connect with 25 miles of additional trails in the Elk State Forest at Brooms Run Road. Go ice fishing, with an annual ice fishing contest held in late January.

A nearby attraction includes Bucktail State Park, located along a 75-mile scenic drive on Pennsylvania 120 between Emporium and Lock Haven. Come to see mountain laurel blooming in the spring and to gain access to several major hiking and backpacking trails. Go fishing in the adjacent state forests.

INFORMATION
Sinnemahoning State Park
R.D. 1, Box 172
Austin, Pennsylvania 16720
814-647-8945

TOBYHANNA STATE PARK
See under GOULDSBORO STATE PARK

TROUGH CREEK STATE PARK
73

LOCATION - Trough Creek State Park is in Trough Creek Gorge, 3 miles north of Trough Creek off Pennsylvania 994 and 5 miles east of Pennsylvania 26.

FEATURES - The park is completely surrounded by Rothrock State Forest and has an old iron furnace plus a Civilian Conservation Corps camp.

ACTIVITIES - Go hiking along a 16-mile trail network through stream bottom hollows and up hillsides for ridge-top vistas. Abbott Run Trail is a popular trail, following Trough Creek to a deep ravine to cross the stream en route to Balanced Rock. In the spring, come here to see the park's waterfalls. Pick up a folder describing Ice Mine, Balanced Rock, and Copperas Rock—all accessible by trail.

Picnickers have access to 325 tables. The park has 30 campsites and a trailer dump station available from the second Friday in April through the end of antlerless deer season in late December.

Tour the visitor center located in one of the historic buildings. Stream fish in Trough Creek for trout, bass, suckers, and sunfish. Hike Lakeside Trail to reach the shoreline of 30-mile-long Raystown Lake where visitors can go boating and camping.

During the winter, go cross-country skiing and snowmobiling. Additional trails are located on state forest lands. Pick up a snowmobile trail map from the park office.

Nearby attractions include Warriors Path State Park, located 12 miles southwest of Trough Creek State Park. This park is near the famous path utilized by the Iroquois Indians while they raided other tribes in southern Pennsylvania. Go fishing, hiking, or have a picnic here.

Take a one-hour tour of Lincoln Caverns in Huntingdon. Annual ghosts and goblins tours are offered in October. For information, call 814-643-0268.

INFORMATION
Trough Creek State Park
R.D. 1
James Creek, Pennsylvania 16657
814-658-3847

TUSCARORA STATE PARK
See under LOCUST LAKE STATE PARK

TYLER STATE PARK
74

LOCATION - Tyler State Park is west of Newtown. From the Pennsylvania Turnpike, take Exit 27 and follow Pennsylvania 332 east from Willow Grove through Richboro. From Exit 28, follow U.S. 1 north to I-95. Follow I-95 north to the Newtown-Yardley Exit. Drive west through Newtown on Pennsylvania 332 to reach the park.

ACTIVITIES - Children have six special play areas designed just for their fun. Two are built to resemble miniature farms, while two others have rustic log observation towers. Go fishing from the banks of Neshaminy Creek or from a canoe for sunnies, crappie, carp, and bass.

Rent a canoe from the concession stand from Memorial Day weekend through Labor Day weekend. Only registered motorboats with electric motors are permitted.

Picnickers have access to over 500 picnic tables located in 7 picnic areas.

Visitors have access to 4 miles of hiking trails, 10.5 miles of paved bicycle trails, and 9 miles of bridle trails. Additional hiking is available across Neshaminy Creek on the park's west side. Also, a youth hostel provides accommodations for hiking and bicycling travelers.

Equestrians have a parking area in a lot on Pennsylvania 332 across from the Spring Garden Mill, off Swamp Road near the county's longest covered bridge.

During the winter, go ice fishing and ice skate near the boathouse warming area. Also enjoy sledding, tobogganing, or cross-country skiing.

INFORMATION
Tyler State Park
Department of Environmental Resources
Newton, Pennsylvania 18940
215-868-2021

WORLDS END STATE PARK
75

LOCATION - The park is 7 miles northwest of Laporte on Pennsylvania 154.

FEATURES - The park is in the narrow S-shaped valley of Loyalsock Creek. Since the first valley road was located high on the steep mountain slope, early travelers felt they were surely at the "end of the world."

ACTIVITIES - Rent one of 19 cabins available for half or full weeks in the spring and fall and for one-week periods only during the summer. Camp in the 70-site campground on Pennsylvania 154. Swim by the small dam where lifeguards are on duty from Memorial Day through Labor Day. Concessions are available.

Whitewater kayakers come to Loyalsock Creek. Be sure to check on water levels prior to arriving. The water is not suitable for open canoes. Anglers can fish the Loyalsock for stocked trout most of the year.

Sightseers go to Canyon Vista via Mineral Spring and Cold Run Roads and to High Knob Overlook to get a good look at the mountainous terrain. If possible, arrive during the June mountain laurel blooming time or when the fall foliage peaks.

Hikers have access to 57-mile Loyalsock Trail which goes from Pennsylvania 87 near Loyalsockville to U.S. 220 north of Laporte. For details, contact the Alpine Hiking Club, P.O. Box 501, Williamsport, Pennsylvania 17701. The park also has several shorter, steep trails.

During the winter, go snowmobiling both in the park and on nearby state forest land. One trailhead is located along Double Run Road to Eagles Mere south of the park. Another trailhead is by the campground.

Cross-country skiers have an 8-mile trail network in the park and on nearby Wyoming State Forest land. Cross-country ski rental equipment is available.

INFORMATION
Worlds End State Park
P.O. Box 62
Forksville, Pennsylvania 18616-0062
717-924-3287

YELLOW CREEK STATE PARK
76

LOCATION - Yellow Creek is 18 miles northwest of Ebensburg on U.S. 422.

FEATURES - The park is located along one of the state's first "highways," the Kittanning Path, which was originally used by the Delaware and Shawnee Indians and later by early settlers. Now U.S. 422 follows this old Indian path.

ACTIVITIES - Yellow Creek Lake is open to boaters with motors not exceeding 10 horsepower, sailboats, canoes, and rowboats. Boat rentals are available. Four boat-launching ramps are available, located on the north and south shores by the Beach/Day-Use Area and at Grampap's Cove.

Swim from the guarded beach Memorial Day through Labor Day. Anglers can fish in Yellow Creek Lake for bass, walleye, muskellunge, pike, perch, and catfish. Laurel Run, Yellow Creek, and Little Yellow Creek are stocked with trout.

Hikers have three trails to explore: .5-mile Laurel Run, 2-mile Ridgetop Trail, and 2.5-mile Damsite Trail.

No family campsites are available, but two private campgrounds are adjacent to the park.

During the winter, ice fish for sunfish, perch, and pike. Visitors can also go sledding, tobogganing, snowmobiling on a trail beginning from the Beach/Day-Use Area, or ice skating, ice boating, cross-country skiing, and snowshoeing.

Incoming pilots can land at Ebensburg Airport, located 3 miles southwest of town. Rental cars are available.

INFORMATION
Yellow Creek State Park
R.D. 1, Box 145-D
Penn Run, Pennsylvania 15765
412-463-3850

RHODE ISLAND

Anglers come to Rhode Island for its great fishing. To catch white marlin, come in July–August; for swordfish in June–July; for school tuna in July–September; for giant tuna from June–October; and year-round for cod. Trout season opens the second Saturday of April at sunrise.

Rhode Island boasts miles of wide, sandy beaches, including Misquamicut, Matunuck, Scarborough, and Narragansett.

Many state parks offer special concerts and theater and dance performances along with their regular naturalist programs. For information, call 401-277-2632.

Drive U.S. 1, a section of the New England Heritage Trail between Westerly and Pawtucket. Pick up a map at any of the state's information centers.

ARCADIA STATE PARK
1

LOCATION - The park is on Arcadia Road off Rhode Island 165, west of Exeter.

ACTIVITIES - Enjoy a picnic, camp in the campground, go boating, fishing, and hike the nature trails. Visit Stepping Stone Falls.

Kenyon Grist Mill, circa 1776, is an historic grist mill located off Rhode Island 138 in Usquepaugh at the Richmond-South Kingstown town line. Tours are offered.

Attend South County Hot Air Balloon Festival in South Kingstown in July.

Go downhill skiing at Rhode Island's only ski area at Yawgoo Valley by Exeter. For information, call 401-295-5366. During the summer, come here to enjoy canoeing and kayaking from March–October.

Fisherville Brook Wildlife Refuge is on Pardon Joslin Road and offers 70 acres with trails winding through the forest to a dammed pond and waterfall.

INFORMATION
Arcadia State Park
Exeter, Rhode Island 02822
401-539-2356

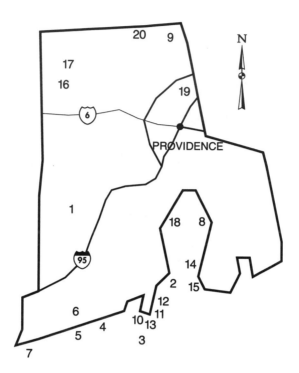

N

BEAVERTAIL STATE PARK
2

LOCATION - From Rhode Island 1 south, take Rhode Island 138 east to North Road. The park is on Beavertail Road in Jamestown.

ACTIVITIES - Visit the granite tower, north of the site for the original lighthouse erected in 1749. From this point, you get a spectacular vista of Rhode Island's Atlantic coastline. Naturalists are on duty from the end of June through the end of August and offer lectures and tours. For information, call 401-423-9920. Tour the Beavertail Lighthouse Museum located in the Assistant Keeper's House, open mid-June through Labor Day on Wednesday–Sunday from 9:00–5:00. For information, call 401-423-9941. Go fishing and hiking.

To see historic Jamestown Windmill, circa 1787, follow North Road off Rhode Island 138. Recently restored, it's open mid-June through September weekends from 1:00–4:00 and by appointment. Call 401-423-1798.

Drive up Prospect Hill off Beavertail Road to reach the island's second highest point and a Revolutionary earthworks battery.

INFORMATION
Beavertail State Park
c/o Goddard Memorial State Park
Ives Road
Warwick, Rhode Island 02818
401-423-9941 (seasonal)

BLOCK ISLAND BEACH STATE PARK
3

LOCATION - The beach is on Block Island.

ACTIVITIES - Catch a car ferry to the island year-round from Galilee. Ferries also depart from Providence and Newport from late June through early September. Reservations for ferries from Galilee and Providence should be made a week in advance. For information, call 401-789-3502 or 401-421-4050.

Enjoy a picnic and go saltwater fishing and swimming in Block Island Sound. Concessions are available. Watch for the many birds flying along the Atlantic Flyway, especially in the spring and fall. Take a hike to Rodman's Hollow, one of the island's five wildlife refuges, to see a deep, cool ravine left behind by glaciers.

Visit Mohegan Bluffs that rise approximately 200 feet above the sea. The Southeast Lighthouse, circa 1875, which is located on the bluffs, has the most powerful electric beacon on the eastern U.S. coast. North Light is located at Sandy Point on the island's northern tip.

Settlers' Rock is on the shore of Cow Cove. The monument lists the names of Block Island's first settlers who landed here in April 1661.

Follow the Maze, an 11-mile path that meanders through pine forests to emerge at cliffs at the northeast end of the island.

Incoming pilots can land at Block Island State Airport, located one mile west of the city. Rental cars are available.

INFORMATION
Block Island State Park
New Shoreham, Rhode Island

BRENTON POINT STATE PARK
See under FORT ADAMS STATE PARK

BURLINGAME STATE PARK
See under CHARLESTOWN BREACHWAY STATE PARK

CHARLESTOWN BREACHWAY STATE PARK
4
EAST BEACH STATE PARK
5
BURLINGAME STATE PARK
6
MISQUAMICUT BEACH STATE PARK
7

LOCATION - East Beach State Park's 3-mile-long beach is off East Beach Road in Charlestown, in the Ninigret Conservation Area. Charlestown Breachway is 5 miles south of Charlestown via U.S. 1 and Charlestown Breachway Road. Burlingame State Park is 5 miles west of Charlestown off U.S. 1.

Misquamicut Beach is 5 miles south of Westerly off Rhode Island 1A.

ACTIVITIES - At Charlestown Breachway, go camping in one of 75 campsites available for self-contained vehicles only from mid-April through the end of October. Go boating from the ramp in the pond which opens to the ocean. Enjoy excellent saltwater and shell fishing and swimming with lifeguards available.

At East Beach, go camping in one of 20 campsites for self-contained units only from mid-April through the end of October. Enjoy a picnic, saltwater and shell fishing, and swimming in the Atlantic Ocean with lifeguards available. Attend naturalist programs.

Additional fishing is available at Quonochontaug Beach. Watch for some prestigious homes along the central part of the beach.

At Burlingame, camp under the trees in the 755-site campground from mid-April through the end of October along the shore of Watchaug Pond. Go boating from the ramp and fishing in Watchaug Pond. Bring along a picnic to enjoy at one of 126 picnic tables. Take a hike along the trails. Go swimming with seasonal lifeguards on duty. Attend summer concerts held by the camp store.

At Misquamicut, go surfing, saltwater fishing, and swimming in Block Island Sound, enjoy a picnic at one of 50 picnic tables, and go swimming from the long, sandy beach. Concessions are available. Ride the carousel. Arrive early to be assured of a parking spot during the summer.

In Westerly, tour the Babcock-Smith House, circa 1732, at 124 Granite Street. For hours, call 401-596-4424.

Children can take a ride aboard the Flying Horse Carousel on Bay Street in Watch Hill. The carousel is America's oldest, used prior to 1879.

The U.S. Coast Guard Light Station, built in 1858, is on Watch Hill, on the east side of the entrance to Little Narragansett Bay. Only exterior viewing is permitted.

Incoming pilots can land at Westerly State Airport off Post Road, 2 miles southeast of town on Rhode Island 1. Rental cars are available.

In Charlestown, visit Ninigret Park off Rhode Island 1A to ride the ten-speed bike course, swim in the spring-fed swimming pool, hike around Drew Memorial Nature Center, and fly model airplanes.

Attend the Charlestown Chamber Seafood Festival held in August.

INFORMATION

Burlingame State Park	Charlestown Breachway State Park
RFD Route 1	East Beach State Park
Bradford, Rhode Island 02808	Misquamicut Beach State Park
401-322-7337 (seasonal)	c/o Burlingame State Park
322-7994 (year-round)	401-364-7000

COLT STATE PARK
8

LOCATION - The park is 2 miles west of Bristol on the east side of Narragansett Bay.

ACTIVITIES - Take a picturesque 3-mile drive along the shoreline of the former Colt family estate. Go saltwater fishing. The park is open from Memorial Day through Labor Day. Attend evening summer concerts Wednesdays by the stone barn. Attend summer nature programs and go hiking, boating, and fishing. Equestrians can ride 2 miles of trails and bicyclists have access to a 3.2-mile bike path. Picnic at one of 300 picnic tables. Concessions are available.

Attend church services at Colt State Park Chapel open year-round.

Tour Coggeshall Farm Museum on Rhode Island 114 with its eighteenth-century working farm and blacksmith's shop. Attend summer weekend programs. For information, call 401-253-9062.

In Bristol, tour Blithewold Gardens and Arboretum at 101 Ferry Road, Rhode Island 114, to see 33 acres of landscaped grounds and gardens bordering Bristol Harbor. The mansion is open May–October from 10:00–4:00, but closed Mondays. For information on tours and summer concerts, call 401-253-8714.

Bristol hosts a Fourth of July parade.

Bicyclists can ride from Bristol to Providence along an abandoned railroad line. Much of the 14.5-mile paved bikepath passes along or near the shoreline of Narragansett Bay. Access is available from the state park. Contact 401-277-2601 or 1-800 556-2484 for information.

INFORMATION
Colt State Park
Bristol, Rhode Island 02809
401-253-7482

DIAMOND HILL STATE PARK
9

LOCATION - The park is one mile north of Diamond Hill on Rhode Island 114.

FEATURES - Diamond Hill has a mile-long face of veined quartz originally deposited by mineral-laden hot water that flowed along a fracture in the Earth's crust.

ACTIVITIES - Have a picnic, hike the trails, and go fishing. Concessions are available.

Tour Diamond Hill Vineyards at 3145 Diamond Hill Road. It's open year-round, but closed Tuesdays. For information, call 401-333-2751.

Former Cistercian Monastery along Rhode Island today offers walking and horseback riding trails.

INFORMATION
Diamond Hill State Park
Cumberland, Rhode Island 02864
401-333-2437

EAST BEACH STATE PARK
See under CHARLESTOWN BREACHWAY STATE PARK

EAST MATUNUCK STATE BEACH
10

LOCATION - The beach is 3 miles southeast of Perryville off U.S. 1.

ACTIVITIES - Have a picnic at one of 25 picnic tables, go saltwater fishing and swimming in Block Island Sound, and purchase a snack at the concession stand.

Take a stroll through Kingston Village. Visit Perryville Trout Hatchery on Old Post Road, open year-round from 8:00–3:30.

In South Kingston, attend the South County Hot Air Balloon Festival in July.

INFORMATION

East Matunuck State Beach
Succotash Road
South Kingstown, Rhode Island 02852
401-783-2058

FISHERMEN'S MEMORIAL STATE PARK
11
SCARBOROUGH STATE BEACH
12
ROGER W. WHEELER STATE BEACH
13

LOCATION - Fishermen's Memorial is 2 miles north of Point Judith on Ocean Road.

Scarborough Beach is east of Galilee off Rhode Island 108.

Roger Wheeler State Beach is east of Galilee via Sand Hill Cove Road off Rhode Island 108.

ACTIVITIES - At Fishermen's Memorial, go surfing, saltwater fishing, and swimming in Block Island Sound. Bring along a picnic to enjoy on the beach at one of 40 picnic tables. Concessions are available. Climb the observation tower or walk the concrete boardwalk for some good ocean views.

At Scarborough, camp in the 182-site campground from mid-April through the end of October, with 107 sites offering electric hookups, 40 with full hookups, and a trailer dump station. Attend summer weekend concerts. Play tennis, basketball, and horseshoes and go fishing and swimming. Attend seasonal naturalist programs.

At Roger Wheeler's have a picnic at one of the 63 picnic tables, go saltwater fishing and swimming, and purchase a snack at the concession stand.

In Narragansett, visit Canonchet Farm on Strathmore Street. This nineteenth-century working mini-farm has a museum, fitness trail, and nature trails to explore.

Point Judith Lighthouse, circa 1816, is at 1460 Ocean Road. Visitors can tour the grounds, but the lighthouse and Coast Guard station aren't open to the public.

INFORMATION
Scarborough State Beach
Fishermen's Memorial State Park
Roger W . Wheeler State Beach
1010 Point Judith Road
Narragansett, Rhode Island 02882-5598
401-789-8374 (Fishermen's)
401-789-2324 (Scarborough)
401-789-3563 (Roger Wheeler)

FORT ADAMS STATE PARK
14
BRENTON POINT STATE PARK
15

LOCATION - Fort Adams is in West Newport, adjoining Narragansett Bay on Ocean Drive. Brenton Point is on Ocean Drive southwest of Newport.

FEATURES - The fort is the second largest bastioned fort in the U.S. and was designed to be the most heavily armed fort in America. Its defenses include listening tunnels, powder magazines, and breast-height walls. It could accommodate 2,400 soldiers with 468 mounted cannons and 3 tiers of guns to defend the East Passage of Narragansett Bay.

ACTIVITIES - At Fort Adams, enjoy a picnic at one of the 40 picnic tables, boat from the ramp, go fishing from the pier, and swimming from the beach. Tour the visitor center and take a guided tour of the fort. Concessions are available. Play soccer and rugby, swim in the ocean from a guarded beach, go boating, wind surfing, and fishing. Attend summer concerts, clambakes, and festivals.

The Continental topsail sloop Providence, a reproduction of the first authorized ship of the Continental navy and the first command of John Paul Jones, is available for group charters. Call 401-846-1776.

Fort Adams Sailing Association within the park offers sailboat instruction and rentals. Tour the Museum of Yachting and walk through Samrock V, a J-class sloop that is open for tours. For information, call 401-847-1018.

Go for a harbor cruise from the marina on America's Cup Avenue.

Fort Wetherill State Park is across the water from Fort Adams and offers scuba diving, boating, fishing, hiking, and picnicking.

At Brenton Point, attend seasonal naturalist programs, go fishing, hiking, and boating from the ramp at King's Beach. Concessions are available.

Newport is the site of the largest number of Colonial buildings found in the U.S., and you can tour several historic mansions dating from 1748–1902. These mansions were built during the "gilded age" by the "400" of America's society. Visitors can purchase combination tickets to tour several of the mansions or pick up a self-guided brochure from the Visitor's Bureau at 23 America's Cup Avenue.

Mansions to tour include the Astors' Beechwood Mansion, built in 1856, at 580 Bellevue Avenue. It's open daily June–October. For information, call 401-816-3774.

Belcourt Castle on Bellevue Avenue is a Louis XIII-style castle with a full-sized gold Coronation Coach and the largest collection of antiques in Newport. For tour information, call 401-846-0669.

Other mansions include the Breakers on Ochre Point Avenue, circa 1895, Chateau Sur Mer on Bellevue Avenue, circa 1852, and Elms on Bellevue Avenue, circa 1901. Kingscote on Bellevue Avenue was built in 1839, the Marble House was built in 1892, and Rosecliff was built in 1902. Rosecliff was modeled after the Grand Trianon at Versailles and features Newport's largest private ballroom. For tour information on these mansions, call 401-847-1000.

Green Animals on Cory's Lane in Portsmouth has 80 sculptured trees and shrubs and formal flower beds that can be seen as part of the mansion tour.

Hammersmith Farm, circa 1887, is on Harrison Avenue along Ocean Drive, adjacent to Fort Adams. This farm was the summer home for the Auchincloss family for four generations and was the setting for Jacqueline Bouvier and John F. Kennedy's wedding reception. For tour information, call 401-846-7346.

Take the Cliff Walk, designated a National Recreation Trail, that begins at Memorial Boulevard along the Atlantic Ocean shoreline where you pass many of the famous Newport summer mansions.

Tour the International Tennis Hall of Fame and Museum at 194 Bellevue Avenue. The world's largest tennis museum is housed in the historic Newport Casino, but the museum is only open to ticket holders during tournaments. However, its fourteen grass courts are open to the public, where major professional tennis tournaments are held. For information, call 401-849-3990.

The Newport Automobile Museum at 1 Casino Terrace at Bellevue Avenue houses the largest collection of antique and classic automobiles in New England. It's open daily during the summer. For information, call 401-846-6688.

Attend the Music Festival and Tennis Week in July. The Newport Jazz Festival and International Horse Jumping Derby, the largest Grand Prix equestrian jumping event in the U.S., is held in August. The Newport International Sailboat Show is held in September.

Incoming pilots can land at Newport State Airport, located 2 miles northeast of town. Rental cars are available.

INFORMATION

Fort Adams State Park
Newport, Rhode Island 02840
401-847-2400

Brenton Point State Park
Ocean Drive
Newport, Rhode Island 02840
401-849-5649

GEORGE WASHINGTON STATE PARK
16
PULASKI MEMORIAL STATE PARK
17

LOCATION - George Washington State Park is 2 miles east of West Glocester on U.S. 44.

Pulaski Memorial State Park is 3 miles north of West Glocester off U.S. 44.

ACTIVITIES - At George Washington, camp in one of 45 campsites and hike the trails. Go boating from the ramp and bass fishing and swimming in Bowdish Reservoir. Picnic at one of 87 picnic tables. Concessions are available.

At Pulaski, have a picnic at one of 264 picnic tables, hike the trails, and go fishing and swimming. Concessions are available. During the winter, go cross-country skiing.

In adjacent Bowdish Lake Campground, campers will find 450 additional campsites, some with water and electricity, and 5 dumping stations. Here you can rent rowboats, paddleboats, and canoes to go fishing, and in July enjoy swimming with supervision.

INFORMATION

George Washington State Park
2185 Putnam Pike
Chepachet, Rhode Island 02814
401-568-2013

Pulaski Memorial State Park
Glocester, Rhode Island 02814
401-568-2013

GODDARD STATE PARK
18

LOCATION - The park is east of East Greenwich on Ives Road.

ACTIVITIES - Call 401-884-9834 to set up a tee-off time to play golf on the nine-hole course from mid-April through the last Saturday in November. Take a horseback ride on 18 miles of bridle paths, enjoy a picnic at one of 200 picnic areas, and hike the trails. Go boating from the ramp, saltwater swimming with lifeguards on duty, and saltwater fishing in Block Island Sound. Picnic at one of 395 picnic tables. Two concession stands are available. Attend a naturalist program or concert at the performing arts center.

In Warwick, tour the John Waterman Arnold House in Roger Williams Circle. Guest speakers appear once a month on Thursday evenings. For details, call 401-467-7647.

Incoming pilots can land at Theodore Francis Green State Airport on U.S. 1.
INFORMATION
Goddard State Park
Ives Road
Warwick, Rhode Island 02818
401-884-2010

LINCOLN WOODS STATE PARK
19

LOCATION - The park is 5 miles north of Providence. Take I-95 north to Rhode Island 146 and then the north exit for Lincoln Woods.

ACTIVITIES - Ride 10 miles of bridle trails, enjoy a picnic at one of 159 picnic tables, and go for a hike. Go boating from the ramp with under 10 horsepower motors allowed. No outboard motors are allowed weekends and holidays during the summer season. Enjoy freshwater fishing and swimming with lifeguards on duty. Concessions are available. During the winter, go snow-mobiling and ice skating.

In Providence, walk the Mile of History, originally an old Indian trail along Benefit Street, to see many original Colonial homes and examples of early Federal and nineteenth-century architecture. Many of the privately owned homes are open to the public during the Festival of Historic Houses. Information on the Mile is available at the Providence Preservation Society located in the Brick School House, circa 1769, 24 Meeting Street, or by calling 401-331-8575.

Take a self-guided tour of historic downtown by picking up a brochure at the Visitor Bureau, 10 Dorrance Street, or call 401-274-1636. The city is hilly, so wear comfortable shoes.

Tour the John Brown House, 52 Power Street, built in 1786 and once described by John Quincy Adams as "the most magnificent mansion I have ever seen on this continent." For information, call 401-331-8575.

Roger Williams Park, Museum, and Zoo is at 950 Elmwood off I-95. For details, call 401-467-9013.

INFORMATION
Lincoln Woods State Park
Great Road, Route 123
Lincoln, Rhode Island 02865
401-723-7892

MISQUAMICUT BEACH STATE PARK
See under CHARLESTOWN BREACHWAY STATE PARK

PULASKI MEMORIAL STATE PARK
See under GEORGE WASHINGTON STATE PARK

ROGER W. WHEELER STATE BEACH
See under FISHERMEN'S MEMORIAL STATE PARK

SCARBOROUGH STATE BEACH
See under FISHERMEN'S MEMORIAL STATE PARK

WORLD WAR II MEMORIAL STATE PARK
20

LOCATION - The park is on Social Street in Woonsocket.
ACTIVITIES - Play tennis, go swimming with lifeguards on duty, and have a picnic. Go fishing and purchase a snack. The park has summer concerts in the bandstand, an annual Autumnfest, plus many summer events.
INFORMATION
World War II Memorial State Park
c/o Lincoln Woods State Park
Great Road, Route 123
Lincoln, Rhode Island 02865
401-762-9717

VERMONT

Vermont has 20 state beaches and 34 state-owned campgrounds with 2,000 campsites without hookups. Many have three-sided lean-tos that accommodate up to five people. Most campgrounds are open from Memorial Day through Labor Day.

Most state parks have hiking trails and several parks have sections of Long Trail and Appalachian Trail passing through. Naturalists are located on the summits of both Camel's Hump and Mount Mansfield. For detailed hiking information, contact the Green Mountain Club, Inc., P.O. Box 889, 43 State Street, Montpelier, Vermont 05602, or call 802-223-3463.

Enjoy canoeing the following rivers: Connecticut, Lamoille, Missisquoi, Winooski, Batten Kill, Lemon Fair, and Otter Creek.

Lake Champlain, the sixth largest body of fresh water in the U.S., has almost 100 mostly uninhabited islands dotting its surface. It provides some of the Northeast's best fishing.

The state boasts over 100 covered bridges, most still in service. Its oldest one, 1820 Pulp Mill Bridge, is located at Middlebury. Scott Covered Bridge in Townshend is the state's longest. A railroad bridge at Wolcott is the only railroad covered bridge still used in the country.

Over 65 state historic districts are listed on the National Register of Historic Places.

Cabins and cottages are located in three state parks: Camp Plymouth, Lake Carmi, and Grand Isle. For information, contact the Department of Forests, Parks, and Recreation, 103 South Main Street, Waterbury, Vermont 05671-0603, or call 802-241-3655.

The Vermont Travel Division operates a 24-hour recorded report on fall foliage conditions beginning the day after Labor Day through late October. For information, call 802-828-3239.

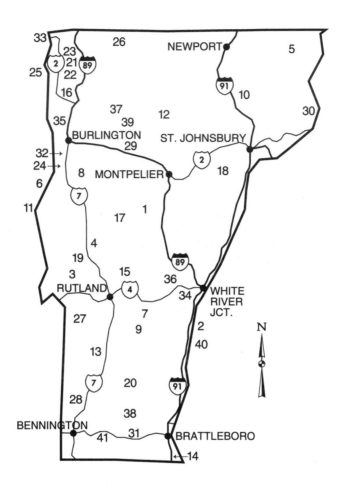

33
23
21
22
16
25
26
NEWPORT
5
89
2
91
10
30
35
37
39
12
BURLINGTON
29
ST. JOHNSBURY
32→
24→
8 MONTPELIER
2
18
6
7
11
17
1
4
19
3
15
36
89
RUTLAND
4
34
WHITE
RIVER
JCT.
27
7
9
2
40
13
7
20
91
28
38
BENNINGTON
41
31
BRATTLEBORO
←14

N

ALLIS STATE PARK
1

LOCATION - From I-89, Exit 5 at Northfield, go 2½ miles west on Vermont 64 to South Northfield, 4 miles south on Vermont 12, and 1½ miles southeast on Vermont 65.

If coming from Randolph, go 12 miles north on Vermont 12 and then 1½ miles east on Vermont 65.

ACTIVITIES - Allis is located on the summit of Bear Mountain. Climb the fire tower in the picnic area for great views of central Vermont. Open mid-May through Labor Day, the 27-site campground has 7 lean-tos and a trailer dump station. Fish in a nearby pond and go hiking.

Rock of Ages is 16 miles from the park in Graniteville, one mile south on Vermont 14 and 3 miles further following signs. Tour Craftsman Center, one of the largest granite plants in the world. Take a self-guided tour from May–October and a quarry shuttle tour from June 1 through mid-October. For information, call 802-476-3115.

INFORMATION
Allis State Park
RFD 2, Box 192
Randolph, Vermont 05060
802-276-3175

ASCUTNEY STATE PARK
2

LOCATION - The park is 2 miles north of Ascutney on U.S. 5 and one mile northwest on Vermont 44A. From I-91, Exit 8, go north 2 miles on U.S. 5, then one mile northwest on Brownsville Road.

ACTIVITIES - Camp in one of 39 wooded campsites with 10 lean-tos and a disposal station from mid-May through Columbus Day. Drive the scenic mountain toll road and hike up 3,144-foot Mount Ascutney from the top parking lot via a .8-mile trail. Hike to Brownsville Rock via a ¼ mile trail northwest of the summit to watch hang gliders taking off. Take along a picnic to enjoy in the shelter part way up the summit road where you overlook the Connecticut River valley. During the winter, snowmobile along park trails.

Visit Old Constitution House's museum in Windsor, 4 miles from the park at 16 North Main. It's open from mid-May through mid-October. For information, call 802-828-3226. One of the longest bridges in the U.S. is in Windsor. Constructed in 1866, it spans the Connecticut River between Windsor and Cornish, New Hampshire.

INFORMATION
Ascutney State Park
HCR 71, Box 186
Windsor, Vermont 05089
802-674-2060

BOMOSEEN STATE PARK
3

LOCATION - The park is on Lake Bomoseen, ½ mile north of West Castleton and 4 miles north of Hydeville on West Shore Road.

ACTIVITIES - Camp in one of 66 wooded sites, including 10 lean-tos, open from mid-May through October. Go fishing for bass, perch, walleye, and record-sized rainbow trout. Go swimming from the beach and boating and canoeing in Lake Bomoseen with boat rentals available. Additional boating is available in nearby Golen Lake. Hike the trails, including slate history's self-guided trail to learn about early slate milling. Come in the fall to "leaf peep" when foliage reaches its peak.

Visit nearby Hubbardton Battlefield 7 miles off U.S. 4 in East Hubbardton. The July 1777 battle began a series of events which led to General Burgoyne's defeat at the Battle of Saratoga. Tour the visitor center's museum and walk along marked points in the battlefield. It's open Memorial Day through Columbus Day from Wednesday through Sunday.

Vermont's Marble Exhibit, the world's largest marble museum, is in Proctor on Main Street. Watch "Marble: The Sparkling Stone" and see marble relief carvings of the presidents. For information, call 802-459-3311, ext. 436.

Wilson Castle is 3½ miles south of Proctor on West Proctor Road. It features 32 rooms with 84 stained glass windows and antiques from Europe and the Far East. For information, call 802-773-3284.

In Pittsford, visit New England Maple Museum, north of town on U.S. 7. For information, call 802-483-9414.

INFORMATION
Bomoseen State Park
Box 2620 RFD 1
Fair Haven, Vermont 05743
802-265-4242

BRANBURY STATE PARK
4

LOCATION - The park is on the eastern shore of Lake Dunmore at the base of Mount Moosalamoo, 3 miles east of Salisbury. From Middlebury, go south 7 miles on U.S. 7, then south another 4 miles on Vermont 53.

ACTIVITIES - Vermont 53 splits Branbury into two sections. Camp in one of 44 campsites, including 5 lean-tos and a disposal station. In Lake Dunmore, go swimming from the beach, bass, northern pike, perch, and trout fishing, and boating from the ramp with rentals available. Hike trails to spectacular views. Attend naturalist programs and tour the nature museum. Food is available at the snack bar.

Go hiking in nearby Green Mountain National Forest. Pick up maps and trail guides at Middlebury in the National Forest office.

Take a guided tour of AVM Morgan Horse Farm. Follow signs from Middlebury, heading 2½ miles to Weybridge. It's open May 1–October 31 from 9:00–4:00. For information, call 802-388-2011.

Take a self-guided tour of historic Middlebury. Pick up a map at the visitor center at 35 Court Street. For information, call 802-388-7579. To learn more about Vermont's early life, tour Sheldon Museum on Park Street. For information, call 802-388-2117.

Tour the Vermont Marble Exhibit on Main Street in Proctor, with the world's largest marble museum. Watch "Marble: The Sparkling Stone" and walk through the Hall of Presidents to see marble relief carvings of past U.S. presidents. For information, call 802-459-3311, ext. 436. En route to Proctor, stop by Pittsford's New England Maple Museum, north of town on U.S. 7. For information, call 802-483-9414.

Take a guided tour of Wilson Castle, 3½ miles south of Proctor on West Proctor Road. It features 32 rooms with 84 stained glass windows and antiques from Europe and the Far East. For information, call 802-773-3284.

INFORMATION
Branbury State Park
RFD 2, Box 2421
Brandon, Vermont 05733
802-247-5925

BRIGHTON STATE PARK
5

LOCATION - The park is 2 miles east of Island Pond on Vermont 105 and then ¾ mile south on a local road.

ACTIVITIES - Camp in the 84-site campground, including 21 lean-tos and a dump station, from mid-May through Columbus Day. Enjoy a picnic, go swimming, and fish for trout, perch, pickerel, and bass. Go boating in Spectacle Lake with rentals available. Hike nature trails, tour the nature museum, and attend naturalist programs. Snacks are sold at the snack bar.

Fairbanks Museum and Planetarium is 35 miles from the park in St. Johnsbury on Main and Prospect. The museum has a U.S. weather observation station and an Outdoor Live Museum. For details, call 802-748-2372. To learn more about maple syrup, tour Maple Grove's Maple Museum one mile east of town on U.S. 2. Tours go through the factory Monday–Friday from 8:00–4:30 during May–October.

INFORMATION
Brighton State Park
Island Pond, Vermont 05846
802-723-4360
802-479-4280 (January–May)

BURTON ISLAND STATE PARK
See under KILL KARE STATE PARK

BUTTON BAY STATE PARK
6

LOCATION - To reach the park from Vergennes, go ½ mile south on Vermont 22A, then northwest for 6½ miles on local roads.

FEATURES - Button Bay is on a bluff along Lake Champlain and was named for the button-like concretions formed by clay deposits found along the shoreline.

ACTIVITIES - Camp in one of 73 campsites, including 13 lean-tos and a disposal station, from mid-May through Columbus Day. The campground overlooks Lake Champlain and the Adirondack Mountains. Go swimming in the guarded pool and fishing, sailing, and boating from the dock on Lake Champlain. Boat rentals are available. Hike marked nature trails through Button Point Natural Area's mature hardwood forest, explore the nature museum, attend naturalist programs, and enjoy a picnic.

Visit Morgan Horse Farm in Middlebury, 20 miles from the park. This world-famous home of Morgans offers daily guided tours from May 1–November 1 from 9:00–4:00. For information, call 802-388-2011.

In Shelburne, 7 miles south of Burlington and 20 miles from the park, tour Shelburne Museum and Heritage Park's 37 historic buildings to learn about early New England life. You'll see eighteenth- and nineteenth-century houses, a hand-crafted circus, and side-wheeler SS *Ticonderoga*. Electra Webb Memorial House features European furnishings and paintings. Walk through formal gardens and enjoy a picnic. For details, call 802-985-3344.

INFORMATION
Button Bay State Park
RFD 3, Box 570
Vergennes, Vermont 05491
802-475-2377

CALVIN COOLIDGE STATE PARK
7

LOCATION - From Plymouth, go north 3 miles on Vermont 100A.

ACTIVITIES - The park is located within Coolidge State Forest. The forest and park have 60 campsites, including 35 lean-tos and a disposal station. Tour the museum, go fishing, and hike the trails. During the winter, snowmobile along park trails.

In Plymouth off Vermont 100A, tour Plymouth Notch, birthplace and homestead of Calvin Coolidge, our thirtieth president. For information, call 802-672-3773.

Go to Killington to ride the gondola and chair lift to the summit of 4,241-foot Killington Peak. Get a snack and hike the nature trail. For information, call 802-422-3333. Ride Pico Alpine Slide west of Killington on U.S. 4. For information, call 802-775-4345.

INFORMATION
Calvin Coolidge State Park
HCR 70, Box 105
Plymouth, Vermont 05056
802-672-3612

CAMEL'S HUMP STATE PARK
8

LOCATION - The park is east of Huntington Center.

FEATURES - Camel's Hump covers 16,654 acres, including the 4,083-foot Camel's Hump, a National Natural Landmark.

ACTIVITIES - Hike one of the many scenic trails to the summit of Camel's Hump. Long Trail, extending the length of Vermont, passes over the open mountain summit and provides a 360-degree view of the surrounding terrain. Enjoy primitive camping by permit. Contact the Vermont Department of Forests, Parks, and Recreation at 802-828-3375. Go cross-country skiing in the winter.

INFORMATION
Camel's Hump State Park
Huntington, Vermont 05462
802-828-3375

CAMP PLYMOUTH STATE PARK
9

LOCATION - The park is in Plymouth. From Vermont 100 in Tyson, cross the concrete bridge and go east one mile uphill to a crossroads. Turn left and go north one mile along the east side of Echo Lake.

ACTIVITIES - In Echo Lake, go swimming, boating with rentals available, and fishing for trout, land-locked salmon, perch, and bass. Enjoy a picnic, hike trails in the undeveloped section of the park, or go gold panning. Concessions are available by the beach house. The park has a camping area on the south side of Buffalo Brook that includes 6 lean-tos. Touring bicyclists often camp here overnight since the park is only 2 miles from Vermont 100, a major bicycle touring route. You can also stay in a fully furnished cottage.

Coolidge State Park, where you can do additional fishing and hiking in the forest, is located 7 miles from here.

For a unique tour, visit Crowley Cheese Factory 5 miles north of Ludlow via Vermont 103 and 2 miles west on Healdville Road, 7 miles from the park. Watch employees making cheese by hand. For details, call 802-259-2340.

INFORMATION
Camp Plymouth State Park
R.D. 1, Box 489
Ludlow, Vermont 05149
802-228-2025

CRYSTAL LAKE STATE PARK
10

LOCATION - The park is off Vermont 16 at the north end of Crystal Lake in Barton Village.

ACTIVITIES - Enjoy a picnic, purchase a snack at the snack bar, and take a hike. Go boating, swimming, and fishing for trout, pickerel, and bass.

Visit Sugarmill Farm, located off I-91, Exit 25, then south ⅛ mile on Vermont 16. Tour the museum and watch their 15-minute film to learn the history of syrup making. Come in the spring to watch sap being collected. For information, call 802-525-3701.

INFORMATION
Crystal Lake State Park
Barton, Vermont 05822
802-525-6205

D.A.R. STATE PARK
11

LOCATION - The park is on the shore of Lake Champlain, one mile north of Chimney Point on Vermont 17. To reach it from Vergennes, go southwest for 6 miles on Vermont 22A to Addison, then southwest for 7 miles on Vermont 17.

ACTIVITIES - Camp in one of 71 grassy campsites, including 24 lean-tos and a trailer dump station, open from mid-May through Labor Day. Go boating, sailing, swimming, and pike fishing in Lake Champlain.

Tour the John Strong Mansion/Museum operated by the D.A.R. and located next to the park.

INFORMATION
D.A.R. State Park
RFD 3, Box 3493
Vergennes, Vermont 05491
802-759-2354

ELMORE STATE PARK
12

LOCATION - From Morrisville, go south 5 miles on Vermont 12.

ACTIVITIES - Camp in one of 60 campsites, including 13 lean-tos and a dump station, from mid-May through Columbus Day. In Lake Elmore, go swimming and fishing for northern pike, perch, bass, and bullhead fishing. Enjoy boating with rentals available. Hike 1¼ miles up 2,608-foot Elmore Mountain to the fire tower and then continue on to Balancing Rock.

INFORMATION
Elmore State Park
P.O. Box 93
Lake Elmore, Vermont 05657
802-888-2982
802-479-4280 (January–May)

EMERALD LAKE STATE PARK
13

LOCATION - The park is in North Dorset on U.S. 7 and 9 miles north of Manchester.

ACTIVITIES - Camp in one of 105 grassy campsites, including 36 lean-tos and a trailer dump station, on a heavily wooded ridge above Emerald Lake. The campground is open from mid-May through Columbus Day. Go swimming, bass fishing, canoeing, and boating with rentals available. No motors are permitted on the lake.

Hike park trails, explore the marked nature trail, and attend naturalist programs. Purchase a snack at the beach snack bar.

Near Manchester, tour Hildene, 1½ miles south of town on U.S. 7A. Hildene was the summer home of Abraham Lincoln's son, Robert, and was later lived in by Lincoln descendants until 1975. Stop by the visitor center to pick up tickets for the house tour. For information, call 802-362-1788.

Drive the toll road up 3,816-foot Mount Equinox. The road begins 5 miles south of Vermont 11 on U.S. 7A.

Anglers will enjoy touring American Museum of Fly Fishing at Seminary Avenue and Vermont 7A. For information, call 802-362-3300.

INFORMATION
Emerald Lake State Park
R.D. Box 485
East Dorset, Vermont 05253
208-362-1655

FORT DUMMER STATE PARK
14

LOCATION - The fort is south of Brattleboro. Take Exit 1 from I-91. Go ¹⁄₁₀ mile north on U.S. 5, then ½ mile east on Fairground Road. Continue south one mile on Main Street, Old Guilford Road.

FEATURES - Fort Dummer in the Connecticut River Valley was established in 1724 and was Vermont's first permanent European settlement.

ACTIVITIES - Camp in one of the 61 gravel campsites, including 10 lean-tos and a trailer dump station, from mid-May through Labor Day. Hike two hiking trails and enjoy a picnic.

In Brattleboro, tour Brattleboro Museum and Art Center, located off I-91. Follow Vermont 5 to Main and Vernon. The museum's five galleries are in the former Union Railroad Station. For information, call 802-257-0124.

Visit Basketville, 5 miles from the park in Putney, with its extensive collection of baskets and wicker furniture. For information, call 802-387-5509.

Bellows Falls, 22 miles from the park, offers a scenic train ride aboard the Green Mountain Flyer. Take a 26-mile excursion in a restored coach pulled by vintage diesels. You'll see Brockways Mills Gorge and two covered bridges. For information, call 802-463-3069.

INFORMATION
Fort Dummer State Park
RR 6, Box 11
Brattleboro, Vermont 05301
802-254-2610

GIFFORD WOODS STATE PARK
15

LOCATION - The park is 2 miles west of Sherburne Center on U.S. 4 and another ½ mile north on Vermont 100.

ACTIVITIES - Camp in one of 48 campsites, including 21 lean-tos and a disposal station, from mid-May through Columbus Day. Go fishing for bass and trout in Kent Pond, Colton Pond, White River, or in one of the numerous ponds located along Vermont 100. Tour the nature center and attend naturalist talks.

Enjoy hiking through the woods on Kent Brook Trail. The Appalachian Trail runs through the park and after 1.5 miles joins Long Trail. Because of the hardwoods, Gifford Woods is a popular spot for "leaf peepers" to visit when the trees assume their colorful fall foliage.

Across from the campground is a 7-acre stand of virgin hardwood, one of the few left in the state.

Ride up Killington Gondola to the summit of 4,241-foot Killington Peak. It's 5 miles east of the park on Vermont 4. For information call 802-422-3333. Ride the Pico Alpine Slide in the Pico Peak Ski Area.

INFORMATION
Gifford Woods State Park
Killington, Vermont 05751
802-775-5354

GRAND ISLE STATE PARK
16

LOCATION - The park is 5 miles north of South Hero off U.S. 2.

FEATURES - Grand Isle, also called South Hero, takes its name from the largest island found in Lake Champlain. The Hero Islands were named to commemorate early Vermonters who served in the American Revolution.

ACTIVITIES - Camp from mid-May through Columbus Day in one of 155 sites, including 33 lean-tos and a dump station. You can also stay in a waterfront cabin. Groceries are available.

Go boating from the ramp with rowboat rentals available and bass fishing in Lake Champlain. Go sailboarding in a designated sailboard area. Practice putting on the putting green, pitch horseshoes in the horseshoe pit, or play volleyball on the sand court. Attend naturalist programs, hike the ¾-mile nature trail or check your fitness on the ⅓-mile fitness trail.

Tour Hyde Log Cabin in Grand Isle, circa 1783, the nation's oldest log cabin still standing in its original condition.

INFORMATION
Grand Isle State Park
Route 1, Box 648
Grand Isle, Vermont 05458
802-372-4300

GRANVILLE GULF STATE PARK
17

LOCATION - The park is between Warren and Granville along the eastern boundary of the Green Mountain National Forest. Mad River runs through the 1,200-acre park, forming Moss Glen Falls.

ACTIVITIES - Drive the 6-mile scenic drive, enjoy a picnic, and fish for trout and bass in the Mad River. The Green Mountains have approximately 512 miles of trails to explore, including part of the Appalachian/Long Trail and Robert Frost National Recreation Trail. Go cross-country skiing during the winter.

INFORMATION
Granville Gulf State Park
c/o Green Mountain National Forest
P.O. Box 519
Rutland, Vermont 05702
802-773-0300

GROTON STATE FOREST
18

LOCATION - The forest occupies nine areas, covering 25,625 acres, and is midway between Montpelier and St. Johnsbury.

ACTIVITIES - Camp in 28-site Big Deer Campground. Go 2 miles west of Groton on U.S. 302, then northwest 6 miles on Vermont 232, and 1½ miles east on Boulder Beach Road. Go fishing in Lake Groton, hiking along miles of trails, and attend naturalist talks.

Boulder Beach Day-Use Area has a nature center, swimming, boating with rentals available, and snacks.

Kettle Pond has year-round camping with 27 lean-tos, some located around the pond. Go fishing for trout and perch. Launch your cartop boat from the launch, go swimming, and explore miles of hiking trails, including one around the lake.

New Discovery Campground is 2 miles west of Groton on U.S. 302, then north for 9½ miles on Vermont 232. It has 61 campsites, including 14 lean-tos, and hiking trails. You can also winter camp here. Ricker Pond Campground has 55 campsites, including 23 lean-tos. Stillwater Campground offers 79 more sites, including 17 lean-tos, a swimming beach, and boat launch/dock facility where rental boats are available.

Go to Osmore Pond to fish for trout. Hike up 1,958-foot Owls Head Mountain or up Little Deer and Big Deer Mountain. Go cross-country skiing along summer hiking trails.

Seyon Recreation Area is beside Noyes Pond and offers boat rentals, flyfishing, and accommodations and meals in Seyon Ranch House. For information, call 802-584-3829 or 802-479-3241.

INFORMATION
Groton State Forest
Marshfield, Vermont 05658
802-584-3823
802-584-3820 (New Discovery Campground)
802-584-3821 (Ricker Pond Campground)
802-584-3822 (Stillwater Campground)

HALF MOON STATE PARK
19

LOCATION - From Hubbardton, go south 2 miles on Vermont 30, west 2 miles on Town Road, and south for 1½ miles. The park is located within Bomoseen State Forest and surrounds Half Moon Pond.

ACTIVITIES - The campground, open from mid-May through Labor Day, has 69 grassy campsites, including 10 lean-tos and a dump station. Go bass, perch, northern pike, and bullhead fishing and go boating with rentals in Half Moon Pond. No motors are permitted. Hike trails to High Pond, Glen Lake, or to Bomoseen State Park. Limited swimming is permitted.

Take a guided tour of Wilson Castle, 3½ miles south of Proctor on West Proctor Road. The castle has 32 rooms and 84 stained glass windows, in addition to antiques and museum pieces. It's open daily, including Sundays, from 9:00–6:00 from late May through mid-October. For information, call 802-773-3284. Hike up 3,957-foot Pico Peak, 11 miles east of the castle on Vermont 4.

In Rutland, tour the Norman Rockwell Museum on U.S. 4, 2 miles east of the intersection of U.S. 4 and U.S. 7. The museum, open from 9:00–6:00 year-round, has over 2,000 reproductions of his work and all 323 of his *Saturday Evening Post* magazine covers. For information, call 802-773-6095.

Vermont's Marble Exhibit is in Proctor. Watch "Marble: The Sparkling Stone" and observe the marble sculptor. For information, call 802-459-3311, ext. 436.

The New England Maple Museum is on Vermont 7 in Pittsford. Watch live demonstrations ranging from candy making to wood bucket construction and sample different syrups at the tasting counter. It's closed January and February. For information, call 802-483-9414.

INFORMATION
Half Moon State Park
RFD 1 Box 2730
Fair Haven, Vermont 05743
802-273-2848

JAMAICA STATE PARK
20

LOCATION - From Jamaica, turn at the inn in the center of the village and continue another ½ mile north on the town road off Vermont 30. It's on a bend of the West River.

ACTIVITIES - Camp in one of the 61 sites, including 18 lean-tos and a disposal station, from early May through Columbus Day. Go canoeing and fishing in West River, and swimming at Salmon Hole, site of a famous Indian massacre in 1776. On spring and fall weekends in late April and late September or early October, water is released from Ball Mountain Dam into the West River heralding the arrival of many kayakers and canoeists.

Hike park trails, including one to Hamilton Falls located upstream on Cobb Brook. The trail along the West River to Ball Mountain Dam follows an old railroad bed used by the Brattleboro Railroad. Attend naturalist programs.

Drive to Hildene, 1½ miles south of Manchester on U.S. 7A to visit the summer home of Robert Todd Lincoln. Purchase tickets at the visitor center to tour the house. Cross-country ski the grounds in the winter. For information, call 802-362-1788.

While you're in the area, drive up U.S. 7A's toll road on 3,816-foot Mount Equinox. It's the highest peak in the Taconic Range and provides a wonderful view.

INFORMATION
Jamaica State Park
P.O. Box 45
Jamaica, Vermont 05342
802-874-4600

KILL KARE STATE PARK
21
BURTON ISLAND STATE PARK
22

WOODS ISLAND STATE PARK
23

LOCATION - To reach Kill Kare State Park from St. Albans Bay, go 4.5 miles west on Vermont 36, then 3½ miles southwest on Point Road. The park is surrounded on three sides by Lake Champlain.

To reach Burton Island State Park, go to Kill Kare State Park and take the passenger ferry from the tip of Hathway Point to Burton Island or go by private boat. No vehicles are permitted on the island. The ferry runs from 8:30 AM until 6:30 PM at 2-hour intervals.

Woods Island State Park is in Lake Champlain, 4 miles north of Burton Island. Access is by private boat only. No ferry service is available.

ACTIVITIES - At Kill Kare go swimming, fishing, sailboarding, or launch your cartop boat into Lake Champlain. Rental rowboats are available. Changing facilities are located in the old hotel where you can see historic photographs of Kill Kare. Enjoy a picnic and purchase a snack at the snack bar.

On Burton Island, camp in one of 44 campsites, including 22 lean-tos. The 100-slip marina has power hookups. Go fishing or boating from the ramp on Lake Champlain with rentals available. The park has 3 miles of shoreline. Hike island trails, including North Shore Trail, Champlain Trail, and Eagle Bay Trail. Tour the nature center and attend naturalist programs. Snacks are available at the snack bar. The park is open mid-May through Labor Day.

On Woods Island, camp in one of five primitive campsites. Obtain your reservation and camping permit through Burton Island State Park. No fires are permitted. Hike the island's perimeter trail. Go fishing and boating in Lake Champlain.

In early April, attend the Vermont Maple Festival held in St. Albans.

INFORMATION
Kill Kare State Park
Burton Island State Park
Woods Island State Park
P.O. Box 123
St. Albans Bay, Vermont 05481
802-933-8383
802-524-6353 (Burton Island and Woods Island)
802-879-5674 (Burton Island and Woods Island: January–May)

KINGSLAND BAY STATE PARK
24

LOCATION - The park is on the shore of Lake Champlain. From Ferrisburg, follow Vermont 7W, Little Chicago Road, approximately one mile and go north another 3½ miles on Slang Road.

ACTIVITIES - Hike scenic trails along the lake and enjoy a picnic along the shoreline. Go fishing, swimming, sailing, and boating with boat rentals available. Play tennis on the tennis court. Attend the annual Lake Champlain Summer Festival held the first weekend in August.

In Ferrisburg, tour Rokeby Museum, home of Rowland E. Robinson, author, naturalist, and illustrator. For tour information, call 802-877-3406.

INFORMATION
Kingsland Bay State Park
Ferrisburg, Vermont 05456
802-877-3445

KNIGHT POINT STATE PARK
25

LOCATION - The park is on North Hero Island in Lake Champlain, 3 miles south of North Hero on U.S. 2. It's 20 miles northeast of Exit 17 off I-89.

FEATURES - Hero Islands were named to commemorate early Vermonters who served in the Revolutionary War. On the east shore, you can still see the old ferry landing used from 1785–1892.

ACTIVITIES - Enjoy a picnic in one of the shelters overlooking the lake or hike the trail around the point to get lake and shore views. Go boating from the ramp with rentals available and fishing and swimming in Lake Champlain.

INFORMATION
Knight Point State Park
R.D. 1, Box 21
North Hero, Vermont 05474
802-372-8389

LAKE CARMI STATE PARK
26

LOCATION - From Enosburg Falls, go west 3 miles on Vermont 105, then north for 3 miles on Vermont 236.

FEATURES - Lake Carmi is Vermont's fourth largest natural lake. The lake has the third largest peat bog in Vermont, with most of it designated as a State Natural Area.

ACTIVITIES - Camp in one of 178 campsites, including 35 lean-tos, or stay in one of two waterfront cabins. Go hiking along the Old Railroad Bed Walking

Path, explore the ½-mile-long nature trail and go swimming from beaches which are located in both camp areas. Go fishing for bass, walleye, and northern pike and boating from the ramp in Lake Carmi with rentals available. Purchase snacks from the park store in the Day-Use Area.

Attend the Dairy Festival held in Enosburg Falls in early June.

Stowe, 35 miles from the park, offers a 5-mile bikepath heading towards Mount Mansfield. Drive up the Stowe Auto Toll Road or take a gondola to the summit to hike trails at the summit. The gondola begins 7½ miles northwest of Stowe on Vermont 108. Hikers and bicyclists can overnight at the Vermont State Ski Dorm and Hostel located at the foot of Mount Mansfield. For reservations, call 802-253-4010.

INFORMATION
Lake Carmi State Park
RR 1, Box 1710
Enosburg Falls, Vermont 05450
802-933-8383
802-879-5671 (January–May)

LAKE ST. CATHERINE STATE PARK
27

LOCATION - The park is 3 miles south of Poultney on Vermont 30.

FEATURES - Lake St. Catherine State Park is known for its former slate quarrying operations.

ACTIVITIES - Camp in one of the 61 campsites, including 10 lean-tos and a trailer dump station, open from mid-May through Columbus Day. Go swimming and boating from the ramp with rental boats available. Anglers find good bass, perch, northern pike, and record-sized trout fishing in Lake St. Catherine. Hike the nature trail and explore the nature museum. Groceries are available in the park store and snacks at the snack bar.

In Manchester, 25 miles from the park, drive up Equinox Mountain. Tour a restored Georgian Revival mansion and gardens in Hildene on Vermont 7A, home of Abraham Lincoln's descendants until 1975. It's open from mid-May through October. Cross-country ski here in the winter. For information, call 802-362-1788.

In Proctor, 20 miles from the park, tour the Vermont Marble Museum, the world's largest marble museum. It's on Main Street and features the Hall of Presidents with past presidents carved in marble. Watch "Marble: The Sparkling Stone." For information, call 802-459-3311, ext. 436. Tour Wilson Castle, a mid-nineteenth-century castle off Vermont 4 on West Proctor Road from mid-May through late October. For information, call 802-773-3284.

INFORMATION
Lake St. Catherine State Park
R.D. 2, Box 230
Poultney, Vermont 05764
802-287-9158

LAKE SHAFTSBURY STATE PARK
28

LOCATION - The park is 10½ miles north of Bennington on U.S. 7A at Shaftsbury.

ACTIVITIES - Wooded group camping is available from mid-May through Labor Day. Go swimming from the beach and boating and fishing in Lake Shaftsbury. Snacks and rental boats are available. Hike the Healing Springs Nature Trail around the lake.

Bennington has three covered bridges. Silk Road and Papermill bridges are off Vermont 67A and Bert Henry Bridge is on Murphy Road.

Pick up a map for a self-guided walking tour of Bennington's historic buildings. They're available from the Chamber of Commerce on Veterans Memorial Drive. For information, call 802-447-3311.

The Battle of Bennington was fought here in 1777 when the Americans defeated the British. The Bennington Battle Monument is ½ mile west of Vermont 9 and U.S. 7 and, when finished in 1891, was the tallest battle monument in the world.

Bennington Museum on West Main has paintings by Grandma Moses, over 5,000 examples of pressed and free-blown glass and early American furniture. For information, call 802-447-1571.

Arlington, 4 miles from the park, has a Norman Rockwell exhibition. Many of his models came from here. Watch the film on his life and stroll through the artist's works. For information, call 802-375-6423.

In Manchester, 13 miles from the park, tour Hildene where Abraham Lincoln's descendants lived until 1975. Tours go from mid-May through October. Go cross-country skiing in the winter. For information, call 802-362-1788.

INFORMATION
Lake Shaftsbury State Park
RFD 1, Box 266
Shaftsbury, Vermont 05262
802-375-9978

LITTLE RIVER STATE PARK
29

LOCATION - The park is near Waterbury. From I-89, Exit 10, go ½ mile south on Vermont 100 and another 1½ miles west on U.S. 2. Continue 3½ miles north on Little River Road.

ACTIVITIES - Little River State Park's campground is central Vermont's largest. You can stay in one of 101 campsites, including 20 lean-tos and a trailer dump station. It's open from mid-May through Columbus Day. Rent a boat to go boating from the ramp in Waterbury Reservoir and go swimming from the beach. Hike marked nature trails or go to Mount Mansfield State Forest and hike up 4,393-foot Mount Mansfield. The state forest also has 38 campsites, including 14 lean-tos in Smugglers Notch, boating, fishing, swimming, and cabins.

Waterbury Center, south of Waterbury Center Village and ¼ mile off Vermont 100, has additional swimming, boating from the ramp, and picnicking. Tour Ben & Jerry's Ice Cream Factory near Waterbury.

Drive up the toll road to the summit of Mount Mansfield. It begins 5 miles northwest of Stowe from Vermont 108. You can also reach the summit via the Stowe Gondola that begins 7.5 miles northwest of Stowe on Vermont 108. For information, call 802-253-7311.

Bicyclists and hikers have access to Stowe's 5-mile recreational path that runs along a stream towards Mount Mansfield. Hikers and cyclists can overnight at Vermont State Ski Dorm and Hostel located at the foot of Mount Mansfield. For information, call 802-253-4010.

Near Barre in Graniteville, 20 miles from the park, tour Rock of Ages, one of the largest granite plants in the world. Shuttle tours are offered from June 1–October 15, weather permitting. For information call 802-476-3115.

INFORMATION
Little River State Park
RFD 1, Box 1150
Waterbury, Vermont 05676
802-244-7103

MAIDSTONE STATE PARK
30

LOCATION - The park is southwest of Bloomfield. Go south 11 miles on Vermont 102 and 5 miles southwest on Madison State Forest Highway.

FEATURES - Maidstone is Vermont's most remote state park. Its lake was created by glacial ice that carved out the deep basin.

ACTIVITIES - Camp in one of 83 campsites, including 37 lean-tos and a disposal station, from mid-May through Labor Day. In Maidstone Lake, go swimming, perch, trout, and salmon fishing, and boating from the ramp with boat rentals. Hike the trails, attend naturalist programs, and enjoy a picnic. Watch for loons on the lake, one of the few lakes still inhabited by this now endangered species.

INFORMATION
Maidstone State Park
R.D. 1, Box 455
Guildhall, Vermont 05905
802-676-3930

MOLLY STARK STATE PARK
31

LOCATION - Molly Stark State Park is 15 miles west of Brattleboro off Vermont 9. From Brattleboro, take Exit 2 from I-91. Continue west 15 miles on Vermont 9. The park is also 3 miles east of Wilmington on Vermont 9.

FEATURES - The park is named for the wife of General John Stark of the Revolutionary War. In 1777, Molly, following her husband's request, rode on horseback to alert 200 men to assist her husband in his fight against the British. Following the Battle of Bennington, General John Stark rode back home over the trail, now called Molly Stark Trail, bringing along one of six brass cannon captured from the British.

ACTIVITIES - Camp in one of 34 campsites, including 10 lean-tos and a disposal station, open from mid-May through Columbus Day. Hike to the summit of 2,415-foot Mount Olga where a fire tower provides a panoramic view of southern Vermont. The 1.4-mile-long trail begins near the park entrance. Enjoy a picnic in the large open shelter. Come in the fall when the fall foliage peaks.

In Wilmington, tour the Maple Grove Honey Museum and the 1836 Country Store Village.

INFORMATION
Molly Stark State Park
Wilmington, Vermont 05363
802-464-5460

MOUNT PHILO STATE PARK
32

LOCATION - The park is located on top of 968-foot Mount Philo, 14 miles south of Burlington off U.S. 7, then one mile east on a local road. From

Vergennes, go north one mile on Vermont 22A, 6 miles north on U.S. 7, and one mile east on the town road. Because of its steep entrance and camp roads, the area is not recommended for trailer use.

FEATURES - Mount Philo State Park overlooks the Lake Champlain Valley and Adirondack Mountains in New York.

ACTIVITIES - Camp in one of 16 sites, including 4 lean-tos and a dump station, open from mid-May through Columbus Day. Go fishing in Ottauquechee River and hike scenic gorge trails. Swimming is available at Kingsland Bay State Park, 6 miles away. You can go boating, fishing, and sailing in nearby Lake Champlain.

Tour Basketville at 152 Cherry Street in Burlington to see a large selection of handmade baskets. It's open year-round. For information, call 802-387-5509.

Take a ferry ride across Lake Champlain to Grand Isle, Vermont, or to Platts-burgh, New York. For times, call 802-864-9804. You can also ride aboard the *Spirit of Ethan Allen*, a replica of a vintage sternwheeler on Lake Champlain. It leaves from Perkins Pier in Burlington. For reservations and information, call 802-862-8300.

Attend the Vermont Mozart Festival held from mid-July through early August in the University's Royall Tyler Theater. In early June–July, attend the Lake Champlain Fishing Derby, Jazz Festival, and a concert by the Vermont Symphony on July 4. Free concerts are given in Battery Park during the summer months.

Take a guided tour through Ethan Allen's restored homestead, 2 miles north of Burlington on Vermont 127. For information, call 802-865-4556.

Drive 7 miles south to Shelburne Museum on U.S. 7 to see 37 historic struc-tures depicting early New England. For information on special events, call 802-985-3344.

INFORMATION
Mount Philo State Park
R.D. 1, Box 1049
North Ferrisburg, Vermont 05473
802-425-2390

NORTH HERO STATE PARK
33

LOCATION - From North Hero, go 8 miles southwest on U.S. 2 and 3 miles northeast on the town road.

FEATURES - North Hero State Park was named after North Hero Island. The islands got their name for the early Vermonters who served in the Revolu-tionary War. Map turtles nest along the park beach.

ACTIVITIES - Camp in one of 117 campsites, including 18 lean-tos and a disposal station, from mid-May through Labor Day. Go swimming or rent a boat or rowboat and go boating and fishing in Lake Champlain. Hike the trails and enjoy a picnic.

Registered campers can enjoy the sand beach at Knight Point State Park, 10 miles away, for free.

Grand Isle, 15 miles from the park, features the Hyde Log Cabin, the oldest found in the U.S. Tour Grand Isle's visitor center and State Fish Culture Station, located near the LCT ferry dock in Grand Isle.

INFORMATION
North Hero State Park
R.D. 1, Box 259
North Hero, Vermont 05474
802-372-8727

QUECHEE GORGE STATE PARK
34

LOCATION - From the intersection of I-89 and U.S. 4, take Exit 1 at White River and go west for 3 miles on U.S. 4.

FEATURES - Quechee Gorge, located along the Ottauquechee River, is called Vermont's Little Grand Canyon. Ottauquechee is an Indian word meaning "swift mountain stream" or "cattails or rushes near a swift current." The gorge was formed near the end of the last glacial era, approximately 13,000 years ago.

ACTIVITIES - Camp in one of the 54 campsites, including 7 lean-tos and a disposal station, from mid-May through Columbus Day. Go fishing in the Ottauquechee River and hike the gorge trails. Cross the bridge 162 feet above the Ottauquechee River. Enjoy a picnic overlooking the waterfalls. Snacks are available next to the park.

Quechee Inn on Clubhouse Road has rental canoes and bicycles, hiking trails, and flyfishing. During the winter, cross-country ski here. For information, call 802-295-3133.

Billings Farm and Museum features implements from the 1800s and is located in Woodstock, 8 miles away and ½ mile on Vermont 12 across Elm Street Bridge. For information, call 802-457-2355.

INFORMATION
Quechee Gorge State Park
190 Dewey Mills Road
White River Junction, Vermont 05001
802-295-2990

SAND BAR STATE PARK
35

LOCATION - The park is 5 miles northwest of Burlington. From I-89, take Exit 17, Champlain Islands Exit, and continue north 4 miles on U.S. 2.

FEATURES - Sand Bar is named for a natural sandbar located between South Hero Island and Milton. The park is located on the eastern end of the sandbar.

ACTIVITIES - The park is for day-use only. Go fishing, swimming from the 2,000-foot sand beach, enjoy a picnic, and go boating with rentals for both boats and sailboards available. Because of its shallow water depth along the shoreline, families enjoy bringing their children to swim here. Concessions are available.

INFORMATION
Sand Bar State Park
Route 2, RFD 1
Milton, Vermont 05468
802-893-2825

SILVER LAKE STATE PARK
36

LOCATION - From Barnard, go north for ¼ mile on Town Road off Vermont 12. It's also 8 miles south of Bethel. The park has 1,100 feet of shore frontage on Silver Lake.

ACTIVITIES - Camp in one of 46 campsites, including 7 lean-tos and a trailer dump station, open from mid-May through Labor Day. In Silver Lake, go swimming, bass, pike, and perch fishing, and boating and canoeing with boat and canoe rentals available. No motors are permitted. Food concessions are available on the beach.

INFORMATION
Silver Lake State Park
Barnard, Vermont 05031
802-234-9451

SMUGGLERS NOTCH STATE PARK
37

LOCATION - From Stowe, go 10 miles northwest on Vermont 108.

FEATURES - Smugglers Notch is a narrow mountain pass with 1,000-foot cliffs rising on either side. The notch was used in the 1800s for illegal trade with Canada when President Thomas Jefferson passed an embargo act forbidding American trade. Later, fugitive slaves crossed through the notch and, during the 1920s prohibition, liquor was smuggled from Canada into the U.S.

ACTIVITIES - Camp in one of 38 campsites, including 14 lean-tos, from mid-May through Columbus Day. Go hiking to the summit of 4,393-foot Mount Mansfield. Enjoy boating, swimming, fishing, bicycling, or picnicking. During the winter, go skiing at Mount Mansfield, Smugglers Notch, or Spruce Peak Ski Area.

State Ski Hostel is adjacent to the park and offers summer lodging for bicyclists and hikers. Reservations are necessary. Call 802-253-4010.

Smugglers Notch Historic Site is 2 miles north of the park on Vermont 108.

Drive up the Stowe toll road to the summit of Mount Mansfield. You can also reach the summit via the Stowe Gondola, located 7.5 miles northwest of Stowe on Vermont 108. For information, call 802-253-7311.

Bicyclists and walkers can enjoy Stowe's 5-mile recreational path that begins in the center of town, following a stream towards Mount Mansfield.

INFORMATION
Smugglers Notch State Park
7248 Mountain Road
RR 1, Box 2040
Stowe, Vermont 05672
802-253-4014

TOWNSHEND STATE PARK
38

LOCATION - The park is 17 miles northwest of Brattleboro via Vermont 30 and then north 3 miles on Town Road. It's at the foot of Bald Mountain on a bend of the West River.

ACTIVITIES - Camp in one of the 34 tent/trailer campsites, including 4 lean-tos, open from late April through Columbus Day. Go fishing and swimming in Townshend Dam, located 2 miles from the park, and trout fishing in West River. Hike the steep 1,110-foot loop trail from the west side of the campground to the summit of Bald Mountain. For an easier route, follow the trail by campsite 25, crossing Negro Brook.

Scott Covered Bridge, built in 1870 over the West River, is one of the state's longest covered bridges.

INFORMATION
Townshend State Park
Route 1, Box 2650
Townshend, Vermont, 05353
802-365-7500

UNDERHILL STATE PARK
39

LOCATION - From Essex Junction, go east 9 miles on Vermont 15 and east 4 miles on paved Town Road, then another 4 miles on a gravel road with a steep grade. No trailers are recommended.

FEATURES - Underhill State Park is located on the western slope of 4,300-foot Mount Mansfield and is part of Mount Mansfield State Forest.

ACTIVITIES - The upper campground has 9 group lean-to sites. The lower campground has 11 tent and 6 lean-to campsites available from mid-May through Columbus Day. The park is not recommended for RV or tent-trailer campers, since campers are required to park in the lot and not at the campsite.

Hike one of four trails ascending 4,393-foot Mount Mansfield's western flank. Sunset Ridge Trail involves a 3-mile climb to the summit. Vermont's Long Trail traverses the summit ridge and, when combined with trails from the other side of the mountain, provides options for hiking loops. Pick up a trail map at the ranger station.

Drive up the privately operated auto road to the mountain summit. The state forest has 38 campsites in Smugglers Notch, hiking trails, fishing, swimming, and boating. Drive up the toll road to the summit of Mount Mansfield. It begins 5 miles northwest of Stowe from Vermont 108.

Bicyclists and hikers can enjoy Stowe's 5-mile recreational path that begins in the center of town and follows a stream north towards Mount Mansfield. Take a ride to the mountain summit on the Stowe Gondola located 7.5 miles west of Stowe on Vermont 108. For information, call 802-253-7311. Bicyclists and hikers can overnight at the Vermont State Ski Dorm and Hostel located at the foot of Mount Mansfield. For information, call 802-253-4010.

INFORMATION
Underhill State Park
Underhill Center, Vermont 05490
802-899-3022

WILGUS STATE PARK
40

LOCATION - The park is on the Connecticut River. From I-91, take Exit 8 and go 1½ miles south of Ascutney on U.S. 5.

ACTIVITIES - Camp in one of 19 tent campsites, including 6 lean-tos and a disposal station, located along the river and open from mid-May through Columbus Day. Go fishing for bass, trout, perch, walleye, and pickerel in the Connecticut River and boating and canoeing with rentals available. Hike the trails and enjoy a picnic. Drive up the road to the summit of 3,144-foot Mount Ascutney and visit the covered bridge at Windsor.

During the winter, go skiing at Mount Ascutney Ski Area.

INFORMATION
Wilgus State Park
P.O. Box 196
Ascutney, Vermont 05030
802-674-5422

WOODFORD STATE PARK
41

LOCATION - The park is on a 2,400-foot mountain plateau encircling Adams Reservoir, surrounded by the Green Mountain National Forest. It's 10 miles east of Bennington on Vermont 9.

ACTIVITIES - Camp in one of 103 campsites with 20 lean-tos and a trailer dump station open from mid-May through Columbus Day. Go boating with rentals available and trout fishing in Adams Reservoir. No motors are permitted. Hike park trails including a 2.7-mile trail around the lake.

During the winter, go snowmobiling or ski Prospect Mountain Ski Area.

Tour Bennington Museum located on West Main Street in downtown Bennington, one mile west of the intersection of Vermont 7 and 9. It has the largest public collection of paintings by Grandma Moses and the schoolhouse she attended as a child. You'll also see over 5,000 examples of pressed and free-blown glass and pottery from the late 1700–1800s. For information, call 802-447-1571.

Pick up a map from the Chamber of Commerce on Veterans Memorial Drive and take a walking tour of historic Bennington. Bennington has three covered bridges. Silk Road and Papermill Village bridges are off Vermont 67A and Bert Henry Bridge is on Murphy Road.

Stop by Bennington Battle Monument, located ½ mile west of Vermont 9 and U.S. 7. When finished in 1891, it was the tallest battle monument in the world.

INFORMATION
Woodford State Park
HCR 65, Box 0928
Bennington, Vermont 05201
208-447-7169

WOODS ISLAND STATE PARK
See under KILL KARE STATE PARK

State Park Index

Name of Park	CG	FS	HK	CO	VC	WA	PG
CONNECTICUT							
Bear Mountain		•	•				3
Bigelow Hollow		•	•			•	5
Black Rock	•	•	•	•		•	6
Bluff Point		•	•				6
Burr Pond	•	•	•	•		•	8
Chatfield Hollow		•	•			•	8
Cockaponset	•	•	•			•	8
Collis Huntington		•	•			•	9
Day Pond		•	•			•	10
Dennis Hill			•				15
Devil's Hopyard	•	•	•				10
Dinosaur			•		•		27
Fort Griswold					•		6
Fort Shantok		•	•				12
Gay City		•	•			•	13
Gillette Castle			•		•	•	10
Haddam Meadows		•				•	13
Hammonasset Beach	•	•		•		•	14
Haystack Mountain			•				15
Hopeville	•	•	•	•		•	16
Housatonic Meadows	•	•	•			•	17
Hurd		•	•				18
Indian Well		•	•	•		•	18

Name of Park	CG	FS	HK	CO	VC	WA	PG
John A. Minetto		•	•			•	15
Kent Falls		•	•				17
Kettletown	•	•	•	•		•	19
Lake Waramaug	•	•		•		•	17
Lover's Leap			•				19
Macedonia Brook	•	•	•				20
Mansfield Hollow		•	•			•	20
Mashamoquet Brook	•	•	•	•		•	21
Mohawk Mountain			•				21
Mount Tom		•	•	•		•	22
Osbornedale		•	•				18
Penwood			•				26
Peoples		•	•				22
Pierrepont		•	•				22
Putnam Memorial		•	•			•	9
Quaddick		•	•	•		•	23
Rocky Neck	•	•	•	•			24
Selden Neck						•	10
Sherwood Island		•		•		•	24
Sleeping Giant		•	•				25
Squantz Pond		•	•	•		•	25
Stoddard Hill		•	•				12
Stratton Brook		•	•			•	26
Talcott Mountain			•				26
Wadsworth Falls		•	•			•	27
West Rock Ridge			•				27
Wharton Brook		•	•	•			28

DELAWARE

Name of Park	CG	FS	HK	CO	VC	WA	PG
Bellevue		•	•	•			29
Brandywine Creek		•	•		•	•	32
Cape Henlopen	•	•	•		•	•	32
Delaware Seashore	•	•				•	33
Fenwick Island		•	•	•		•	34
Fort Delaware		•	•		•		35
Holts Landing		•				•	35
Killens Pons State Park	•	•	•		•	•	36
Lums Pond	•	•	•	•	•	•	36
Trap Pond	•	•	•			•	37
Walter S. Carpenter		•	•				37

MAINE

Name of Park	CG	FS	HK	CO	VC	WA	PG
Aroostook		•	•	•		•	39

Name of Park	CG	FS	HK	CO	VC	WA	PG
Point Lookout	•	•	•		•	•	72
Pocomoke River	•	•	•	•	•	•	73
Rocks		•	•				74
Rocky Gap	•	•	•	•		•	74
Sandy Point		•	•	•		•	75
Seneca Creek		•	•	•	•	•	75
Smallwood		•	•	•	•	•	76
St. Mary's River		•	•			•	77
Susquehanna	•	•	•		•	•	77
Swallow Falls	•	•	•				78
Tuckahoe	•	•	•		•	•	78
Washington Monument	•		•		•		79
Wye Oak					•		80

MASSACHUSETTS

Name of Park	CG	FS	HK	CO	VC	WA	PG
Ames Nowell		•	•			•	83
Ashland		•	•			•	83
Bash Bish Falls/Mt. Washington	•	•	•			•	83
Battleship Cove							84
Blackstone/Canal Heritage		•	•			•	85
Borderland	•	•				•	85
Boston Harbor	•	•	•	•		•	86
Bradley Palmer			•				88
Callahan			•				89
Clarksburg	•	•	•			•	89
Cochituate		•		•		•	89
Demerest Lloyd		•				•	90
F. Gilbert Hills			•				90
Fall River Heritage					•		91
Gardner Heritage			•		•	•	91
Georgetown–Rowley			•				88
Great Brook Farm		•	•			•	92
Halibut Point			•				93
Hampton Ponds		•				•	100
Harold Parker	•	•	•			•	94
Holyoke Heritage		•	•		•		94
Hopkinton		•				•	83
Lake Dennison	•	•	•			•	95
Lawrence Heritage					•		96
Lowell					•	•	97
Lynn Heritage					•	•	98
Massasoit	•	•				•	98
Maudslay			•				99

Name of Park	CG	FS	HK	CO	VC	WA	PG
Mohawk Trail	•	•	•		•	•	100
Moore		•				•	106
Mount Tom		•	•			•	100
Mount Chicopee		•					100
Myles Standish	•	•	•			•	101
Natural Bridge		•					102
Nickerson	•	•	•			•	102
Otter River	•	•	•			•	95
Pearl Hill	•	•	•			•	103
Pilgrim Memorial		•				•	104
Quinsigamond	•	•				•	105
Robinson		•	•				105
Rutland		•	•			•	106
Skinner			•		•		106
Springfield Heritage							107
Wahconah Falls			•				107
Walden Pond		•	•			•	108
Wells	•	•	•			•	109
Wendell		•	•			•	109
Western Gateway					•		109
Willowdale			•				88
Wompatuck		•	•		•	•	110

NEW HAMPSHIRE

Name of Park	CG	FS	HK	CO	VC	WA	PG
Bear Brook	•	•	•	•			113
Cardigan			•				114
Clough		•				•	114
Coleman	•	•	•			•	115
Crawford Notch	•	•	•	•	•		115
Dixville Notch		•					116
Echo Lake			•			•	117
Ellacoya	•	•				•	117
Franconia Notch	•	•	•	•	•	•	118
Greenfield	•	•	•	•		•	120
Hampton Beach	•	•	•	•		•	121
Lake Francis	•	•				•	121
Miller			•				122
Moose Brook	•	•	•			•	122
Mount Monadnock	•		•		•		123
Mount Sunapee		•	•			•	123
Mount Washington			•				124
Odiorne Point		•	•			•	125
Pawtuckaway	•	•	•			•	127

Name of Park	CG	FS	HK	CO	VC	WA	PG
Pillsbury	•	•	•			•	128
Pisgah		•	•				128
Rhododendron			•				129
Rollins			•				130
Wellington			•	•		•	129
Wentworth–Coolidge							125
White Lake	•	•	•	•		•	130
Winslow			•				130

NEW JERSEY

Name of Park	CG	FS	HK	CO	VC	WA	PG
Allaire	•	•	•	•	•		133
Allamuchy	•	•	•				134
Barnegat Lighthouse		•		•		•	135
Bass River	•	•	•	•		•	135
Cape May Point		•	•		•		136
Cheesequake	•	•	•	•		•	137
Delaware and Raritan Canal		•	•			•	138
Fort Mott		•				•	139
High Point	•	•	•	•	•	•	140
Hopatcong		•	•	•		•	140
Island Beach		•	•	•		•	141
Lebanon	•		•			•	141
Liberty			•	•	•	•	142
Monmouth Battlefield					•		143
Parvin	•	•	•	•	•	•	143
Ringwood		•	•	•		•	144
Round Valley	•	•	•	•		•	144
Spruce Run	•	•	•	•		•	145
Swartswood	•	•	•	•		•	145
Voorhees	•		•				146
Washington Crossing			•		•		146
Wawayanda		•	•	•		•	147
Wharton	•	•	•	•	•	•	147

NEW YORK

Name of Park	CG	FS	HK	CO	VC	WA	PG
Allegany	•	•	•	•	•	•	151
Bear Mountain		•	•	•		•	188
Bethpage			•	•		•	152
Bowman Lake	•	•	•	•		•	153
Burnham Point	•	•				•	153
Cayuga Lake	•	•	•	•		•	197
Cedar Point	•	•	•			•	154
Chenango Valley	•	•	•	•		•	153

Name of Park	CG	FS	HK	CO	VC	WA	PG
Evansburg		•	•				217
Fort Washington		•	•		•		218
Frances Slocum		•	•	•		•	219
French Creek	•	•	•	•		•	219
Gifford Pinchot	•	•	•	•	•	•	220
Gouldsboro		•	•	•		•	221
Greenwood Furnace	•		•	•	•		223
Hickory Run	•	•	•	•	•	•	224
Hills Creek	•	•	•	•	•	•	225
Hyner Run	•	•	•	•	•	•	225
Jacobsburg		•	•				226
Kettle Creek	•	•	•	•	•	•	226
Keystone	•	•	•	•	•	•	227
Kinzua Bridge		•	•	•			228
Kooser	•	•	•	•		•	228
Lackawanna	•	•	•	•		•	229
Laurel Hill	•	•	•	•		•	230
Laurel Ridge	•		•				231
Laurel Summit			•				233
Lehigh Gorge		•	•			•	232
Leonard Harrison	•	•	•	•			232
Linn Run		•	•				233
Little Buffalo		•	•	•	•	•	234
Little Pine	•	•	•			•	234
Locust Lake	•	•	•			•	235
Lyman Run	•	•	•	•		•	236
Marsh Creek		•	•	•		•	237
Maurice Goddard		•	•	•		•	238
McConnells Mill		•	•		•		238
Memorial Lake		•	•			•	239
Moraine		•	•	•		•	240
Mount Pisgah		•	•	•		•	241
Nockamixon		•	•	•		•	242
Ohiopyle	•	•	•	•		•	243
Oil Creek		•	•	•	•	•	244
Ole Bull	•	•	•			•	245
Parker Dam	•	•	•	•	•	•	246
Pine Grove Furnace	•	•	•	•	•	•	247
Poe Valley	•	•	•	•	•	•	248
Point						•	249
Presque Isle		•	•	•	•	•	250
Prince Gallitzin	•	•	•	•	•	•	251
Promised Land	•	•	•	•	•	•	252

Name of Park	CG	FS	HK	CO	VC	WA	PG
Bomoseen	•	•	•	•		•	280
Branbury	•	•	•	•		•	280
Brighton	•	•	•			•	281
Burton Island	•	•	•	•		•	290
Button Bay							282
Calvin Coolidge	•	•	•				283
Camel's Hump	•		•				283
Camp Plymouth		•	•	•		•	283
Crystal Lake		•	•	•		•	284
D.A.R.	•	•	•			•	284
Elmore	•	•	•	•		•	285
Emerald Lake	•	•	•	•		•	285
Fort Dummer	•		•				286
Gifford Woods	•	•	•				287
Grand Isle	•	•	•	•		•	287
Granville Gulf		•	•				288
Groton	•	•	•	•		•	288
Half Moon	•	•	•			•	289
Jamaica	•	•	•	•		•	290
Kill Kare		•	•	•		•	290
Kingsland Bay	•	•				•	291
Knight Point		•	•			•	292
Lake Carmi	•	•	•	•		•	292
Lake St. Catherine	•	•	•	•		•	293
Lake Shaftsbury	•	•	•	•		•	294
Little River	•	•	•			•	295
Maidstone	•	•	•			•	295
Molly Stark	•		•				296
Mount Philo	•		•				296
North Hero	•	•	•			•	297
Quechee Gorge	•	•	•				298
Sand Bar		•			•	•	299
Silver Lake	•	•	•	•		•	299
Smugglers Notch	•	•	•			•	299
Townshend	•	•	•				300
Underhill	•		•				301
Wilgus	•	•	•			•	301
Woodford	•	•	•			•	302
Woods Island		•	•			•	291

About the Author

Vici DeHaan was an elementary schoolteacher in the Boulder Valley Schools for thirty-one years where she has taught grades kindergarten through sixth. She is the author of nine other books: *Bicycling the Colorado Rockies, Hiking Trails of the Boulder Mountain Parks and Plains, Moving Through the Ratings: Passing from Private to Professional Pilot, The Runner's Guide to Boulder County, Bike Rides of the Colorado Front Range, Pilot's Cross-Country Guide to National Parks and Historical Monuments, The Pilot's Cross-Country Guide to National Parks, State Parks of the West,* and *State Parks of the Midwest.*

Vici DeHaan is an avid outdoorsperson who has hiked in the Colorado Rockies all her life. She also plays handbells with the Boulder Valley Retired Teachers and with the First United Methodist Bell Choir. She has been singing actively for forty-two years, performing with the Boulder Chorale, the Rocky Mountain Chorale, and the Boulder Bach Festival Choir, and she also plays the piano as time permits.

Vici holds a private pilot's license and a ground instructor's rating. She and her husband, Warren, have flown their light plane all over the United States, Canada, and Mexico. They live in Boulder, Colorado, and have five children and two grandchildren.